Psychoanalysis and Female Sexuality

PSYCHOANALYSIS

AND

FEMALE SEXUALITY

Edited with an Introduction by

DR. HENDRIK M. RUITENBEEK

COLLEGE & UNIVERSITY PRESS · *Publishers*
NEW HAVEN, CONN.

Library of Congress Catalog Card Number: 66:14820

For
CORRY LANGSTAFF-VAN DER ROTTE
with fond memories of Leyden and our childhood

MANUFACTURED IN THE UNITED STATES OF AMERICA BY
UNITED PRINTING SERVICES, INC.
NEW HAVEN, CONN.

Acknowledgments

The International Journal of Psychoanalysis granted permission to reprint the following articles:

Ernest Jones, "The Early Development of Female Sexuality," Vol. VIII, 1927.

J. Lampl-de Groot, "The Evolution of the Oedipus Complex in Women," Vol. IX, 1928.

J. H. W. van Ophuijsen, "Contributions to the Masculinity Complex in Women," Vol. V, 1924.

Karen Horney, "The Denial of the Vagina," Vol. XIV, 1933.

Helene Deutsch, "On Female Homosexuality," Vol. XIV, 1933.

Joan Riviere, "Womanliness as a Masquerade," Vol. X, 1929.

Sandor Lorand, "Contribution to the Problem of Vaginal Orgasm," Vol. XX, 1939.

Marie Bonaparte, "Passivity, Masochism and Femininity," Vol. XVI, 1935.

With the permission of *Psychiatry*:

Clara Thompson, "Penis-Envy," Vol. VI, 1943.

Clara Thompson, "Some Effects of the Derogatory Attitude towards Female Sexuality," Vol. XIII, 1950.

David Freedman, "On Women Who Hate their Husbands," Vol. XXIV, 1961.

With the permission of Basic Books, New York:

Sigmund Freud, "Female Sexuality," *Collected Papers*, Vol. V.

With the permission of *Psychosomatic Medicine*:

Judd Marmor, "Some Considerations Concerning Orgasm in the Female," Vol. XVI, no. 3, 1954.

With the permission of the *Journal of Social Psychology*:

A. H. Maslow, "Self-Esteem (Dominance-Feeling) and Sexuality in Women," Vol. XVI, 1942.

With the permission of the International Universities Press, New York:

Phyllis Greenacre, "Special Problems of Early Female Sexual Development," *Psychoanalytic Study of the Child*, V, 1950.

Contents

Introduction

Much as has been written about female sexuality, little is actually understood about its dynamics and character. The frigid female, the domineering female, the asexual female, the single female, the castrating female, and the competitive female have been bruited about until each of the terms is emptied of meaning, a mere cliché. Yet little thought is given to the total sexual situation of the American female.

When we look at the total sexual situation of the American female or male, the picture becomes rather disturbing. Or, perhaps, one might say the picture becomes mirror-like, with the manifestations of sexuality reflecting the attitudes characteristic of American culture as a whole. Our society is technically oriented and competitive, as is the sexual expression of many people in it. Sex, which once was a forbidden topic, is now all too much a staple of conversation, and all too often the participants compete to boast about their prowess.

Betty Friedan says that sex "is becoming a strangely joyless national compulsion, if not a contemptuous mockery." Rollo May points to the emphasis on technique in sexual performance and notes how, when carried beyond a certain point, that emphasis tends to foster "a mechanistic attitude toward love-making"; such attitudes are consistent with feelings of loneliness, with alienation, and with the depersonalization common today.

Contemporary American women enjoy a level of social and economic liberty which would have astonished their grandmothers. Middle-class women can enter most lucrative occupations and professions. They are actually expected to devote a major portion of their lives to their careers, despite the greater trend toward early marriage and large families than was common in the 1920's or 1930's. American mothers and daughters continue to govern and dominate the household.

American women have become emancipated. Whereas they had once been expected to disclaim and repudiate their sexuality, they are now expected to acknowledge, express, and enjoy it. And—as in many other respects—heaven help the American who does not enjoy as expected. For the American woman, "freedom" to make sexual pleasure a part of her life has been transformed into an imperative: on pain of regarding herself as either inadequate or abused, she must experience vaginal orgasm. If she does not—or rather, if she cannot match her experience with that of her neighbors and the novels she reads—then she considers herself defeated; she is a sort of cripple and not a fulfilled woman. When feelings of this kind are present, and the therapist in practice sees them often enough, then it can be maintained, as Bruno Bettelheim[1] does, that, in respect to their sexuality, many contemporary women may be worse off than even their Victorian predecessors. Those women could not feel genuinely respectable if they admitted, even to themselves, their sexual needs or desires. In our day, it has become disreputable, or at least humiliating, for a woman to acknowledge to herself or anyone else that her sexual experiences have never constituted a truly shattering eroticism.

Freud divided females into three principal types, each related to a different pattern of response to the shock every small girl experiences when she finds out that she is automatically different from the little boys she has encountered. The first type of female response substitutes the child for the unobtainable penis. This response produces what Marie Bonaparte has called "true woman: normal, vaginal, maternal." The second type of female response recognizes the absence of the penis, but abandons hope of obtaining any external love object as substitute. The third type of female response denies reality; unconsciously, such a woman asserts that she has a penis and clings to the male organic and psychical elements—the clitoris and its responsiveness and the masculinity complex—which are present in all women.

In many respects, female sexuality is the outgrowth of a peculiar struggle, and that basic psychological struggle has been reinforced and even intensified by the changing conditions of life which women encounter in present-day American society.

[1] See his "Growing-up Female" in Hendrik Ruitenbeek, *Psychoanalysis and Contemporary American Culture* (New York, 1964).

Like boys, little girls have their mothers as their first love objects. Like boys, they lose this love object to the father, but unlike boys, they cannot repossess it, as it were, in their final, proper sexual object. Girls must shift to a second infantile love object and lose that too, since the father is also forbidden. Furthermore, the active little girl must change into a far more passive creature if she is to assume her appointed sexual and social role. The female must thus travel a twisted road in order to reach her "true nature."

The female movement to passivity has been made more difficult in our time, which has reached a high point in a continuing social shift. During most of humanity's historical experience, people have been expected to remain what and where they were born, to continue in their parents' social and economic class; now they are not only able but often expected to move, and to move upward. In our American society, expectation has become demand. Women, too, experience this demand to move upward and succeed; and they are no longer ready to meet the demand vicariously: they want to do or to get something for themselves rather than merely to reflect the achievement of their husbands. It might be argued that this is scarcely true of the contemporary middle-class young woman who avoids the exacting kinds of professional training that are open to her because she plans to marry early and have a large family. She, surely, has successfully made the transition to proper female passivity. One may question this, not merely from the statistics on the incidence of alcoholism and other signs of emotional distress evident among reasonably prosperous young women, but from the symptoms which are presented by patients of this sort who come into psychotherapy, and particularly by the quality of the anxiety they manifest in respect to their capacity for orgasm. Many patients treat this aspect of their sexual experience as if it were a kind of touchstone of success, and of a success which seems to be defined in terms not unlike those a man might use.

In a world where male activity sets the standards of worth—and analysts point out that both physiologically and psychologically, male sexual performance is an achievement—female experience in sex as in other aspects of life takes on the character of a peculiarly ambiguous struggle against male domination. That domination is expected. It is even accepted in the sense that the male sets the standard. For just as we say *mankind* to mean all human beings, so we regard the male as the human norm; what differs from that norm is necessarily inferior. But the male, whose prime importance has never been seriously questioned even in American culture, is active. Hence many women perceive the demand for passivity as a demand that they accept a status of inferiority.

Some women submit; they do not rebel; they do not become aggressive and therefore a threat to the men in their lives, but their inability either to enjoy their assigned role or to react against it leads to feelings of despair and to a kind of disintegration of the self. The English novelist Doris Lessing (South Africa might claim her, but she would scarcely acknowledge the claim) paints a vivid portrait of this type of woman in *A Man and Two Women*,[2] notably in the story "To Room Nineteen." Here, she describes a young woman, happily married, with an attractive husband, children, friends, and money. Yet the woman's whole existence is a lie. The only reality she can envision is the time she spends alone at a seedy hotel. Finally even this experience loses meaning. Life is no longer endurable and the woman turns on the gas; she was "quite content lying there, listening to the faint soft hiss of the gas that poured into the room, into her lungs, into her brain, as she drifted off into the dark river."

Thus, even fortunately situated women who do not use aggressiveness as a way of expressing resentment feel resentment and respond to it. They may turn to sex as a means of relief, which they often find inadequate. Sexual encounter has been divorced from a sense of personal relatedness without becoming a wholly satisfying although limited experience. As Betty Friedan stated about one woman[3]: "I need sex to feel alive, but I never really feel him."

Many contemporary women are thus in a state of rebellion against the passivity which nature and society impose on them. Their rebellion is several generations old, we should remember, but it has reached a kind of climax in our time. In reaction to male domination, even though the pre-World War I kind of feminism is rarely evident, women have become more aggressive,

[2] *A Man and Two Women* (New York, 1963), p. 316.
[3] *The Feminine Mystique* (New York, 1963), p. 258.

especially sexually. For in sexual as in economic life, there has been a "revolution of rising expectations."

Fifty years ago, many women not only waited to be sought in marriage (or at least tried very hard not to show that they were in pursuit of a husband) but, once married, regarded their role as that of serving their husband's pleasure, not of being pleased themselves. Contemporary women are no longer content to give men satisfaction; they want satisfaction, too. Perhaps women have always wanted satisfaction; after all, the author of Ecclesiastes does call the womb the horse-leech's daughter, and the folklore of many people includes the insatiable female. Now, however, women not only want and expect sexual satisfaction in marriage and elsewhere, but hold themselves and their men to blame if they do not experience that satisfaction—and in prescribed ways.

Thus formulated, the demand for satisfying sexual experience creates problems both for men and for women. American men, in marriage and outside, find themselves having to deal with knowledgeable women who at least think they know what they want and have every intention of getting it. Some men find this stimulating, no doubt, but a sizable number feel the sexually active woman to be a threat. They become passive in response—or perhaps in retaliation—and women find themselves involved with men who do not provide the kind of sexual experience they have come to feel to be their birthright. Yet, at the same time, the woman tends to blame herself for not being "woman enough" to rouse the man out of passivity.

Increasing social liberty further complicates the orientation of female sexuality. Once, and particularly for American middle-class women, sexual experience was limited to what could be had in marriage and with the marriage partner alone. Now, pre-marital and extramarital sexual experience is increasingly common. A surplus of women has contributed to a new emphasis on the sex life of the adult woman who either has not married or is "between" marriages. Single women, too, demand sexual experience. Such a woman may now have that without forfeiting "respectability"; but this liberty involves her in another set of complications which she might not have encountered at an earlier time. First, her partner may be unsatisfactory, a passive person, more pursued than pursuing and often, apparently, little worth the pursuit. Secondly, the single woman may be confused about the goals of her sexual expression and experience since, however free she may be to collect men, she is not socially free to have children. Is sexual play her most satisfying outlet, or is orgasm the *sine qua non?*

In listening to female patients, married or not, the analyst may well wonder whether orgasm has not been transformed into a fetish. As men feel increasingly challenged to elicit an orgasmic response, women, too, feel obligated to have the expected response. If the woman does not respond, she may be charged with acting to castrate her partner. Thus, a patient may feel both wrong and wronged. Without orgasm, she feels unsuccessful, even humiliatingly immature; yet she also feels deprived, cheated by her partner of her share of reward in the relationship.

In my opinion, too many contemporary women tend to forget that satisfactory sexual experience entails something more than orgasm. Now as in the past, a woman can know sexual gratification by satisfying the component drives of her ego: awareness that she is desirable, ability to excite the man sexually, childbearing, and the aim-deflected sexual pleasures of affection and tenderness. It should be noted that, contrary to expectation, women who are severely disturbed emotionally may have vaginal orgasm. Perhaps clitoridal sexuality should be stressed, for a high degree of sexual contentment actually can be reached by this means. Carl Sulzberger has suggested a possible shift of the area of maximal sexual sensitivity in the contemporary woman. As women secure more economic and social liberty and more of the rewards which men enjoy, Sulzberger observes, their sex habits and responses may tend to approach the male's—since, as we have said, all that is male is considered the more human and normal. Consequently, clitoridal satisfaction may be both easier to achieve and more satisfying than vaginal excitation.

Whether Sulzberger's contention is physiologically tenable is of less interest to us than is the attitude which so many female patients—and women not in therapy—have: their self-esteem is invested in being a well-functioning female and functioning well as a female requires that sexual relations produce the experience of vaginal orgasm. In this fashion, the anticipated "liberation" of female sexuality has become a new kind of sexual restraint for many women.

II

The essays in this anthology examine the problem of female sexuality both as it is affected by patterns of development and as it is affected by the peculiar conditions of women's life in our time.

The anthology opens with a paper by Ernest Jones which deals with the Oedipus conflict of the young female, with her experience of a partial castration threat, and with the phenomenon of *aphanisis*, the extinction of sexuality. In a paper on the evolution of the Oedipus complex in women, the Dutch psychoanalyst Jeanne Lampl-de Groot deals with essentially the same problem as Jones does. She, however, treats the material mainly in terms of the negative and positive Oedipus complex and illustrates the points she makes with data derived from the analysis of two female patients.

Clara Thompson, who is a well-known member of the neo-Freudian school, differs from Jones and Lampl-de Groot. Thompson questions the significance of penis-envy for understanding female sexuality and doubts that this has much effect on the psychology of the contemporary woman. Woman's real problem, Thompson asserts, does not lie "in becoming reconciled to having no penis but in accepting her own sexuality in its own right." Karen Horney, too, departs from the Freudian view. In her classic paper, "The Denial of the Vagina," Horney contends that Freud's concept "of the failure to discover the vagina" should be further explored. For, Horney continues, "behind the 'failure to discover' the vagina is a denial of its existence." The female, in other words, is thus deprived of any proper sexual organ; she is not merely castrated, she is de-sexed.

Another Dutch analyst, Van Ophuijsen, returns to the original Freudian view that women are deeply affected by the notion of their own castration; the masculinity complex in women, in his opinion, is closely connected with infantile masturbation of the clitoris and with urethral erotism.

Freud's own interpretation of female sexuality appears here in a paper in which he stresses the importance of the pre-Oedipal stage in the girl's development. For a female, this stage is far more important than it is for a male.

Two of Freud's women disciples are represented in this anthology, Helene Deutsch with an essay on female homosexuality and Marie Bonaparte with a discussion of the relationship of passivity, masochism, and femininity. Deutsch's paper is based on the analysis of eleven women. From this clinical experience, she concludes that the phallic masculine attitude is the outstanding aspect of homosexual behavior in these patients. At the pregenital level, the mother-child relationship was the most important element in the patient's affective life. The wish for activity, typical for the phallic phase of child development, is carried along into the adult's neurotic regression and culminates in the need to behave homosexually.

Marie Bonaparte was one of Freud's favorite pupils. In this paper, she relates the little girl's concept of coitus as a sadistic act to the development of masochism, on the one hand, and of more normal passive receptive attitudes on the other.

Three papers deal with the problem of clitoridal and vaginal sensitivity and their relation to orgasm. Phyllis Greenacre discusses clitoral stimulation and early vaginal sensations in the phallic phase of the girl's development. In his discussion of orgasm in the female, Judd Marmor throws considerable doubt on the assumption that genital erogenicity in the female normally is transferred from the clitoris to the vagina. Clitoral sensation continues to be an important factor in the sexuality of the adult female and, by implication, should be recognized as an adult response. Sandor Lorand rejects the thesis that clitoridal sensations are transferred to the vagina. Rather, he insists, vaginal orgasm exists as an independent phenomenon. Vaginal sensation gains new importance when the maturing girl rediscovers and relearns to experience the sensations in the vagina which she once knew, but repressed and forgot.

In contrast to these papers on sexual sensation are three others which regard sexual expression and experience as problems of relatedness rather than of pure sensation. A. H. Maslow thinks that women's sexual behavior is more related to dominance-feeling than to more simple sexual drives. One should remember, here, that dominance-feeling, as Maslow interprets it, is an evaluation of one's own self. Somewhat akin to this interpretation is David Freedman's essay "On Women Who Hate Their Husbands." Working with data drawn from the analysis of three women patients, Freedman decides that the patient's choice of a mate was directed by a specific defect in her ego. She could not see herself "as a person of sufficient potential significance and ability to hold a man she really admired," and therefore she married someone she disliked. In "Womanliness as a Masquerade," Joan Riviere deals with one disguise of the wish for masculinity: the female who dons womanliness as a mask to conceal her anxiety and to ward off the retribution she fears from the men whose prerogative she wishes to usurp.

In the final essay in this anthology, Clara Thompson returns to the problem of penis-envy. This feeling is not based upon perception of biological difference, as Freud maintained. Men have a privileged position in the culture, Thompson declares; it is their status that women envy, not their penises. Women's feeling of inferiority may be symbolized as penis-envy, but the phrase is merely metaphoric; what women want is less the male organ than the kind of social recognition and privileges which the possessors of the organ get as a right.

Psychoanalysis and Female Sexuality

I

The Early Development of Female Sexuality*

By Ernest Jones

Freud has more than once commented on the fact that our knowledge of the early stages in female development is much more obscure and imperfect than that of male development, and Karen Horney has forcibly, though justly, pointed out that this must be connected with the greater tendency to bias that exists on the former subject. It is probable that this tendency to bias is common to the two sexes, and it would be well if every writer on the subject kept this consideration in the foreground of his mind throughout. Better still, it is to be hoped that analytic investigation will gradually throw light on the nature of the prejudice in question and ultimately dispel it. There is a healthy suspicion growing that men analysts have been led to adopt an unduly phallo-centric view of the problems in question, the importance of the female organs being correspondingly underestimated. Women have on their side contributed to the general mystification by their secretive attitude toward their own genitals and by displaying a hardly disguised preference for interest in the male organ.

The immediate stimulus to the investigation on which the present paper is mainly based was provided by the unusual experience, a couple of years ago, of having to analyze at the same time five cases of manifest homosexuality in women. The

* Read at the Tenth International Congress of Psycho-Analysis, Innsbruck, September 1, 1927.

analyses were all deep ones and lasted from three to five years; they have been completed in three of the cases and carried to a far stage in the other two. Among the numerous problems thus aroused two particular ones may serve as a starting point for the considerations I wish to bring forward here. They were: what precisely in women corresponds with the fear of castration in men? and what differentiates the development of homosexual from that of heterosexual women? It will be noticed that these two questions are closely related, the word "penis" indicating the point of connection between them.

A few clinical facts about these cases may be of interest, though I do not propose to relate any casuistic material. Three of the patients were in the twenties and two in the thirties. Only two of the five had an entirely negative attitude toward men. It was not possible to establish any consistent rule in respect of their conscious attitude toward the parents: all varieties occurred, negative toward the father with either negative or positive toward the mother, and vice versa. In all five cases, however, it proved that the unconscious attitude toward both parents was strongly ambivalent. In all cases there was evidence of an unusually strong infantile fixation in regard to the mother, this being definitely connected with the oral stage. This was always succeeded by a strong father fixation, whether it was temporary or permanent in consciousness.

The first of the two questions mentioned above might also be formulated as follows: when the girl feels that she has already suffered castration, what imagined future event can evoke dread proportionate to the dread of castration? In attempting to answer this question, that is, to account for the fact that women suffer from dread at least as much as men, I came to the conclusion that the concept "castration" has in some respects hindered our appreciation of the fundamental conflicts. We have here in fact an example of what Horney has indicated as an unconscious bias from approaching such studies too much from the male point of view. In his illuminating discussion of the penis complex in women, Abraham[1] had remarked that there was no reason for not applying the word "castration" there as well as with men, for wishes and fears about the penis of a parallel order occur in

[1] Karl Abraham, *Selected Papers*, 1927, p. 339.

both. To agree with this statement, however, does not involve overlooking the differences in the two cases, nor should it blind us to the danger of importing into the one considerations with which we are already familiar in the other. Freud has justly remarked in connection with the pregenital precursors of castration (weaning and defecation, pointed out by Stärcke and myself, respectively) that the psychoanalytical concept of castration, as distinguished from the corresponding biological one, refers definitely to the penis alone—the testicles at most being included in addition.

Now the fallacy to which I wish to draw attention here is this. The all-important part normally played in male sexuality by the genital organs naturally tends to make us equate castration with the abolition of sexuality altogether. This fallacy often creeps into our arguments even though we know that many men wish to be castrated for, among others, erotic reasons, so that their sexuality certainly does not disappear with the surrender of the penis. With women, where the whole penis idea is always partial and mostly secondary in nature, this should be still more evident. In other words, the prominence of castration fears among men tends sometimes to make us forget that in both sexes castration is only a *partial* threat, however important a one, against sexual capacity and enjoyment as a whole. For the main blow of total extinction we might do well to use a separate term, such as the Greek word "aphanisis."

If we pursue to its roots the fundamental fear which lies at the basis of all neuroses we are driven, in my opinion, to the conclusion that what it really signifies in this aphanisis, the total, and of course permanent, extinction of the capacity (including opportunity) for sexual enjoyment. After all, this is the consciously avowed intention of most adults toward children. Their attitude is quite uncompromising: children are not to be permitted *any* sexual gratification. And we know that to the child the idea of indefinite postponement is much the same as that of permanent refusal. We cannot, of course, expect that the unconscious, with its highly concrete nature, will express itself for us in these abstract terms, which admittedly represent a generalization. The nearest approach to the idea of aphanisis that we meet with clinically is that of castration and of death thoughts (conscious dread of death and unconscious death wishes). I may cite here an obsessional case in a young man which illustrates the same point. He had substituted as his *summum bonum* the idea of aesthetic enjoyment for that of sexual gratification, and his castration fears took the form of apprehension lest he should lose his capacity for this enjoyment, behind them being of course the concrete idea of the loss of the penis.

From this point of view we see that the question under discussion was wrongly put. The male dread of being castrated may or may not have a precise female counterpart, but what is more important is to realize that this dread is only a special case and that both sexes ultimately dread exactly the same thing, aphanisis. The mechanism whereby this is supposed to be brought about shows important differences in the two sexes. If we neglect for the moment the sphere of auto-erotism—on the justifiable ground that conflicts here owe their main importance to the subsequent allo-erotic cathexis of it—and thus confine our attention to allo-erotism itself, we may say that the reconstructed train of thought in the male is somewhat as follows: "I wish to obtain gratification by committing a particular act, but I dare not do so because I fear that it would be followed by the punishment of aphanisis, by castration that would mean for me the permanent extinction of sexual pleasure." The corresponding thought in the female, with her more passive nature, is characteristically somewhat different: "I wish to obtain gratification through a particular experience, but I dare not take any steps toward bringing it about, such as asking for it and thus confessing my guilty wish, because I fear that to do so would be followed by aphanisis." It is, of course, plain that this difference not only is not invariable, but is in any event only one of degree. In both cases there is activity, though it is more overt and vigorous with the male. This is not, however, the main difference in accent; a more important one depends on the fact that, for obvious physiological reasons, the female is much more dependent on her partner for her gratification than is the male on his. Venus had much more trouble with Adonis, for example, than Pluto with Persephone.

The last consideration mentioned provides the biological reason for the most important psychological differences in the behavior and attitude of the sexes. It leads directly to a greater dependence (as distinct from desire) of the female on the willingness and moral approbation of the partner than we usually find with the male, where the corresponding sensitiveness occurs in respect of another, authoritative male. Hence, among other things, the more characteristic reproaches and need for reassurance on the woman's part. Among the important social consequences the following may be mentioned. It is well known that the morality of the world is essentially a male creation, and —what is much more curious—that the moral ideals of women are mainly copied from those of men. This must certainly be connected with the fact, pointed out by Helene Deutsch,[2] that the superego of women is, like that of men, predominantly derived from reactions to the father. Another consequence, which brings us back to our main discussion, is that the mechanism of aphanisis tends to differ in the two sexes. Whereas with the male this is typically conceived of in the active form of castration, with the female the primary fear would appear to be that of separation. This can be imagined as coming about through the rival mother intervening between the girl and the father, or even through her sending the girl away forever, or else through the father simply withholding the desired gratification. The deep fear of being deserted that most women have is a derivative of the latter.

At this point it is possible to obtain from the analysis of women a deeper insight than from that of men into the important question of the relation between privation and guilt, in other words into the genesis of the superego. In his paper on the passing of the Oedipus complex, Freud suggested that this happened in the female as the direct result of continued disappointment (privation), and we know that the superego is as much the heir of this complex in the female as in the male where it is the product of the guilt derived from the dread of castration. It follows, and my analytical experience fully confirms the conclusion,[3] that sheer privation comes, of course in both sexes, to have just the same meaning as deliberate deprivation on the part of the human environment. We thus reach the formula: *Privation is equivalent to frustration.* It is even likely that, as may be inferred from

[2] Helene Deutsch, *Zur Psychologie der weiblichen Sexualfunktionen,* 1925, p. 9.
[3] This was reached partly in conjunction with Mrs. Riviere, whose views are expounded in another context, *International Journal of Psychoanalysis,* Vol. VIII, pp. 374-75.

Freud's remarks on the passing of the female Oedipus complex, privation alone may be an adequate cause for the genesis of guilt. To discuss this further would take us too far into the structure of the superego and away from the present theme, but I should like just to mention a view I have reached which is sufficiently germane to the latter. It is that guilt, and with it the superego, is as it were artificially built up for the purpose of protecting the child from the stress of privation, i.e., of un-gratified libido, and so warding off the dread of aphanisis that always goes with this; it does so, of course, by damping down the wishes that are not destined to be gratified. I even think that the external disapproval, to which the whole of this process used to be ascribed, is largely an affair of exploitation on the child's part; that is to say, non-gratification primarily means danger, and the child projects this into the outer world, as it does with all internal dangers, and then makes use of any disapproval that comes to meet it there (*moralisches Entgegenkommen*) to signalize the danger and to help it in constructing a barrier against this.

To return once more to the young girl, we are faced with the task of tracing the various stages in development from the initial oral one. The view commonly accepted is that the nipple, or artificial teat, is replaced, after a little dallying with the thumb, by the clitoris as the chief source of pleasure, just as it is with boys by the penis. Freud[4] holds that it is the compara-tive unsatisfactoriness of this solution which automatically guides the child to seek a better external penis, and thus ushers in the Oedipus situation where the wish for a baby[5] gradually re-places that for a penis. My own analyses, as do Melanie Klein's "early analyses," indicate that in addition to this there are more direct transitions between the oral and the Oedipus stages. It would seem to me that the tendencies derived from the former stage bifurcate early into clitoris and fellatio directions, i.e., into digital plucking at the clitoris and fellatio phantasies respective-ly; the proportion between the two would naturally be different

[4] Freud, *International Journal of Psychoanalysis*, Vol. VIII, p. 140.

[5] Little is said throughout this paper about the wish for a baby because I am mainly dealing with early stages. I regard the wish as a later deriva-tive of the anal and phallic trends.

in different cases, and this may be expected to have fateful consequences for the later development.

We have now to follow these lines of development in closer
detail, and I will first sketch what I conceive to be the more
normal mode of development, that leading to heterosexuality.
Here the sadistic phase sets in late, and so neither the oral nor
the clitoris stage receives any strong sadistic cathexis. In consequence, the clitoris does not become associated with a particularly active masculine attitude (thrusting forward, etc.), nor
on the other hand is the oral-sadistic fantasy of biting off the
male penis at all highly developed. The oral attitude is mainly
a sucking one and passes by the well-known developmental
transition into the anal stage. The two alimentary orifices thus
constitute the receptive female organ. The anus is evidently
identified with the vagina to begin with, and the differentiation
of the two is an extremely obscure process, more so perhaps
than any other in female development; I surmise, however, that
it takes place in part at an earlier age than is generally supposed.
A variable amount of sadism is always developed in connection
with the anal stage and is revealed in the familiar fantasies of
anal rape which may or may not pass over into beating fantasies.
The Oedipus relationship is here in full activity; and the anal fantasies, as we shall show later, are already a compromise between
libidinal and self-punishment tendencies. This mouth-anus-vagina
stage, therefore, represents an identification with the mother.

What in the meantime has been the attitude toward the penis?
It is likely enough that the initial one is purely positive,[6]
manifested by the desire to suck it. But penis-envy soon sets in
and apparently always. The primary, so to speak auto-erotic,
reasons for this have been well set out by Karen Horney[7] in her
discussion of the part played by the organ in urinary, exhibitionistic, scoptophilic and masturbatory activities. The wish to
possess a penis as the male does passes normally, however, into
the wish to share his penis in some coitus-like action by means of
the mouth, anus or vagina. Various sublimations and reactions

[6] Deutsch, op. cit., p. 19, records an interesting observation in a girl-
child of eighteen months who viewed a penis with apparent indifference
at that time, and who only later developed affective reactions.

[7] Karen Horney, International Journal of Psychoanalysis, Vol. V, pp.
52-54.

show that no woman escapes the early penis-envy stage, but I fully agree with Karen Horney,[8] Helene Deutsch,[9] Melanie Klein,[10] and other workers in their view that what we meet with clinically as penis-envy in the neurosis is only in small part derived from this source. We have to distinguish between what may perhaps be termed pre-Oedipus and post-Oedipus penis-envy (more accurately, auto-erotic and allo-erotic penis-envy), and I am convinced that clinically the latter is much the more significant of the two. Just as masturbatory and other auto-erotic activities owe their main importance to reinvestment from allo-erotic sources, so we have to recognize that many clinical phenomena depend on the defensive function of regression, recently insisted on by Freud.[11] It is the privation resulting from the continued disappointment at never being allowed to share the penis in coitus with the father, or thereby to obtain a baby, that reactivates the girl's early wish to possess a penis of her own. According to the theory put forward above, it is this privation that is primarily the unendurable situation, the reason being that it is tantamount to the fundamental dread of aphanisis. Guilt, and the building-up of the superego, is, as was explained above, the first and invariable defense against the unendurable privation. But this is too negative a solution in itself; the libido must come to expression somehow as well.

There are only two possible ways in which the libido can flow in this situation, though both may, of course, be attempted. The girl must choose, broadly speaking, between sacrificing her erotic attachment to her father and sacrificing her femininity, i.e., her anal identification with the mother. Either the object must be exchanged for another one or the wish must be; it is impossible to retain both. Either the father or the vagina (including pregenital vaginas) must be renounced. In the first case feminine wishes are developed on the adult plane—diffuse erotic charm (narcissism), positive vaginal attitude toward coitus, culminating in pregnancy and child-birth—and are transferred to more accessible objects. In the second case the bond with the

---

[8] *Ibid.*, p. 64.

[9] Deutsch, *op. cit.*, pp. 16-18.

[10] Melanie Klein, communications to the British Psycho-Analytical Society.

[11] Freud, *Hemmung, Symptom und Angst,* 1926, p. 48.

father is retained, but the object-relationship in it is converted into identification, i.e., a penis complex is developed.

More will be said in the next section about the precise way in which this identification defense operates, but what I should like to lay stress on at the moment is the interesting parallelism thus established, already hinted at by Horney,[12] between the solutions of the Oedipus conflict in the two sexes. The boy also is threatened with aphanisis, the familiar castration fear, by the inevitable privation of his incest wishes. He also has to make the choice between changing the wish and changing the object, between renouncing his mother and renouncing his masculinity, i.e., his penis. We have thus obtained a generalization which applies in a unitary manner to boy and girl alike: *faced with aphanisis as the result of inevitable privation, they must renounce either their sex or their incest;* what cannot be retained, except at the price of neurosis, is hetero-erotic and allo-erotic incest, i.e., an incestuous object-relationship. In both cases the situation of prime difficulty is the simple, but fundamental, one of union between penis and vagina. Normally this union is made possible by the overcoming of the Oedipus complex. When, on the other hand, the solution of inversion is attempted every effort is made to avoid the union, because it is bound up with the dread of aphanisis. The individual, whether male or female, then identifies his sexual integrity with possessing the organ of the opposite sex and becomes pathologically dependent on it. With boys this can be done either by using their mouth or anus as the necessary female organ (toward either a man or a masculine woman) or else by vicariously adopting the genitalia of a woman with whom they identify themselves; in the latter case they are dependent on the woman who carries the precious object and develop anxiety if she is absent or if anything in her attitude makes the organ difficult of access. With girls the same alternative presents itself, and they become pathologically dependent on either possessing a penis themselves in their imagination or on having unobstructed access to that of the man with whom they have identified themselves. If the "condition of dependence" (cf. Freud's phrase "Liebesbedingung") is not fulfilled the individuals, man or woman, approach an aphanistic state, or, in

---

[12] Horney, *op. cit.*, p. 64.

looser terminology, "feel castrated." They alternate, therefore, between potency on the basis of inverted gratification and aphanisis. To put it more simply, they either have an organ of the opposite sex or none at all; to have one of their own sex is out of the question.

We have next to turn to the second of our two questions, the difference in the development of heterosexual and homosexual women. This difference was indicated in our discussion of the two alternative solutions of the Oedipus conflict, but it has now to be pursued in further detail. The divergence there mentioned —which, it need hardly be said, is always a matter of degree— between those who surrender the position of their object-libido (father) and those who surrender the position of their subject-libido (sex), can be followed into the field of homosexuality itself. One can distinguish two broad groups here. (1) Those who retain their interest in men, but who set their hearts on being accepted by men as one of themselves. To this group belongs the familiar types of women who ceaselessly complain of the unfairness of women's lot and their unjust ill-treatment by men. (2) Those who have little or no interest in men, but whose libido centers on women. Analysis shows that this interest in women is a vicarious way of enjoying femininity; they merely employ other women to exhibit it for them.[13]

It is not hard to see that the former group corresponds with the class in our previous division where the sex of the subject is surrendered, while the latter group corresponds with those who surrender the object (the father), replacing him by themselves through identification. I will amplify this condensed statement for the sake of greater clarity. The members of the first group exchange their own sex, but retain their first love-object; the object-relationship, however, becomes replaced by identification, and the aim of the libido is to procure recognition of this identification by the former object. The members of the second

---

[13] For the sake of simplicity an interesting third form is omitted in the text, but should be mentioned. Some women obtained gratification of feminine desires provided two conditions are present: (1) that the penis is replaced by a surrogate such as the tongue or finger, and (2) that the partner using this organ is a woman instead of a man. Though clinically they may appear in the guise of complete inversion, such cases are evidently nearer to the normal than either of the two mentioned in the text.

group also identify themselves with the love-object, but then lose further interest in him; their external object-relationship to the other woman is very imperfect, for she merely represents their own femininity through identification, and their aim is vicariously to enjoy the gratification of this at the hand of an unseen man (the father incorporated in themselves).

Identification with the father is thus common to all forms of homosexuality, though it proceeds to a more complete degree in the first group than in the second, where, in a vicarious way, some femininity is after all retained. There is little doubt that this identification serves the function of keeping feminine wishes in repression. It constitutes the most complete denial imaginable of the accusation of harboring guilty feminine wishes, for it asserts, "I cannot possibly desire a man's penis for my gratification, since I already possess one of my own, or at all events I want nothing else than one of my own." Expressed in terms of the theory developed earlier in this paper, it assures the most complete defense against the aphanistic danger of privation from the non-gratification of the incest wishes. The defense is in fact so well designed that it is little wonder that indications of it can be detected in all girls passing through the Oedipus stage of development, though the extent to which it is retained later is extremely variable. I would even venture the opinion that when Freud postulated a "phallic" stage in female development corresponding with that in the male, that is a stage in which all the interest appears to relate to the male organ only with obliteration of the vaginal or pre-vaginal organs, he was giving a clinical description of what may be observed rather than a final analysis of the actual libidinal position at that stage; for it seems to me likely that the phallic stage in normal girls is but a mild form of the father-penis identification of female homosexuals, and, like it, of an essentially secondary and defensive nature.

Horney[14] has pointed out that for a girl to maintain a feminine position and to accept the absence of a penis in herself often signifies not only the daring to have incestuous object-wishes, but also the fantasy that her physical state is the result of a castrating rape once actually performed by the father. The penis identification, therefore, implies a denial of both forms of

---

[14] *Idem, loc. cit.*

guilt, the wish that the incestuous deed may happen in the future and the wish-fulfillment fantasy that it has already happened in the past. She further points out the greater advantage that this heterosexual identification presents to girls than to boys, because the defensive advantage common to both is strengthened with the former by the reinforcement of narcissism derived from the old pre-Oedipus sources of envy (urinary, exhibitionistic and masturbatory) and weakened with the latter by the blow to narcissism involved in the acceptance of castration.

As this identification is to be regarded as a universal phenomenon among young girls, we have to seek further for the motives that heighten it so extraordinarily and in such a characteristic way among those who later become homosexual. Here I must present my conclusions on this point even more briefly than those on the former ones. The fundamental—and, so far as one can see, inborn—factors that are decisive in this connection appear to be two—namely, an unusual intensity of oral erotism and of sadism respectively. These converge in an *intensification of the oral-sadistic stage*, which I would regard, in a word, as *the central characteristic of homosexual development in women*.

The sadism shows itself not only in the familiar muscular manifestations, with the corresponding derivatives of these in character, but also in imparting a specially active (thrusting) quality to the clitoris impulses, which naturally heightens the value of any penis that may be acquired in fantasy. Its most characteristic manifestation, however, is to be found in the oral-sadistic impulse forcibly to wrench the penis from the man by the act of biting. When, as is often found, the sadistic temperament is accompanied by a ready reversal of love to hate, with the familiar ideas of injustice, resentment and revenge, then the biting fantasies gratify both the desire to obtain a penis by force and also the impulse to revenge themselves on the man by castrating him.

The high development of the oral erotism is manifested in the numerous ways well known through the researches of Abraham[15] and Edward Glover;[16] they may be positive or negative in con-

---

[15] Abraham, *op. cit.*, ch. xii.
[16] Edward Glover, "Notes on Oral Character Formation," *International Journal of Psychoanalysis*, Vol. VI, p. 131.

sciousness. A special feature, however, to which attention should be called is the importance of the tongue in such cases. The identification of tongue with penis, with which Flügel[17] and I[18] have dealt at length, reaches with some female homosexuals a quite extraordinary degree of completeness. I have seen cases where the tongue was an almost entirely satisfactory substitute for the penis in homosexual activities. It is evident that the nipple fixation here implied favors the development of homosexuality in two ways. It makes it harder for the girl to pass from the fellatio position to that of vaginal coitus, and it also makes it easier to have recourse once more to a woman as the object of libido.

A further interesting correlation may be effected at this point. The two factors mentioned above of oral erotism and sadism appear to correspond very well with the two classes of homosexuals. Where the oral erotism is the more prominent of the two the individual will probably belong to the second group (interest in women) and where the sadism is the more prominent to the first group (interest in men).

A word should be said about the important factors that influence the *later* development of female homosexuality. We have said that, to protect herself against aphanisis, the girl erects various barriers, notably penis identification, against her femininity. Prominent among these is a strong sense of guilt and condemnation concerning feminine wishes; most often this is for the greater part unconscious. As an aid to this barrier of guilt the idea is developed of "men" (i.e., the father) being strongly opposed to feminine wishes. To help her own condemnation of it she is forced to believe that all men in their hearts disapprove of femininity. To meet this comes the unfortunate circumstance that many men do really evince disparagement of women's sexuality together with dread of the female organ. There are several reasons for this, into which we need not enter here; they all center around the male castration complex. The homosexual woman, however, seizes with avidity on any manifestations of this attitude and can by means of them sometimes convert her deep belief into a complete delusional system. Even in milder forms it is quite common to find both men and women ascribing

[17] J. C. Flügel, "A Note on the Phallic Significance of the Tongue," *International Journal of Psychoanalysis,* Vol. VI, p. 209.

[18] Ernest Jones, *Essays in Applied Psycho-Analysis,* 1923, ch. viii.

the whole of the supposed inferiority of women[19] to the social influences which the deeper tendencies have exploited in the way just indicated.

I will conclude with a few remarks on the subjects of dread and punishment among women in general. The ideas relating to these may be connected mainly with the mother or mainly with the father. In my experience the former is more characteristic of the heterosexual and the latter more of the homosexual. The former appears to be a simple retaliation for the death wishes against the mother, who will punish the girl by coming between her and the father, by sending the girl away forever, or by in any other way seeing to it that her incestuous wishes remain ungratified. The girl's answer is partly to retain her femininity at the cost of renouncing the father and partly to obtain vicarious gratification of her incest wishes in her imagination through identification with the mother.

When the dread mainly relates to the father the punishment takes the obvious form of his withholding gratification of her wishes, and this rapidly passes over into the idea of his disapproval of them. Rebuff and desertion are the common conscious expressions of this punishment. If this privation takes place on the oral plane the answer is resentment and castrating (biting) fantasies. If it takes place on the later anal plane the outcome is rather more favorable. Here the girl manages to combine her erotic wishes with the idea of being punished in a single act —namely, of anal-vaginal rape; the familiar fantasies of being beaten are, of course, a derivative of this. As was remarked above, this is one of the ways in which incest gets equated with castration, so that the penis fantasy is a protection against both.

We may now recapitulate the main conclusions reached here. For different reasons both boys and girls tend to view sexuality in terms of the penis alone, and it is necessary for analysts to be sceptical in this direction. The concept "castration" should be reserved, as Freud pointed out, for the penis alone and should not be confounded with that of "extinction of sexuality," for which the term "aphanisis" is proposed. Privation in respect of sexual wishes evokes with the child the fear of aphanisis, i.e., is equivalent to the dread of frustration. Guilt arises rather from

[19] Really, their inferiority *as* women.

within as a defense against this situation than as an imposition from without, though the child exploits any *moralisches Entgegenkommen* in the outer world.

The oral-erotic stage in the young girl passes directly into the fellatio and clitoris stages, and the former of these then into the anal-erotic stage; the mouth, anus and vagina thus form an equivalent series for the female organ. The repression of the incest wishes results in regression to the pre-Oedipus, or auto-erotic, penis-envy as a defense against them. The penis-envy met with clinically is principally derived from this reaction on the allo-erotic plane, the identification with the father essentially representing denial of femininity. Freud's "phallic phase" in girls is probably a secondary, defensive construction rather than a true developmental stage.

To avoid neurosis both the boy and the girl have to overcome the Oedipus conflict in the same way: they can surrender either the love-object or their own sex. In the latter, homosexual solution they become dependent on imagined possession of the organ of the opposite sex, either directly or through identification with another person of that sex. This yields the two main forms of homosexuality.

The essential factors that decide whether a girl will develop the father-identification in such a high degree as to constitute a clinical inversion are specially intense oral erotism and sadism, which typically combine in an intense oral-sadistic stage. If the former of these two factors is the more prominent one the inversion takes the form of dependence on another woman, with lack of interest in men; the subject is male, but enjoys femininity also through identification with a feminine woman whom she gratifies by a penis substitute, most typically the tongue. Prominence of the second factor leads to occupation with men, the wish being to obtain from them recognition of the subject's male attributes; it is this type that shows so often resentment against men, with castrating (biting) fantasies in respect of them.

The heterosexual woman dreads the mother more than the homosexual woman does, whose dread centers around the father. The punishment feared in the latter case is withdrawal (desertion) on the oral level, beating on the anal one (rectal assault).

II

The Evolution of the Oedipus Complex in Women

By Jeanne Lampl-de Groot

One of the earliest discoveries of psychoanalysis was the existence of the Oedipus complex. Freud found the libidinal relations to the parents to be the center and the acme of the development of childish sexuality and soon recognized in them the nucleus of the neuroses. Many years of psychoanalytical work greatly enriched his knowledge of the developmental processes in this period of childhood; it gradually became clear to him that in both sexes there is both a positive and a negative Oedipus complex and that at this time the libido finds physical outlet in the practice of onanism. Hence the Oedipus complex makes its appearance only when the phallic phase of libido-development is reached and, when the tide of infantile sexuality recedes, that complex must pass in order to make way for the period of latency during which the instinctual tendencies are inhibited in their aim. Nevertheless, in spite of the many observations and studies by Freud and other authors, it has been remarkable how many obscure problems have remained for many years unsolved.[1]

[1] Karl Abraham, "Manifestations of the Female Castration Complex," 1920, *International Journal of Psychoanalysis*, Vol. III, 1922. Franz Alexander, "The Castration Complex in the Formation of Character," *ibid.*, Vol. IV, 1923. Helene Deutsch: *Psychoanalyse der weiblichen Sexualfunktionen*. Neue Arbeiten zur ärztlichen Psychoanalyse, No. V. Karen Horney, "On the Genesis of the Castration Complex in Women," *ibid.*, Vol. V, 1924; "The Flight from Womanhood," *ibid.*, Vol. VII, 1926. J. H. W. Van Ophuijsen, "Contributions to the Masculinity Complex in Women" (1917), *ibid.*, Vol. V, 1924.

It seemed that one very important factor was the connection between the Oedipus and the castration complexes, and there were many points about this which were obscure. Again, understanding of the processes in male children has been carried much further than with the analogous processes in females. Freud ascribed the difficulties in elucidating the early infantile love-relations to the difficulty of getting at the material relating to them: he thought that this was due to the profound repression to which these impulses are subjected. The greater difficulty of understanding these particular mental processes in little girls may arise on the one hand from the fact that they are in themselves more complicated than the analogous processes in boys and, on the other, from the greater intensity with which the libido is repressed in women. Horney thinks that another reason is that, so far, analytical observations have been made principally by men.

In 1924 and 1925 Freud published two works which threw much light on the origin of the Oedipus complex and its connection with the castration complex. The first of these, "The Passing of the Oedipus Complex,"[2] shows what happens to that complex in little boys. It is true that several years previously in the "History of an Infantile Neurosis"[2] and again, in 1923, in the paper entitled "A Neurosis of Demoniacal Possession in the Seventeenth Century,"[2] its fate in certain individual cases had been described. But in "The Passing of the Oedipus Complex" we have the general application and the theoretical appreciation of this discovery and also the further conclusions to be deduced from it. The result arrived at in this paper is as follows: the Oedipus complex in male children receives its death-blow from the castration complex, that is to say, that both in the positive and the negative Oedipus attitude the boy has to fear castration by his father, whose strength is superior to his own. In the first case castration is the punishment for the inadmissible incest-wish and, in the second, it is the necessary condition of the boy's adopting the feminine role in relation to his father. Thus, in order to escape castration and to retain his genital he must renounce his love-relations with both parents. We see the peculiarly important part which this organ plays in boys and the

[2] *Collected Papers.*

enormous psychic significance it acquires in their mental life. Further, analytic experience has shown how extraordinarily difficult it is for a child to give up the possession of the mother, who has been his love-object since he was capable of object-love at all. This reflection leads us to wonder whether the victory of the castration complex over the Oedipus complex, together with the narcissistic interest in the highly prized bodily organ, may not be due also to yet another factor, namely, the tenacity of this first love-relation. Possibly, too, the following train of thought may have some significance: If the boy gives up his ownership of the penis, it means that the possession of the mother (or mother-substitute) becomes forever impossible to him. If, however, forced by the superior power of that far stronger rival, his father, he renounces the fulfillment of his desire, the way remains open to him at some later period to fight his father with greater success and to return to his first love-object, or, more correctly, to her substitute. It seems not impossible that this knowledge of a future chance of fulfilling his wish (a knowledge probably phylogenetically acquired and, of course, unconscious) may be a contributing motive in the boy's temporary renunciation of the prohibited love-craving. This would also explain why before, or just at the beginning of, the latency-period a little boy longs so intensely to be "big" and "grown-up."

In this work, then, Freud largely explains the connections between the Oedipus and the castration-complex in little boys, but he does not tell us much that is new about the same processes in little girls. Hence his paper, published in 1925, "Some Psychological Consequences of the Anatomical Distinction between the Sexes,"[3] throws all the more light on the fate of the early infantile love-impulses of the little girl. Freud holds that in girls the Oedipus complex (he is speaking of the attitude which for the girl is positive: love for the father and rivalry with the mother) is a secondary formation, first introduced by the castration-complex; that is to say, that it arises after the little girl has become aware of the difference between the sexes and has accepted the fact of her own castration. This theory throws a new light on many hitherto obscure problems. By this assump-

---

[3] *International Journal of Psychoanalysis*, Vol. VIII, 1927.

tion Freud explains many later developmental characteristics, various differences in the further vicissitudes of the Oedipus complex in girls and in boys, and in the superego formation in the two sexes, and so forth.

Nevertheless, even after his connection has been discovered, there are several problems which remain unsolved. Freud mentions that, when the castration-complex has become operative in the girl, that is, when she has accepted her lack of the penis and therewith become a victim of penis-envy, "a loosening of the tender relation with the mother as love-object" begins to take place. He thinks that one possible reason for this may be the fact that the girl ultimately holds her mother responsible for her own lack of the penis and, further, quotes a historical factor in the case, namely, that often jealousy is conceived later on against a second child who is more beloved by the mother. But, Freud says, "we do not very clearly understand the connection." According to him another remarkable effect of penis-envy is the girl's struggle against onanism, which is more intense than that of the boy and which, in general, still makes itself felt at a later age. Freud's view is that the reason why the little girl revolts so strongly against phallic onanism is the blow dealt to her narcissism in connection with her penis-envy: she suspects that in this matter it is no use to compete with the boy and therefore it is best not to enter into rivalry with him. This statement gives rise to the involuntary thought: How should the little girl who never possessed a penis and therefore never knew its value from her own experience, regard it as so precious?

Why has the discovery of this lack in herself such far-reaching mental consequences and, above all, why should it begin to produce a mental effect at a certain moment, when it is probable that the bodily difference between herself and little boys has already been perceived countless times without any reaction? Probably the little girl produces pleasurable physical sensations in the clitoris in the same way and presumably with the same degree of intensity as the boy does in the penis, and perhaps she feels them in the vagina too. About this latter fact we received a communication by Josine Müller in the German Psycho-Analytical Society, and I have been told of it by an acquaintance, the mother of two little girls. Why, then, should there be this mental reaction in the girl to the discovery that her own member is smaller than the boy's or is lacking altogether? I should like to try whether the following considerations, which have been suggested to me by experiences in my analytic practice (to be narrated hereafter), may bring us a little nearer to answering these questions.

I think that several points will be clearer to us if we consider the previous history of the castration-complex or penis-envy in little girls. But, before doing so, it will be advisable to examine once more the analogous process in boys. As soon as the little boy is capable of an object-relation he takes as his first love-object the mother who feeds and tends him. As he passes through the pregenital phases of libidinal development he retains always the same object. When he reaches the phallic stage he adopts the typical Oedipus attitude, i.e., he loves his mother and desires to possess her and to get rid of his rival, the father. Throughout this development the love-object remains the same. An alteration in his love-attitude, an alteration characteristic of his sex, occurs at the moment when he accepts the possibility of castration as a punishment threatened by his powerful father for these libidinal desires of his. It is not impossible, indeed it is very probable, that the boy, even before he reaches the phallic stage and adopts the Oedipus attitude which coincides with it, has perceived the difference between the sexes by observing either a sister or a girl playfellow. But we assume that this perception has no further significance to him. If, however, such a perception occurs when he is already in the Oedipus situation and has recognized the possibility of castration as a punishment with which he is threatened, we know how great its significance may be in his mind. The child's first reaction is an endeavor to deny the actuality of castration and to hold very tenaciously to his first love-object. After violent inward struggles, however, the little fellow makes a virtue of necessity; he renounces his love-object in order to retain his penis. Possibly he thus ensures for himself the chance of a renewed and more successful battle with his father at some later date—a possibility which I suggested earlier in this paper. For we know that, when the young man reaches maturity, he succeeds in wresting the victory from his father, normally in relation to a mother-substitute.

Now what happens in the little girl? She, too, takes as her first object-love the mother who feeds and tends her. She, too, retains the same object as she passes through the pregenital phases of libidinal evolution. She, too, enters upon the phallic stage of libido-development. Moreover, the little girl has a bodily organ analogous to the little boy's penis, namely, the clitoris, which gives her pleasurable feelings in masturbation. Physically she behaves exactly like the little boy. We may suppose that in the psychic realm also, children of either sex develop up to this point in an entirely similar manner; that is to say, that girls as well as boys, when they reach the phallic stage enter into the Oedipus situation, i.e., that which for the girl is negative. She wants to conquer the mother for herself and to get rid of the father. Up to this point, too, a chance observation of the difference between the sexes may have been without significance; now, however, a perception of this sort is fraught with serious consequences for the little girl. It strikes her that the boy's genital is larger, stronger and more visible than her own and that he can use it actively in urinating, a process which for the child has a sexual significance. When she makes this comparison, the little girl must feel her own organ to be inferior. She imagines that hers was once like the boy's and that it has been taken from her as a punishment for her prohibited love-cravings in relation to the mother. At first the little girl tries, as does the boy, to deny the fact of castration or to comfort herself with the idea that she will grow a genital. The acceptance of castration has for her the same consequences as for the boy. Not only does her narcissism suffer a blow on account of her physical inferiority, but she is forced to renounce the fulfillment of her first love-longings. Now at this point the difference in the psychic development of the two sexes sets in, in connection, that is, with the perception of the anatomical difference between male and female. To the boy castration was only a threat, which can be escaped by a suitable modification of behavior. To the girl it is an accomplished fact, which is irrevocable, but the recognition of which compels her finally to renounce her first love-object and to taste to the full the bitterness of its loss. Normally, the female child is bound at some time to come to this recognition: she is forced thereby completely to abandon her negative Oedipus attitude, and with it the onanism which is its accompaniment. The object-libidinal relation to the mother is transformed into an identification with her; the father is chosen as a love-object, the enemy becomes the beloved. Now, too, there arises the desire for the child in the place of the wish for the penis. A child of her own acquires for the girl a similar narcissistic value to that which the penis possesses for the boy; for only a woman, and never a man, can have children.

The little girl, then, has now adopted the positive Oedipus attitude with the very far-reaching after-results of which we are so familiar. Freud has explained more than once that there is no motive for the shattering of the positive Oedipus complex in the female such as we have in the threat of castration in the case of the boy. Hence, the female Oedipus complex vanishes only gradually, is largely incorporated in the normal development of the woman, and explains many of the differences between the mental life of women and of men.

We may now sum up by saying that the little girl's castration complex (or her discovery of the anatomical difference between the sexes) which, according to Freud, ushers in and renders possible her normal, positive Oedipus attitude, has its psychic correlative just as that of the boy, and it is only this correlative which lends it its enormous significance for the mental evolution of the female child. In the first years of her development as an individual (leaving out of account the phylogenetic influences which, of course, are undeniable) she behaves exactly like a boy not only in the matter of onanism but in other respects in her mental life: in her love-aim and object-choice she is actually a little man. When she has discovered and fully accepted the fact that castration has taken place, the little girl is forced once and for all to renounce her mother as love-object and therewith to give up the active, conquering tendency of her love-aim as well as the practice of clitoral onanism. Perhaps here, too, we have the explanation of a fact with which we have long been familiar, namely, that the woman who is wholly feminine does not know object-love in the true sense of the word: she can only "let herself be loved." Thus it is to the mental accompaniments of phallic onanism that we must ascribe the fact that the little girl normally represses this practice much more energetically and has to make a far more intense struggle against it than the boy. For she has to forget with it the first love-disappointment, the pain of the first loss of a love-object.

We know how often this repression of the little girl's negative

Oedipus attitude is wholly or partly unsuccessful. For the female as well as for the male child it is very hard to give up the first love-object: in many cases the little girl clings to it for an abnormally long time. She tries to deny the punishment (castration) which would inevitably convince her of the forbidden nature of her desires. She firmly refuses to give up her masculine position. If later her love-longing is disappointed a second time, this time in relation to the father who does not give way to her passive wooing of his love, she often tries to return to her former situation and to resume a masculine attitude. In extreme cases this leads to the manifest homosexuality of which Freud gives so excellent and clear an account in "A Case of Female Homosexuality."[4] The patient about whom Freud tells us in this work made a faint effort on entering puberty to adopt a feminine love attitude but, later in the period of puberty, she behaved toward an elder woman whom she loved exactly like a young man in love. At the same time she was a pronounced feminist, denying the difference between man and woman; thus she had gone right back to the first, negative phase of the Oedipus complex.

There is another process which is perhaps commoner. The girl does not entirely deny the fact of castration, but she seeks for overcompensation for her bodily inferiority on some plane other than the sexual (in her work, her profession). But in so doing she represses sexual desires altogether, that is, remains sexually unmoved. It is as if she wished to say: "I may not and cannot love my mother, and so I must give up any further attempt to love at all." Her belief in her possession of the penis has then been shifted to the intellectual sphere; there the woman can be masculine and compete with the man.

We may observe as a third possible outcome that a woman may form relationships with a man, and yet remain nevertheless inwardly attached to the first object of her love, her mother. She is obliged to be frigid in coitus because she does not really desire the father or his substitute, but the mother. Now these considerations place in a somewhat different light the fantasies of prostitution so common amongst women. According to this view they would be an act of revenge, not so much against the father as against the mother. The fact that prostitutes are so

[4] *Collected Papers.*

often manifest or disguised homosexuals might be explained in analogous fashion as follows: the prostitute turns to the man out of revenge against the mother, but her attitude is not that of passive feminine surrender but of masculine activity; she captures the man on the street, castrates him by taking his money and thus makes herself the masculine and him the feminine partner in the sexual act.

I think that in considering these disturbances in the woman's development to complete femininity we must keep two possibilities in view. Either the little girl has never been able wholly to give up her longing to possess her mother and thus has formed only a weak attachment to her father, or she has made an energetic attempt to substitute her father for her mother as love-object but, after suffering a fresh disappointment at his hands, has returned to her first position.

In the paper "Some Psychological Consequences of the Anatomical Distinction between the Sexes," Freud draws attention to the fact that jealousy plays a far greater part in the mental life of women than in that of men. He thinks that the reason for this is that in the former jealousy is reinforced by deflected penis-envy. Perhaps one might add that a woman's jealousy is stronger than a man's because she can never succeed in securing her first love-object, while the man, when he grows up, has the possibility of doing so.

In another paragraph Freud traces the fantasy "A child is being beaten" ultimately to the masturbation of the little girl when in the phallic phase. The child which is beaten or caressed is at bottom the clitoris (i.e., the penis); the being beaten is on one hand the punishment for the forbidden genital relation and on the other a regressive substitute for it. But in this phase the punishment for prohibited libidinal relations is precisely castration. Thus the formula "A child is being beaten" means "a child is being castrated." In the fantasies in which the child beaten is a stranger, the idea of its being castrated is intelligible at the first glance. It means: "No one else shall have what I have not got." Now we know that in the fantasies of puberty, which are often greatly metamorphosed and condensed, the child beaten by the father always represents as well the girl herself. Thus she is constantly subjecting herself to castration, for this is the necessary condition of being loved by the father; she is making a fresh effort to get clear of her old love-relations and reconcile herself to her womanhood. In spite of the many punishments, pains and tortures which the hero has to undergo, the fantasies always end happily,[5] i.e., the sacrifice having been made, the passive, feminine love is victorious. Sometimes this immolation permits the return to masturbation, the first forbidden love-tendency having been duly expiated. Often, however, onanism remains none the less prohibited, or it becomes unconscious and is practiced in some disguised form, sometimes accompanied by a deep sense of guilt. It seems as though the repeated submission to the punishment of castration signifies not only the expiation due to the feelings of guilt but also a form of wooing the father, whereby the subject experiences also masochistic pleasure.

To sum up what I have said above: In little boys who develop normally, the positive Oedipus attitude is by far the more prevalent, for by adopting it the child through his temporary renunciation of the mother-object can retain his genital and perhaps ensure for himself thereby the possibility of winning later in life a mother-substitute; if he adopted the negative attitude, it would mean that he must renounce both from the outset. Little girls, however, normally pass through both situations in the Oedipus complex: first the negative, which occurs under precisely the same conditions as in boys, but which they are compelled finally to abandon when they discover and accept the fact of their castration. Now, the girl's attitude changes; she identifies herself with the lost love-object and puts in its place her former rival, the father, thus passing into the positive Oedipus situation. Thus, in female children the castration-complex deals a death-blow to the negative Oedipus attitude and ushers in the positive Oedipus complex.

This view confirms Freud's hypothesis that the (positive) Oedipus complex in women is made possible and ushered in by the castration-complex. But, in contradistinction to Freud, we are assuming that the castration-complex in female children is a secondary formation and that its precursor is the negative Oedipus situation. Further, that it is only from the latter that the castration-complex derives its great psychic significance, and it is probably this negative attitude which enables us to explain

[5] Compare Anna Freud: *Schlagephantasie und Tagtraum, Imago,* VIII, 1922.

in greater detail many peculiarities subsequently met with in the mental life of women.

I am afraid it will be objected that all this looks like speculation and is lacking in any empirical basis. I must reply that this objection may be just as regards part of what I have said, but that nevertheless the whole argument is built up on a foundation of practical experience, although unfortunately this is still but meager. I shall now give a short account of the material which has led me to my conclusions.

Some time ago I was treating a young girl who had been handed over to me by a male colleague. He had analyzed her for some years already, but there were certain difficulties connected with the transference which resisted solution. This girl had suffered from a somewhat severe hysterical neurosis. Her analysis had already been carried a good way. The normal, positive Oedipus complex, her rivalry with her sister and her envy of her younger brother's penis had been dealt with thoroughly, and the patient had understood and accepted them. Many of her symptoms had disappeared, but nevertheless she remained to her great regret unfit for work. When she came to me, the unresolved, ambivalent transference to the male analyst was playing a principal part in the situation. It was difficult to determine which was the stronger: her passionate love or her no less passionate hate. I knew this patient personally before she came to me for treatment, and the analysis began with a strong positive transference to me. Her attitude was rather that of a child who goes to its mother for protection. But after a short time a profound change began to take place. The patient's behavior became first rebellious and hostile and soon, behind this attitude, there was revealed a very deepseated and wholly active tendency to woo my love. She behaved just like a young man in love, displaying, for instance, a violent jealousy of a young man whom she suspected of being her rival in real life. One day she came to analysis with the idea that she would like to read all Freud's writing and become an analyst herself. The obvious interpretation which we tried first, namely, that she wanted to identify herself with me, proved inadequate. A series of dreams showed an unmistakable desire to get rid of my own analyst, to "castrate" him and take his place, so as to be able to analyze (possess) me. In this connection the patient remembered various situations in her childhood when her parents quarrelled and she assumed a defensive and protective attitude toward her mother, and also times when they displayed mutual affection and she detested her father and wished to have her mother to herself. The analysis had long ago revealed a strong positive attachment to the father and also the experience which put an end to this. As a child the patient slept in a room next to her parents' and was in the habit of calling them at night when she had to urinate; of course, the intention was to disturb them. At first she generally demanded that her mother should come but, later on, her father.

She said that, when she was five years old, this once happened again and her father came to her and quite unexpectedly boxed her ears. From that moment the child resolved to hate him. The patient produced yet another recollection: when she was four years old she dreamed that she was lying in bed with her mother beside her and that she had a sense of supreme bliss. In her dream her mother said: "That is right, that is how it ought to be." The patient awoke and found that she had passed urine in bed; she was greatly disappointed and felt very unhappy.

She had various recollections of the time when she still slept in her parents' room. She said she used often to awake in the night and sit up in bed. These recollections are a fairly certain indication that she observed her parents' coitus. The dream she had as a child may very well have been dreamt after such an observation. It clearly represents coitus with her mother, accompanied by a sense of bliss. Even in later life urethral erotism played a particularly important part in this patient. Her disappointment on awaking showed that she was already conscious of her inability to possess her mother: she had long ago discovered the male genital in her younger brother. The bed-wetting can be construed either as a substitute for or a continuation of masturbation; the dream shows how intense must have been her emotional relation to her mother at that time. Hence it is clear that the patient, after the disappointment with her faher (the box on the ears) tried to return to the earlier object, whom she had loved at the time of the dream, i.e., to her mother. When she grew up she made a similar attempt. After an unsuccessful love-affair with a younger brother of her father's she had for a short time a homosexual relation. This situation was repeated in her analysis when she came from the male analyst to me.

This patient stated that she had had a special form of the beating fantasy when she was from eight to ten years old. She described it as "the hospital fantasy." The gist of it was as follows: A large number of patients went to a hospital to get well. But they had to endure the most frightful pains and tortures. One of the most frequent practices was that they were flayed alive. The patient had a feeling of shuddering pleasure when she imagined their painful, bleeding wounds. Her associations brought recollections of how her younger brother sometimes pushed back the foreskin of his penis, whereupon she saw something red, which she thought of as a wound. The method of cure in her fantasy was therefore obviously a representation of castration. She identified herself on one occasion with the patients, who at the end always got well and left the hospital with great gratitude. But generally she had a different role. She was the protecting, compassionate Christ, who flew over the beds in the ward, in order to bring relief and comfort to the sick people. In this fantasy, which reveals its sexual-symbolic character in the detail of *flying*, the patient is the man who alone possesses his mother (for Christ was born without father), but who finally, in order to atone for the guilt and to be able to reach God the Father, offered the sacrifice of crucifixion (castration). After we broke off the analysis, which the patient gave up in a state of negative transference, a reaction to the disappointment of her love, she tried to translate this fantasy into reality by deciding to become a nurse. After a year, however, she abandoned this new profession for her earlier one, which was more masculine in character and much more suited to her temperament. Gradually, too, her feelings of hate toward me disappeared.

I had a second patient in whom I discovered similar processes with regard to the transference. In the first two months of treatment this patient produced very strong resistances. She acted the part of a naughty, defiant child and would utter nothing but monotonous compaints to the effect that she was forsaken and that her husband treated her badly. After we had succeeded in discovering that her resistance arose from feelings of hate toward me, due to envy and jealousy, the full, positive, feminine Oedipus attitude gradually developed in her—there entered into it both love for the father and the wish for a child. Soon, too, penis-envy began to show itself. She produced a recollection from her fifth or sixth year. She said that she had once put on her elder brother's clothes and displayed herself proudly to all and sundry. Besides this she had made repeated efforts to urinate like a boy. At a later period she always felt that she was very stupid and inferior and thought that the other members of her family treated her as if this were the case. During puberty she conceived a remarkably strong aversion from every sort of sexual interest. She would listen to none of the mysterious conversations in which her girl-friends joined. She was interested only in intellectual subjects, literature, etc. When she married she was frigid. During her analysis she experienced a desire to have some profession; this stood to her for being male. But her feelings of inferiority forbade any real attempt to compass this ambition. Up to this point the analysis had made splendid progress. The patient had one peculiarity: she remembered very little, but she enacted all the more in her behavior. Envy and jealousy and the desire to do away with the mother were repeated in the most diverse guises in the transference. After this position had been worked through, a new resistance presented itself; we discovered behind it deep homosexual desires having reference to myself. The patient now began to woo my love in a thoroughly masculine manner. The times of these declarations of love, during which in her dreams and fantasies she always pictured herself with a male genital, invariably coincided with some active behavior in real life. They alternated, however, with periods in which her behavior was wholly passive. At such times the patient was once more incapable of anything; she failed in everything, suffered from her inferiority and was tortured with feelings of guilt. The meaning of this was that every time she conquered the mother, she was impelled to castrate herself in order to get free from her sense of guilt. Her attitude to masturbation also was noteworthy. Before analysis she had never consciously practiced this habit; during the period when she was being treated she began clitoral masturbation. At first this onanism was accompanied by a strong sense of guilt; later, at times when her love-wishes in relation to her father were most vehemently manifested, the feelings of guilt abated. They were succeeded by the fear that the onanism might do her some physical harm: "weaken her genitals." At the stage when she was in love with me the sense of guilt reappeared and she gave up masturbating, because this fear became in her mind a certainty. Now this "weakening" of the genital organs signified castration. Thus the patient constantly oscillated between a heterosexual and homosexual love. She had a tendency to regress to her first love-relation—with the mother—and at this stage tried to deny the fact of castration. To make up, however, she had to refrain from onanism and sexual gratification of any kind. She could not derive satisfaction from her husband, because she herself really wanted to be a man in order to be able to possess the mother.

Thus, in both the cases which I have quoted it was plain that behind the woman's positive Oedipus attitude there lay a negative attitude, with the mother as love-object, which revealed itself later in the analysis and therefore had been experienced at an earlier stage of development. Whether this evolution is typical cannot, of course, be asserted with any certainty from the observation of two cases. I should be inclined to believe that in other female patients the Oedipus complex has had a similar previous history, but I have not been able to gather enough material from their analyses to establish this beyond question. The phase of the negative Oedipus attitude, lying, as it does, so far back in the patient's mental history, cannot be reached until the analysis has made very considerable progress. Perhaps with a male analyst it may be very hard to bring this period to light at all. For it is difficult for a female patient to enter into rivalry with the father-analyst, so that possibly treatment under these conditions cannot get beyond the analysis of the positive Oedipus attitude. The homosexual tendency, which can hardly be missed in any analyses, may then merely give the impression of a later reaction to the disappointment experienced at the father's hands. In our cases, however, it was clearly a regression to an earlier phase—one which may help us to understand better the enormous psychic significance that the lack of a penis has in the erotic life of women. I do not know whether in the future it will turn out that my exposition in this paper explains only the development of these two patients of mine. I think it not impossible that it may be found to have a more general significance. Only the gathering of further material will enable us to decide this question.

III

Some Effects of the Derogatory Attitude Toward Female Sexuality*

In an earlier paper[1] I stressed the fact that the actual envy of the penis as such is not as important in the psychology of women as their envy of the position of the male in our society. This position of privilege and alleged superiority is symbolized by the possession of a penis. The owner of this badge of power has special opportunities while those without have more limited possibilities. I questioned in that paper whether the penis in its own right as a sexual organ was necessarily an object of envy at all.

That there are innate biological differences between the sexual life of man and woman is so obvious that one must apologize for mentioning it. Yet those who stress this aspect most are too often among the first to claim knowledge of the psychic experiences and feelings of the opposite sex. Thus for many centuries male writers have been busy trying to explain the female. In recent years a few women have attempted to present the inner life of their own sex, but they themselves seem to have had difficulty in freeing their thinking from the male orientation. Psychoanalysts, female as well as male, seem for

---

* Read at a Symposium on Feminine Psychology, given under the auspices of the Department of Psychiatry of the New York Medical College, March 19, 1950.
[1] Clara Thompson, "Penis Envy in Women," *Psychiatry* VI (1943), 123-25.

the most part still to be dominated by Freud's thinking about women.

Freud was a very perceptive thinker but he was a male, and a male quite ready to subscribe to the theory of male superiority prevalent in the culture. This must have definitely hampered his understanding of experiences in a woman's life, especially those specifically associated with her feminine role.

Of course this thinking can be carried to extreme lengths and one can say that no human being can really know what another human being actually experiences about anything. However, the presence of similar organs justifies us in thinking that we can at least approximate an understanding of another person's experiences in many cases. A headache, a cough, a pain in the heart, intestinal cramps, weeping, laughter, joy, a sense of well-being—we assume that all of these feel to other people very similar to what we ourselves experience under those titles.

In the case of sexual experiences, however, one sex has no adequate means of identifying with the experience of the other sex. A woman, for instance, cannot possibly be sure that she knows what the subjective experience of an erection and male orgasm is. Nor can a man identify with the tension and sensations of menstruation, or female genital excitation, or childbirth. Since for many years most of the psychoanalysts were men this may account for the prevalence of some misconceptions about female sexuality. Horney pointed out in 1926 that Freud's theory that little girls believed they had been castrated and that they envied boys their penises is definitely a male orientation to the subject.[2] In this paper she listed several ideas which little boys have about girls' genitals. These ideas, she shows, are practically identical with the classical psychoanalytic conception of the female. The little boys' ideas are based on the assumption that girls also have penises, which results in a shock at the discovery of their absence. A boy, reasoning from his own life experience, assumes this is a multilation, as a punishment for sexual misdemeanor. This makes more vivid to him any castration threats which have been made to him. He concludes that the girl must feel inferior and envy him because she must have come to the same conclusions about her state. In short, the little boy, in-

[2] Karen Horney, "Flight from Womanhood," International Journal of Psycho-Analysis, VII (1926), 324-39.

capable of imagining that one could feel complete without a penis, assumes that the little girl must feel deprived. It is doubtless true that her lack of a penis can activate any latent anxiety the boy may have about the security of his own organ, but it does not necessarily follow that the girl feels more insecure because of it.

In the "Economic Problem of Masochism"[3] Freud assumes that masochism is a part of female sexuality, but he gives as his evidence the fantasies of passive male homosexuals. What a passive male homosexual imagines about the experience of being a woman is not necessarily similar to female sexual experience. In fact, a healthy woman's sexual life is probably not remotely similar to the fantasies and longings of a highly disturbed passive male personality.

Recently I heard to my amazement that a well-known psychiatrist had told a group of students that in the female sexual life there is no orgasm. I can only explain such a statement by assuming that this man could not conceive of orgasm in the absence of ejaculation. If he had speculated that the female orgasm must be a qualitatively different experience from that of the male because of the absence of ejaculation, one could agree that this may well be the case. I think these examples suffice to show that many current ideas about female psychosexual life may be distorted by being seen through male eyes.

In "Sex and Character"[4] Fromm has pointed out that the biological differences in the sexual experience may contribute to greater emphasis on one or the other character trends in the two sexes. Thus he notes that for the male it is necessary to be able to perform, while no achievement is required of the female. This, he believes, can have a definite effect on the general character trends. This gives the man a greater need to demonstrate, to produce, to have power, while the woman's need is more in the direction of being accepted, being desirable. Since her satisfaction is dependent on the man's ability to produce, her fear is in being abandoned, being frustrated, while his is fear of failure. Fromm points out that the woman can make herself available at any time and give satisfaction to the man, but

[3] Freud, *Collected Papers*, II, 225-68; London: Hogarth Press, 1925.
[4] Erich Fromm, "Sex and Character," *Psychiatry*, VI (1943), 21-31.

the man's possibility of satisfying her is not entirely within his control. He cannot always produce an erection at will.

The effect of basic sexual differences on the character structure is not pertinent to this paper. Fromm's thesis that the ability to perform is important in male sexual life, that it is espcially a matter of concern to the male because it is not entirely within his control, and that the female may perform at all times if she so wishes, are points of importance in my thesis. But I should like to develop somewhat different aspects of the situation. Fromm shows that the woman can at any time satisfy the male, and he mentions the male's concern over successfully performing for the female, but he does not at any point discuss how important obtaining satisfaction for themselves is in the total reaction.

In general the male gets at least some physiological satisfaction out of his sexual performance. Some experiences are more pleasurable than others, to be sure, and there are cases of orgasm without pleasure. However, for the very reason that he cannot force himself to perform, he is less likely to find himself in the midst of a totally uncongenial situation.

The female, however, who permits herself to be used when she is not sexually interested or is at most only mildly aroused frequently finds herself in the midst of an unsatisfactory experience. At most she can have only a vicarious satisfaction in the male's pleasure. I might mention parenthetically here that some male analysts, for example Ferenczi, are inclined to think that identification with the male in his orgasm constitutes a woman's true sexual fulfillment. This I would question.

One frequently finds resentment in women who have for some reason consented to being used for the male's pleasure. This is in many cases covered by an attitude of resignation. A frequent answer from women when they are asked about marital sexual relations is: "It is all right. He doesn't bother me much." This attitude may hold even when in other respects the husband and wife like each other; that is, such an attitude may exist even when the woman has not been intimidated by threats or violence. She simply assumes that her interests are not an important consideration.

Obviously the sexual act is satisfactory to the woman only when she actively and from choice participates in her own characteristic way. If she considered herself free to choose, she would refuse the male except when she actually did desire to participate.

This being the case, it might be fruitful to examine the situation in which the woman submits with little or no interest. There are, of course, occasions when she genuinely wishes to do this for the man's sake; this does not create a problem. More frequently the cause is a feeling of insecurity in the relationship; this insecurity may arise from external factors—that is, the male concerned may insist on his satisfaction or else! The insecurity may also arise from within because of the woman's own feelings of inadequacy. These feelings may arise simply from the fact that the woman subscribes to the cultural attitude that her needs are not as insistent as the man's; but in addition she may have personal neurotic difficulties.

The question arises, How has it become socially acceptable for a man to insist on his sexual rights whenever he desires? Is this because rape is a possibility, and the woman is physically relatively defenseless? This must have had some influence in the course of society's development. However, it has often been proved that even rape is not easy without some cooperation from the woman. The neurotic condition of vaginismus illustrates that in some conditions even unconscious unwillingness on the part of the woman may effectively block male performance. So while the superior physical power of the male may be an important factor in the frequency of passive compliance, there must be other factors. These other factors are not of a biological nature, for the participation in sexual relations without accompanying excitement is most obviously possible in human females, although not definitely impossible in other animals.

One must look to cultural attitudes for the answer. There are two general concepts which are significant here, and to which both men and women subscribe in our culture. One is that the female sexual drive is not as pressing or important as the male. Therefore there is less need to be concerned in satisfying it or considering it. The other is the analytically much discussed thesis that the female sex organs are considered inferior to those of the male.

In recent years there has been a definite tendency to move away from the first idea as far as actual sexual performance is concerned. With the increasing tendency to be more open in observing facts about sex, women in many groups have become able to admit not only to themselves but also to men that their sexual needs are important. However, this is still not true of all groups. Moreover, at almost the same time another important aspect of woman's sexual life has diminished in importance; that is, the bearing of children. Woman's specific type of creativeness is no longer highly desired in many situations. This is an important subject in itself and will not be discussed here.

As we know, during the Victorian era a woman's sexual needs were supposed to be practically nonexistent. A woman was expected to be able to control her sexual desires at all times. Thus an extramarital pregnancy was allegedly entirely due to the woman's weakness or depravity. The man's participation in such an extramarital relationship was looked upon with more tolerance, and there was little or no social disgrace attached to him. The double standard of sexual morality also implied an assumption that woman's sexual drive was not as insistent as the male's.

The fact that evidence of erotic excitement could be concealed much better by a woman than by a man made the development of such thinking possible. Since she was not supposed to be erotic and since the man must have his satisfaction, a pattern was developed in which the dutiful wife offered herself to her husband without actively participating in the act herself. I am sure many women were sufficiently normal to find nonparticipation difficult, and doubtless many men did not subscribe to the feeling that they should be horrified at any evidence of passion in their wives. Nevertheless as recently as twenty years ago a woman, who consulted me about her marital difficulties, reported that her husband felt disgust, it seemed, whenever she responded sexually to him. She tried to conceal her sexual responses, including orgasm, from him, then would lie awake the rest of the night in misery and rage. Since I saw this woman only twice, I am not in a position to say how much this situation contributed to her suicide about a year later. Undoubtedly there were many other difficulties in her relation to her husband of which the sexual may have been only one expression. Certainly this extreme denial of sexual interest is seldom required of women today, but an attenuated form still remains, especially in marriage. Here it is found not only in frigid women who, realizing their inadequacy as mates, make amends as best they can by a nonparticipating offering of themselves. But one also finds the attitude even in women with adequate sexual responsiveness in many situations. They have accepted the idea that the male's needs are greater than their own and that therefore his wishes and needs are paramount.

So the feeling that woman's sexual life is not as important or insistent as the male's may produce two unfortunate situations. It may inhibit the woman's natural expression of desire for fear of appearing unwomanly, or it may lead her to feel she must be ready to accommodate on all occasions—that is, she has no rights of her own. Both extremes mean an interference with her natural self-expression and spontaneity with resulting resentment and discontent.

Moreover, since the male has often been indoctrinated with the idea that woman's sexual life is not important, he may not exert himself much to make her interested. He fails to see the importance of the art of love.

When an important aspect of a person's life becomes undervalued, this has a negative effect on the self-esteem. What a woman actually has to offer in sexual responsiveness becomes undervalued, and this in turn affects her own evaluation of herself as a person.

The second way in which our culture has minimized woman's sexual assets is in the derogation of her genitals. This in classical terminology is connected with the idea of penis envy. I wish to approach the problem differently. As I said earlier, the idea of penis envy is a male concept. It is the male who experiences the penis as a valuable organ and he assumes that women also must feel that way about it. But a woman cannot really imagine the sexual pleasure of the penis—she can only appreciate the social advantages its possessor has.[5] What a woman needs rather is a feeling of the importance of her own organs. I believe that much more important than penis envy in the psychology of woman is her reaction to the undervaluation of her own organs. I think we can concede that the acceptance of one's body and all its func-

[5] I do not wish to leave the impression that there is never a woman who thinks she desires to possess the male genital as such, but I believe such women are found relatively rarely.

tions is a basic need in the establishment of self-respect and self-esteem.

The short plump brunette girl may feel that she would be more acceptable if she were a tall thin blonde—in other words, if she were somebody else. The solution of her problem lies not in becoming a blonde but in finding out why she is not accepting of what she is. The history will show either that some significant person in her early life preferred a tall blonde or that being a brunette has become associated with other unacceptable characteristics. Thus in one case in which this envy of the blonde type was present, being brunette meant being sexy, and being sexy was frowned upon.

Sex in general has come under the disapproval of two kinds of thinking in our culture. The Puritan ideal is denial of body pleasure, and this makes sexual needs something of which to be ashamed. Traces of this attitude still remain today in the feelings of both sexes.

We also have another attitude which derogates sexuality, especially female sexuality. We are people with great emphasis on cleanliness. In many people's minds the genital organs are classed with the organs of excretion and thus become associated with the idea of being unclean. With the male some of the curse is removed because he gets rid of the objectionable product. The female, however, receives it, and when her attitude is strongly influenced by the dirty excretion concept, this increases her feeling of unacceptability. Moreover, the men who feel the sexual product is unclean reinforce the woman's feeling that her genitals are unclean.

The child's unrestrained pleasure in his body and its products begins to be curbed at an early age. This is such a fundamental part of our basic training that most of us would have difficulty imagining the effect on our psychic and emotional life of a more permissive attitude. What has happened is that this training has created a kind of moral attitude toward our body products. Sphincter morality, as Ferenczi has called it, extends to more than the control of urine and feces. To some extent genital products come also under the idea of sphincter morality. Obviously this especially has an influence on attitudes toward the female genitals where no sphincter control is possible. My attention was first called to this by a paper written in German by Bertram Lewin twenty years ago.[6] In this paper he presented, among other things, clinical data in which the menses were compared to an unwanted loss of feces and urine due to lack of sphincter control. In one case which he reported the woman had become very proficient at contracting the vaginal muscles so that she attained some semblance of control of the quantity of menstrual flow. Although in my own practice I have never encountered a patient who actually tried to produce a sphincter, I have frequent evidence that the inability to control not only menstruation but all secretions of the female genitals has contributed to a feeling of unacceptability and dirtiness. One patient on being presented by her mother with a perineal napkin on the occasion of her first menses refused to use it. To her it meant a baby's diaper, and she felt completely humiliated. Obviously she presently felt even more humiliated because of the inevitable consequences of her refusal.

Also because of the culture's overevaluation of cleanliness another attribute of the female genital can be a source of distress, that is, the fact that it has an odor. Thus one of the chief means by which the female attracts the male among animals has been labeled unpleasant, to many even disgusting. For example, a female patient whose profession requires her appearing before audiences has been greatly handicapped for many years by a feeling of being "stinking" which is greatly augmented whenever she is in a position to have her body observed. Thus she can talk over the radio but not before an audience. Another patient felt for years that she could never marry because she would not be able to keep her body clean at every moment in the presence of her husband. Whenever she had a date with a man she prepared for it by a very vigorous cleansing of the genitals, especially trying to make them dry. When she finally had sexual relations she was surprised and greatly helped in her estimation of her body by discovering that this highly prized dryness was just the opposite of what was pleasing to the man.

In two cases the feeling of genital unacceptability had been a factor in promiscuity. In each case an experience with a man who kissed her genitals in an obviously accepting way was the

---

[6] B. Lewin, "Kotschmieren, Menses und weibliches Über-Ich," *Internat. Zschr. Psychoanal*, XVI (1930), 43-56.

final step in bringing about a complete transformation of feeling. In both cases all need to be promiscuous disappeared, and each of the women felt loved for the first time.

I am obviously oversimplifying these cases in order to make my point clear. I do not wish to leave the impression that the feeling of dirtiness connected with the genitals was the sole cause of a feeling of unacceptability in these patients. There was in each case a feeling from early childhood of not being acceptable, produced by specific attitudes in the parents. The feeling of unacceptability became focused on the genitals eventually for different reasons in each case. For example, in three cases the woman had risen above the lowly social position of her parents and with each of these three women the feeling of having dirty genitals became symbolic of her lowly origin of which she was ashamed. The parents had not placed such an emphasis on baths as they found to be the case in the new social milieu. Therefore any evidence of body secretion or odor betrayed them, and this made sex itself evidence of lower-class origin. On the other hand two other patients suffered from their own mothers' overemphasis on body cleanliness. In each of these two cases the mother was cold and puritanical as well as overclean, and the patient felt humiliated because she had a more healthy sexual drive which she felt was proclaimed to the world by her body's odors and secretions.

From these observations I hope I have emphasized the fact that the problem of a woman's sexual life is not in becoming reconciled to having no penis but in accepting her own sexuality in its own right. In this she is hampered by certain attitudes in the culture such as that her sexual drive is not important and her genitals are not clean. With these two deprecatory cultural attitudes in the background of women's lives it is to be expected that both are important points at which difficulties in interpersonal relations may be expressed.

IV

Contributions to the Masculinity Complex in Women[*]

By J. H. W. VAN OPHUIJSEN

In his essay on "Some Character-Types Met with in Psycho-Analysis," Freud writes: "As we learn from our psycho-analytic work all women feel that they have been injured in their infancy, and that through no fault of their own they have been slighted and robbed of a part of their body; and the bitterness of many a daughter towards her mother has as its ultimate cause the reproach that the mother has brought her into the world as a woman instead of a man."[1] These lines came to my notice at the very moment when my attention had been directed in a small sequence of cases to a particular form of reaction to the complex referred to, and when I believed that in one case I also had determined some of the conditions of its origin. In the following paper I will give an account of my conclusions.

The type of reaction with which we are concerned is, in common with the castration complex in women, founded on a belief in the possibility of possessing a male genital organ. The chief difference between the two lies in the fact that a consciousness of guilt belongs to the castration complex. The loss, the damage, or the faulty development of the genital organ is supposed to be the result of wrongdoing, often punishment for a sexual lapse. The feeling of guilt is absent in the cases of which I shall speak here—not always, of course, completely, but the feeling of having

[*] From a paper delivered before the Dutch Psycho-Analytical Society, June 23, 1917.
[1] *Sammlung Kleiner Schriften.* Vierte Folge.

been ill-treated and the consequent reaction of bitterness is in all very strongly developed. In view of this second group of cases, in which the protest (which seeks to make up for the want) is predominant, I propose to introduce the term masculinity complex.

The origin of the masculinity complex is, of course, to be traced to the sight of a male organ, belonging either to the father or the brother, or some other man; and in the history of most women patients, and without exception in those with a strongly marked masculinity complex, there is found the memory of such an observation and of the comparison of the patient's own body with that of a man. In one of the cases I have analyzed, the patient, D., tells me quite clearly that the wish to be a boy developed from the desire to be able to urinate like a boy, after she once saw a boy perform this act. This incident has determined till today the manner of her sexual satisfaction through masturbation. Another patient, H., was able to observe her father and uncle, who were not ashamed to urinate before her.

Yet the question arises, by what instincts the fantasy of masculinity is nourished, and how it is that the fantasy, in spite of later experience and information, not only continues to exist but even causes women frequently to behave as though they possessed male genitals. A patient, P., tells me that for some time past in urinating she has given up a sitting for a standing position, nominally because her hip-joints have become too stiff. She also sits down as though she had to guard against crushing her genitals, as if they were male organs.

Recollection of the masculinity complex does not always exist in consciousness, at any rate in the primitive form of a belief in the possession of a male genital. Often the recollection only becomes conscious during discussion of the so-called masculine attitude. But in every case it requires close study to establish that the complex is still effective in its original form, in spite of repression or experience.

The small sequence of cases which first turned my attention to the complex consists of five patients, who were suffering from psychasthenia with obsessions, otherwise called obsessional neurosis. I have been able to observe four of them for quite a long period; the fifth, however, gave up the analysis very soon. But this fifth patient came to me for treatment just after I had learned to take sufficient notice of the fantasy of being a man. All the facts of her case pointed to her as the type sketched by Freud in the lines quoted above; and I think, therefore, it will be agreed that there can be no misunderstanding about this statement of hers: "Often when I am restless and don't know what to do with myself I have a feeling that I would like to ask my mother to give me something that she cannot give me."

The behavior of one of the four other patients had for a long time inclined me to think that in her case also the problem was the influence of her unconscious wish to be a man. For instance, her obsessional movements in lying or sitting down are of such a kind as to give one the impression that she has to make the same overtures to the sofa or chair that a cock makes to his hens. Only a short time ago she said to me, "I feel as though I coquetted with the sofa."

It might perhaps be not without significance that three of the five patients informed me of their own accord that they possessed "Hottentot nymphae"; this fact, which they had already noticed very early in their lives, led them to the conviction that they were different from other women. I did not find to any great extent in any of these cases what is called a masculine disposition; nor indeed a masculine appearance and expression, a contempt for men, or a predilection for masculine activities. I would rather define the attitude present as one of rivalry with men in the intellectual and artistic spheres. A pronounced homosexual component makes no difference to this, as the resulting rivalry in sexual matters expresses itself only in symptoms and symptomatic acts.

Returning to the question put above, we may state that we have already learned from experience, when the recollection of an observation or of an event is being retained and used as the starting point for a new fantasy-system (screen-memory), that we then have to do with the return of a repressed wish under fresh distortion. We are tempted to surmise such a return from the unconscious when a girl reacts to the experience of seeing or observing a male genital organ with the violent, embittered thought, "Why haven't I anything like that?" or "I ought to have had one too"; or on the other hand with anxiety and a consciousness of guilt, "I might have had one too—what a pity that I injured myself to such an extent"; or with the expectation, "It won't be long before I grow one too"; or even with the re-assurance, "Yet I do possess one!" These are only examples of such a reaction; there are still a number of another kind, and the form of the bodily symptoms almost always present changes with these reactions. For instance in place of the genital so passionately desired, there is usually felt to be a "wound," which is either painful or irritating, according to the manner in which the patient regards the lack of the organ.

Now what are the repressed impulses which, after the trauma of seeing a male organ, can find an outlet in the newly appearing idea of having such an organ? We may assume that these bear a certain relation or likeness to the content of the masculinity idea. In an allusive way the patients speak of this themselves, by making vague contrasts—and this often happens—between their masculine traits and their feminine inclinations, also quite well known to them. Even when they do not mention the thing they seek, the meaning of their expressions is quite clear to the analyst. That is to say, they usually express a wish to take possession of a person, instead of devoting and subjecting themselves to him, or they have the feeling that they wish to penetrate someone else, instead of themselves being penetrated; or they remark that a state of tension would disappear if they could but give out something instead of taking something in. Such expressions are of course used then in a hyperbolical sense; but not seldom associations of this kind afford evidence that they should be taken to a certain extent literally—in fact, it is one of the several ways in which one can discover the masculinity complex in analysis.

At the central point of the childhood reminiscences of one of my patients, whom I shall call H., and of whose analysis I shall give the most detailed account, there stands the following dream; it dates from about her fourth year when she still slept in her parents' bedroom. She dreamed—it may perhaps be a mere fantasy—that she lay in bed and her mother stood near her. She had a surprisingly pleasant bodily sensation and her mother told her it was quite all right, there was no harm in it. Thereupon she experienced a kind of orgasm and awoke. To her astonishment and horror she found that she had soiled the bed. She called her mother, who came to her assistance without being angry. Since that time the patient has always remained shy, has had anxiety during the night, has suffered to an increasing extent from sleeplessness, and so has gradually developed a neurosis; this neurosis grew very much worse at the age of thirteen, when she lost her mother, and again at nineteen, when she lost her brother; its chief symptom is shyness with men. We may suppose that the sensations which the patient had in her dream were derived from her filled bladder, and that the emptying of it corresponds to the orgasm of the dream. Her feeling of shame and astonishment on waking prove to us that the girl must already have learned to control the bladder function. As a contrast there is in the dream a return to an earlier period before she had learned this control, associated with the idea of the methods of teaching her cleanliness: the mother near the bed, who tells her to let it happen, is obviously the mother who makes her use the chamber. Urinating into a chamber has had considerable significance to her; her father also helped her with this function later, and imitated the noise to her in order to make her urinate. And in addition she had in her early youth heard the sound of her father urinating in the next room.

The patient is very gifted musically and composed music even as a child. It often happened that while she sat on the closet she let a stream of water run from a tap in order to catch a melody from the noise. When she plays at a concert she often feels as though through her playing she were to put an end to the tension which she feels in the public or in an individual listener—sometimes the public is replaced by the composer. If she succeeds in feeling in this way, she plays well. From her associations there appeared an analogy in this with the childhood situation in which by urinating she produced the noise which her father had either produced for her with his mouth or by urinating in another room; she transfers this detail, therefore, of her father-complex to the composer: the tension either actually felt or unconsciously existing in herself is projected into the audience or again into the composer. In addition her father has always encouraged her musical ambitions, with the result that the patient has identified herself with him in the musical sphere and has regarded herself as the instrument of his will. One very primitive expression of this identification is the idea of being her father's genital organ.[2] One has only to remember

[2] This fantasy connects with infantile birth-theories.

her attitude at concerts, which I have just mentioned; she is to be the organ which provides relief for the tension she feels in the audience. The association of music with urination led to this fantasy. Moreover, she has already inferred a connection between the symptom of congestion (due to the pressure from constipation) and the reddened glans penis she had seen in her brother's genitals, and had interpreted her convulsions of weeping as ejaculations. The sobbing and sighing which accompanies such a convulsion reminded her of what she used to hear in her parent's bedroom.

In this connection the following fact is also of importance. The patient was awaiting her last examination at the Conservatoire and had considerable anxiety about it. A vision, as she calls it, came to her rescue in her need: someone standing near her bed speaks to her during the night about her attitude to music and to her examination; she is to forget herself and to surrender herself entirely to the intentions of the composer, and give herself free rein. After the vision she fell into a state of exaltation, slept no more, but played very well at her examination. The agreement of this vision with the dream in childhood must of course occur to everyone; the identification with her father to which I have alluded above was also in operation in this experience.

It is natural to conclude that *hearing* has played a large part in the development of this interest in little H. We have already mentioned the fact that she listened when anyone passed water in the room, or in the next room. The patient suffered quite early from sleeplessness. At night she always felt obliged to listen, either to the music that was going on in the house, or lest burglars were in the room, or to hear what her parents were saying on the other side of the wall against which her own bed stood. This habit of listening had begun when she ceased to sleep in her parents' room. I cannot prove that she had observed, or tried to observe, parental coitus on one or more occasions, but from what has been said above it is obvious that she had been greatly interested in what went on in her parents' bedroom or bed. The reason for her sleeplessness was the tension produced by sexual curiosity.

The patient herself suggested that the childhood dream might be due to her having witnessed parental coitus and that she probably identified herself with her father. It is a fact that many associations pointed to a possibility of this sort, but no recollection of it has come into consciousness. We know that children sometimes imagine that the man passes urine into the woman; it would be in agreement with this idea if we looked upon this dream as a homosexual coitus dream. Of course the material used to represent the fulfillment of the desire to perform coitus with the mother (or rather, to do with her what the patient thought her father did) is taken from an earlier period.

A whole series of recollections bear witness to infantile intimacy with the mother, and particularly to occasions when they went to the closet together and her mother passed urine as did she, herself. We may assume that the child's wish to see what her mother looked like and how she did this was a preliminary phase of the later curiosity. Sometimes, too, little H. had difficulty in defecation; she suffered from constipation, and she clearly remembered that when she strained very hard her mother told her not to do so. When straining in this way she had a curious sensation in her head, a kind of giddiness, which recurred later accompanying her shyness. Here, the infantile situation in the closet has been transferred to later situations when she has been overcome by shyness. By means of displacement from below upwards, into which I do not wish to enter here, the mouth has become an anus and that which proceeds from the mouth, namely speech, is feces and flatus. For instance, in talking to anyone, she is compelled to notice whether any odor proceeds from that particular person's mouth. In the same way there has been a transference of details connected with the bladder function, and to this is to be traced the struggle with fits of crying which is another of the symptoms connected with shyness.

Quite suddenly these intimate relations with her mother were stopped; she was no longer allowed to go to the closet with her, and so on. Suddenly, too, her relations with her father in these matters were forcibly interrupted. She was already suffering from sleeplessness, probably at the beginning of her fifth year, and she had formed a habit of calling her parents, whereupon she was helped on to the chamber. One night she called more than once and her father came in angrily and gave the unsuspecting child a box on the ear. She was much embittered by this and vowed to herself that she would never call out again. In order to attract her parents' attention, or possibly to disturb them, she then bethought her of the plan of shaking her bed.

It is quite likely that being suddenly forced to give up her infantile pleasure for which no substitute was provided may have had a traumatic effect and have produced an embittered frame of mind, which might have been avoided if the parents had gone about her training in a less abrupt manner. We find something similar if we leave this period of the patient's life and observe her in the following period when she was in the infants' school and the first class of a preparatory school. She was compelled to go to school, and once more, at least so she thinks, the order was given quite unexpectedly. On one fateful day she was restless and lay down on a table and rolled about on it, without any definite idea of what she wanted. Thereupon she was suddenly told: "Now you will have to go to school." She has always felt this conduct on the part of her mother as a great injustice and it left its traces of resentment and anxiety—anxiety due to an uncertainty of what unpleasant thing might happen next because of something she quite innocently did or said. It was as if something had been taken from her, which she herself could not put into any definite words. But from that day on she inwardly resisted the rules made by those who brought her up, even though she seemed to submit and obey them. Her mental picture of the infants' school is linked up with the recollection of several forbidden things, two of which I will mention. Her mother forbade her to go to the closet at school, but she once did so all the same, out of curiosity. Moreover, she has never quite lost her curiosity in relation to the functions of the bladder and bowel or her interest in excrement, which is in agreement with what has been said above. Secondly, when sitting on the form she played with her genitals and then, afraid lest the smell on her hand should be detected, she licked her fingers till no smell could be noticed. It is a remarkable thing that the patient cannot say whether she had masturbated before that as well. Analysis has not been able to decide this point either. But it is quite possible that the childhood dream indicates the beginning, the first perception, of clitoris sensations, For the feeling of gratification was, as the patient expressly said, hitherto unknown to her, and after this experience she felt different from what she was before, as though she possessed something special, a kind of secret, which from that time on made her different from other people. In general, a connection between the function of the bladder and that of the clitoris is established very early; probably this is partly due to the anatomical condition. Freud in one of his writings emphasizes the connection between strongly developed urethral erotism and ambition. Certainly my patient was ambitious in every direction; her ambition was fostered, moreover, by her father's expectations based on her musical talent, and it culminated in a fantasy which I do not wish to go into in detail here: the so-called "hospital fantasy" in which she figured to some extent as a healer but treated people with extraordinarily cruel remedies. In the same way her ambition was fed by rivalry with a sister a year older than herself but less talented. She succeeded too in apparently excelling her in almost every respect, but on the other hand there were various relations, especially that with her father, in which she was inhibited, constrained and shy. In later years impulses of rivalry caused her to attach rather to her brother, who was some years her junior— at first as his school-fellow, and afterwards, when their mother died, with a mother's devotion.

She often heard it said that, before she was born, her parents wanted a boy and that they were somewhat disappointed when another girl was born. She noticed too how proud they were of their son. Here again was an injustice which she never forgot. She could not say whether at that time the thought already occurred to her—at any rate it was a familiar thought—that she too might have been a boy if only she had been born rather later. She regarded herself as having been born too soon. The same bitterness was displayed in her analysis in a striking way when, for certain reasons, I fixed a time for the treatment to end —I, too, then, was making her go before she was ready. I think that the idea of being born to early is somehow connected with the experience, several times undergone by the patient, that something was ordered or forbidden, some renunciation imposed upon her or the fulfillment of a duty required of her, before she had enjoyed the infantile modes of gratification long enough. Here of course there may also be the wish to retain a form of gratification as long as possible, an attitude originating in strongly developed anal erotism.

The patient observed the male genital principally in her brother, but also in her father and an uncle, with whom many years later she fell in love; this unfortunate love affair was the direct cause of her illness growing worse and of treatment being undertaken. In those early days she made comparisons of the male organ with her own genitals, and once more I found in her case, too, the familiar expectation that an organ would grow out from within. This expectation was supported by the Hottentot nymphae, which she noticed very early and construed as something peculiar to herself. Her conviction that she was an exception found plenty of evidence in this respect.

The expectation I have just mentioned, that a penis would grow out from within, was also for a time transferred to the intestines. I have several times had the opportunity of observing a similar process in girls who had witnessed coitus in dogs. Fantasies occur too of an auto-erotic coitus in which the rectum stands for the vagina and the feces for the penis. The discovery of fantasies of this sort has led me to wonder whether the vaginal sensations which should develop later are not derivable from anal feelings. It is not surprising that the patient developed strong homosexual tendencies, for in the first place her intimate relations with her mother and later the identification with her father were a most favorable soil for such tendencies. But, of course, here too gratification was denied her, or else the tendencies always became inhibited by strong negative feelings. Only when her incestuous love for her uncle, at the beginning of her illness, threatened to overwhelm her did she take refuge in a homosexual relation which in a short time resulted in an acute confusional condition.

If we sum up what we know of this patient we may say briefly that here is a case where the idea of being a male, an idea based on identification with the father or the brother, is the central feature of the picture. The idea of masculinity, so closely bound up with clitoris erotism, finds congenial soil in the repression of the strongly developed bladder and urethral erotism. Because of the failure to effect a permanent and satisfactory transference to homosexual and heterosexual objects there is regression to the auto-erotic stage of libido development, principally to that of urethral erotism.

In the other patient, too, the connection between the masculinity complex and urethral erotism is perfectly plain.

The patient D., of whom I have already said that the masculinity complex manifested itself in her in the desire to urinate like a man, either tries to lengthen the urethra, for instance by passing her urine through a tube, or she passes it into vessels not intended for that purpose. Tricks of this sort, occasioned by an already existing sexual tension, then invariably lead to masturbation. This patient has marked homosexual tendencies, which are displayed far more strongly than her heterosexual desires. The latter are confined to innumerable fleeting experiences of being in love—underneath there is a firm fixation to a childish love-relation which continues to exercise a powerful inhibitory influence. Her psychasthenic symptoms are those of obsessive doubt and speculating. These probably originate in a strongly developed childish curiosity, which in this particular case culminated in the question: "How do men do it?" i.e., how does he (the father) perform the act of defecation? The patient is the only daughter of an elderly couple; her father died when she was about sixteen. At one time she had turned from him and had thoughts of hatred and death-wishes against him; after his death she reproached herself for feeling it to be a deliverance rather than a loss, and was troubled with doubts whether her thoughts could have caused him to die. Later she also developed negative feelings toward her mother, and asked whether she were to blame for her mother's illness, a kind of athritis deformans. We understand the meaning of such wishes, especially when we know further that the patient had to help her mother in everything because the latter could hardly move at all. The attachment to the incestuous homosexual object was thus not threatened by prohibitions from without, and this gave ample scope for a large amount of infantile libido to come into action. The patient never sucked, either at the breast or from a bottle; she always drank her milk from a cup or a spoon. She herself now uses this fact as a pretext for regarding herself as an exception.

I mentioned a third patient, P., as an example of a woman who behaves as though she were a man, or at least as though she had a male genital. In this case I have not been able to prove the connection with urethral erotism so clearly as in the other. But this is not very surprising, for the patient in question is somewhat older. In any case I could not prove that there was any other form of infantile auto-erotic sexual activity corresponding to the extreme development of the masculinity complex, and there was not much difficulty in discovering the connection with the earlier masturbation which was generally accompanied by homosexual fantasies of an incestuous sadistic-masochistic type. In this case, however, the masculinity complex had long been conscious. As a child the patient used to enjoy making bread or dough into figures shaped like a phallus and recognized them as such. As late as her tenth or twelfth year she used to play a kind of shadow-game with her sisters, and used to like to make her own shadow project in the region of the genitals. Her principal symptoms represented the fulfillment of the wish to have a male organ, and were accompanied by a feeling of envy of men for their possession of it, and by an attitude to women which must be regarded as an overcompensation for her embitterment against her mother for withholding it from her.

I feel as if I had not really succeeded in making it clear how strong an impression I have received in my analytic work of the intimate connection between the masculinity complex, infantile masturbation of the clitoris, and urethral erotism. I have said to myself that the observations which I happened to make all at one time might be merely accidental findings. Nevertheless I decided to publish them, because I am convinced that publication of the result of any careful observations may be of some value.

V

The Denial of the Vagina

A Contribution to the Problem of the Genital Anxieties Specific to Women

By Karen Horney

The fundamental conclusions to which Freud's investigations of the specific character of feminine development have led him are as follows: first, that in little girls the early development of instinct takes the same course as in boys, both in respect of the erotogenic zones (in the two sexes only one genital organ, the penis, plays a part, the vagina remaining undiscovered) and also in respect of the first choice of object (for both the mother is the first love-object). Secondly, that the great differences which nevertheless exist between the two sexes arise from the fact that this similarity of libidinal trend does not go with similar anatomical and biological foundations. From this premise it follows logically that girls feel themselves inadequately equipped for this phallic orientation of their libido and cannot but envy boys their superior endowment in that respect. Over and above the conflicts with the mother which the girl shares with the boy, she adds a crucial one of her own; she lays at her mother's door the blame for her lack of a penis. This conflict is crucial because it is just this reproach which is essential for her detachment from her mother and her turning to her father.

Hence, Freud has chosen a happy phrase to designate the period of blossoming of childish sexuality, the period of infantile genital primacy in girls as well as boys, which he calls the "phallic phase."

I can imagine that a man of science who was not familiar with analysis would in reading this account pass over it as merely one of the many strange and peculiar notions which analysis expects the world to believe. Only those who accept the point of view of Freud's theories can gauge the importance of this particular thesis for the understanding of feminine psychology as a whole. Its full bearings emerge in the light of one of the most momentous discoveries of Freud's one of those achievements which, we may suppose, will prove lasting. I refer to the realization of the crucial importance for the whole subsequent life of the individual of the impressions, experiences and conflicts of early childhood. If we accept this proposition in its entirety, that is, if we recognize the formative influence of early experience on the subject's capacity for dealing with his later experience and the way in which he does so, there ensue at least potentially, the following consequences as regards the specific psychic life of women:

(1) With the onset of each fresh phase in the functioning of the female organs—menstruation, coitus, pregnancy, parturition, suckling and the menopause—even a normal woman (as Helene Deutsch[1] has in fact assumed) would have to overcome impulses of a masculine trend before she could adopt an attitude of whole-hearted affirmation toward the processes taking place within her body.

(2) Again, even in normal women, irrespective of race and of social and individual conditions, it would happen altogether more readily than in men that the libido adhered, or came to be turned, to persons of her own sex. In a word: *homosexuality* would be incomparably and unmistakably more common amongst women than amongst men. Confronted with difficulties in relation to the opposite sex, a woman would plainly fall back more readily than a man into a homosexual attitude. For, according to Freud, not only are the most important years of her childhood dominated by such an attachment to one of her own sex but, when she first turns to a man (the father), it is in the main only by way of the narrow bridge of resentment. "Since I cannot have a penis I want a child instead and 'for this purpose' I turn

[1] Helene Deutsch: *Psychoanalyse der weiblichen Sexualfunktionen.*

to my father. Since I have a grudge against my mother because of the anatomical inferiority for which I hold her responsible, I give her up and turn to my father." Just because we are convinced of the formative influence of the first years of life we should feel it a contradiction if the relation of woman to man did not retain throughout life some tinge of this enforced choice of a substitute for that which was really desired.

(3) The same character of something remote from instinct, secondary and substitutive, would, even in normal women, adhere to the *wish for motherhood,* or at least would very easily manifest itself.

Freud by no means fails to realize the strength of the desire for children: in his view it represents on the one hand the principal legacy of the little girl's strongest instinctual object-relation, i.e., to the mother, in the shape of a reversal of the original child-mother relationship. On the other hand, it is also the principal legacy of the early, elementary wish for the penis. The special point about Freud's conception is rather that it views the wish for motherhood not as an innate formation, but as something that can be reduced psychologically to its onto-genetic elements and draws its energy originally from homosexual or phallic instinctual desires.

(4) If we accept a second axiom of psychoanalysis, namely, that the individual's attitude in sexual matters is the prototype of his attitude toward the rest of life, it would follow, finally, that woman's whole reaction to life would be based on a strong, subterranean resentment. For, according to Freud, the little girl's penis-envy corresponds to a sense of being at a radical disadvantage in respect of the most vital and most elementary instinctual desires. Here we have the typical basis upon which a general resentment is wont to be built up. It is true that such an attitude would not follow inevitably; Freud says expressly that, *where development proceeds favorably,* the girl finds her own way to the man and to motherhood. But here, again, it would contradict all our analytical theory and experience if an attitude of resentment so early and so deeply rooted did not manifest itself extremely easily—by comparison much more easily than in men under similar conditions—or at any rate were not readily set going as an undercurrent detrimental to the vital feeling-tone of women.

These are the very weighty conclusions with regard to the whole psychology of women which follow from Freud's account of early feminine sexuality. When we consider them, we may well feel that it behooves us to apply again and again the tests of observation and theoretical reflection to the facts on which they are based and to their proper appraisal.

It seems to me that analytic experience alone does not sufficiently enable us to judge the soundness of some of the fundamental ideas which Freud has made the basis of his theory. I think that a final verdict about them must be postponed until we have at our disposal systematic observations of *normal* children, carried out on a large scale by persons trained in analysis. Among the views in question I include Freud's statement that "it is well known that a clearly defined differentiation between the male and the female character is first established after puberty." The few observations which I have made myself do not go to confirm this statement. On the contrary I have always been struck by the marked way in which little girls between their second and fifth years exhibit specifically feminine traits. For instance, they often behave with a certain spontaneous feminine coquetry toward men, or display characteristic traits of maternal solicitude. From the beginning I have found it difficult to reconcile these impressions with Freud's view of the initial masculine trend of the little girl's sexuality.

We might suppose that Freud intended his thesis of the original similarity of the libidinal trend in the two sexes to be confined to the sphere of sex. But then we should come into conflict with the maxim that the individual's sexuality sets the pattern for the rest of his behavior. To clear up this point we should require a large number of exact observations of the differences between the behavior of normal boys and that of normal girls during their first five or six years.

Now it is true that, in these first years, little girls who have not been intimidated very often express themselves in ways which admit of interpretation as early penis-envy; they ask questions, they make comparisons to their own disadvantage, they say they want one too, they express admiration of the penis or comfort themselves with the idea that they will have one later on. Supposing for the moment that such manifestations occurred very frequently or even regularly, it would still be an open question what weight and place in our theoretical structure we should give them. Consistently with his total view, Freud utilizes them to show how much even the little girl's instinctual life is dominated already by the wish to possess a penis herself.

Against this view I would urge the following three considerations:

(1) In boys of the same age, too, we meet with parallel expressions in the form of wishes to possess breasts or to have a child.

(2) In neither sex have these manifestations *any influence on the child's behavior as a whole.* A boy who wishes vehemently to have a breast like his mother's may at the same time behave in general with thoroughgoing boyish aggressiveness. A little girl who casts glances of admiration and envy at her brother's genital may simultaneously behave as a true little woman. Thus it seems to me still an open question whether such manifestations at this early age are to be deemed expressions of elementary instinctual demands or whether we should not perhaps place them in a different category.

(3) Another possible category suggests itself if we accept the assumption that there is in every human being a bisexual disposition. The importance of this for our understanding of the mind has, indeed, always been stressed by Freud himself. We may suppose that though at birth the definitive sex of each individual is already fixed physically, the result of the bisexual disposition which is always present and merely inhibited in its development, is that *psychologically* the attitude of children to their own sexual role is at first uncertain and tentative. They have no consciousness of it and therefore naturally give naïve expression to bisexual wishes. We might go further and conjecture that this uncertainty only disappears in proportion as stronger feelings of love, directed to objects, arise.

To elucidate what I have just said, I may point to the marked difference which exists between these diffuse bisexual manifestations of earliest childhood, with their playful, volatile character, and those of the so-called latency-period. If, at *this* age, a girl wishes to be a boy—but here again the frequency with which these wishes occur and the social factors by which they are conditioned should be investigated—the manner in which this determines her whole behavior (preference for boyish games and ways, repudiation of feminine traits) reveals that such wishes emanate from quite another depth of the mind. This picture, so different from the earlier one, represents, however, already the outcome of mental conflicts[2] that she has been through and cannot therefore, without special theoretical assumptions, be claimed as a manifestation of masculinity wishes which had been laid down biologically.

Another of the premises on which Freud builds up his view relates to the erotogenic zones. He assumes that the girl's early genital sensations and activities function essentially in the clitoris. He regards it as very doubtful whether any early vaginal masturbation takes place and even holds that the vagina remains altogether "undiscovered."

To decide this very important question we should once more require extensive and exact observation of normal children. Josine Müller[3] and I, myself, as long ago as 1925, expressed doubts on the subject. Moreover, most of the information we occasionally get from gynecologists and children's physicians interested in psychology suggests that, just in the early years of childhood, vaginal masturbation is at least as common as clitoral. The various data which give rise to this impression are: the frequent observation of signs of vaginal irritation, such as reddening and discharge, the relatively frequent occurrence of the introduction of foreign bodies into the vagina and, finally, the fairly common complaints by mothers that their children put their fingers into the vagina. The well-known gynecologist, Wilhelm Liepmann, has stated[4] that his experience as a whole has led him to believe that, in early childhood and even in the first years of infancy, vaginal masturbation is much more common than clitoral, and that only in the later years of childhood are the relations reversed in favor of clitoral masturbation.

These general impressions cannot take the place of systematic observations, nor therefore can they lead to a final conclusion. But they do show that the exceptions which Freud himself admits seem to be of frequent occurrence.

[2] Karen Horney, "On the Genesis of the Castration Complex in Women," *International Journal of Psychoanalysis*, 1924, Vol. V.

[3] Josine Müller, "The Problem of Libidinal Development of the Genital Phase in Girls," *International Journal of Psychoanalysis*, 1932, Vol. XIII.

[4] In a private conversation.

Our most natural course would be to try to throw light upon this question from our analyses, but this is difficult. At the very best the material of the patient's conscious recollections or the memories which emerge in analysis cannot be treated as unequivocal evidence, because, here as everywhere else, we must also take into account the work of repression. In other words: the patient may have good reason for not remembering vaginal sensations or masturbation, just as conversely we must feel skeptical about her ignorance of clitoral sensations.[5]

A further difficulty is that the women who come for analysis are just those from whom one cannot expect even an average naturalness about vaginal processes. For they are always women whose sexual development has departed somehow from the normal and whose *vaginal* sensibility is disturbed in a greater or lesser degree. At the same time it does seem as if even accidental differences in the material play their part. In approximately two-thirds of my cases I have found the following state of affairs:

(1) Marked vaginal orgasm produced by manual vaginal masturbation prior to any coitus. Frigidity in the form of vaginismus and defective secretion in coitus. I have seen only two cases of this sort which were quite unmistakable. I think that, in general, preference is shown for the clitoris or the labia in manual genital masturbation.

(2) Spontaneous vaginal sensations, for the most part with noticeable secretion, aroused by unconsciously stimulating situations, such as that of listening of music, motoring, swinging, having the hair combed, and certain transference-situations. No manual vaginal masturbation; frigidity in coitus.

(3) Spontaneous vaginal sensations produced by extra-genital masturbation, e.g., by certain motions of the body, by tight-lacing, or by particular sadistic-masochistic fantasies. No coitus, because of the overpowering anxiety aroused whenever the vagina is about to be touched, whether by a man in coitus, by a physician in a gynecological examination, or by the subject her-

---

[5] In a discussion following the reading of my paper on the phallic phase, before the German Psycho-Analytical Society, in 1931, Boehm cited several cases in which only vaginal sensations and vaginal masturbation were recollected and the clitoris had apparently remained "undiscovered."

self in manual masturbation, or in any douching prescribed medically.

For the time being, then, my impressions may be summed up as follows: in manual genital masturbation the clitoris is more commonly selected than the vagina, *but spontaneous genital sensations resulting from general sexual excitations are more frequently located in the vagina.*

From a theoretical standpoint I think that great importance should be attached to this relatively frequent occurrence of spontaneous vaginal excitations even in patients who were ignorant, or had only a very vague knowledge, of the existence of the vagina, and whose subsequent analysis did not bring to light memories or other evidence of any sort of vaginal seduction, nor any recollection of vaginal masturbation. For this phenomenon suggests the question *whether from the very beginning sexual excitations may not have expressed themselves perceptibly in vaginal sensations.*

In order to answer this question we should have to wait for very much more extensive material than any single analyst can obtain from his own observations. Meanwhile there are a number of considerations which seem to me to favor my view.

In the first place there are the fantasies of rape which occur before coitus has taken place at all, and indeed long before puberty, and are frequent enough to merit wider interest. I can see no possible way of accounting for the origin and content of these fantasies if we are to assume the non-existence of vaginal sexuality. For these fantasies do not in fact stop short at quite indefinite ideas of an act of violence, through which one gets a child. On the contrary, fantasies, dreams, and anxiety of this type usually betray quite unmistakably an instinctive "knowledge" of the actual sexual processes. The guises they assume are so numerous that I need only indicate a few of them: criminals who break in through windows or doors; men with guns who threaten to shoot; animals which creep, fly or run inside some place (e.g., snakes, mice, moths); animals or women stabbed with knives; or trains running into a station or tunnel.

I speak of an "instinctive" knowledge of the sexual processes because we meet typically with ideas of this sort, e.g., in the anxieties and dreams of early childhood, at a period when as yet there is no intellectual knowledge derived from observation or from explanations by others. It may be asked whether such instinctive knowledge of the processes of penetration into the female body necessarily presupposes an instinctive knowledge of the existence of the vagina as the organ of reception. I think that the answer is in the affirmative if we accept Freud's view that "the child's sexual theories are modeled on the child's own sexual constitution." For this can only mean that the path traversed by the sexual theories of children is marked out and determined by spontaneously experienced impulses and sensations in its organs. If we accept this origin for the sexual theories, which already embody an attempt at rational elaboration, we must all the more admit it in the case of that instinctive knowledge which finds symbolic expression in play, dreams, and various forms of anxiety, and which obviously has not reached the sphere of reasoning and the elaboration which takes place there. In other words, we must assume that both the dread of rape, characteristic of puberty, and the infantile anxieties of little girls are based on vaginal organ sensations (or the instinctual impulses issuing from these), which imply that something ought to penetrate into that part of the body.

I think we have here the answer to an objection which may be raised, namely, that many dreams indicate the idea that an opening was only created when first the penis brutally penetrated the body. For such fantasies would not arise at all but for the previous existence of instincts—and the organ sensations underlying them—having the passive aim of reception. Sometimes the connection in which dreams of this type occur indicates quite clearly the origin of this particular idea. For it occasionally happens that, when a general anxiety about the injurious consequences of masturbation makes its appearance, the patient has dreams with the following typical content: she is doing a piece of needlework and all at once a hole appears, of which she feels ashamed; or she is crossing a bridge which suddenly breaks off in the middle, above a river or a chasm; or she is walking along a slippery incline and all at once begins to slide and is in danger of falling over a precipice. From such dreams we may conjecture that when these patients were children and indulged in onanistic play, they were led by vaginal sensations to the discovery of the vagina itself, and that their anxiety took the very form of the dread that they had made a hole where no hole ought to be. I would here emphasize that I have never been wholly convinced by Freud's explanation why girls suppress direct genital masturbation more easily and frequently than boys. As we know, Freud supposes[6] that (clitoral) masturbation becomes odious to little girls because comparison with the penis strikes a blow at their narcissism. When we consider the strength of the drive behind the onanistic impulses, a narcissistic mortification does not seem altogether adequate in weight to produce suppression. On the other hand, the dread that she has done herself an irreparable injury in that region might well be powerful enough to prevent vaginal masturbation, and either to compel the girl to restrict the practice to the clitoris, or else permanently to set her against all manual genital masturbation. I believe that we have further evidence of this early dread of vaginal injury in the envious comparison with the man which we frequently hear from patients of this type, who say that men are "so nicely closed up" underneath. Similarly, that deepest anxiety which springs out of masturbation for a woman, the dread that it has made her unable to have children, seems to relate to the inside of the body rather than to the clitoris.

This is another point in favor of the existence and the significance of early vaginal excitations. We know that observation of sexual acts has a tremendously exciting effect upon children. If we accept Freud's view we must assume that such excitation produces in little girls in the main the same phallic impulses to penetrate as are evoked in little boys. But then we must ask: whence comes the anxiety met with almost universally in the analyses of female patients—the dread of the gigantic penis which might pierce her? The origin of the idea of an excessively large penis can surely not be sought anywhere but in childhood, when the father's penis must actually have appeared menacingly large and terrifying. Or again, whence comes that understanding of the female sexual role, evinced in the symbolism of sexual anxiety, in which those early excitations once more vibrate? And how can we account at all for the unbounded jealous fury with the mother, which commonly manifests itself in the analyses of women when memories of the "primal scene" are affectively re-

---

[6] Sigmund Freud, "Some Psychological Consequences of the Anatomical Distinction between the Sexes," *International Journal of Psychoanalysis*, 1927, Vol. VIII.

vived? How does this come about if at that time the subject could only share in the excitations of the father?

Let me bring together the sum-total of the above data. We have reports of powerful vaginal orgasm going with frigidity in subsequent coitus; spontaneous vaginal excitation without local stimulus, but frigidity in intercourse; reflections and questions arising out of the need to understand the whole content of early sexual games, dreams, and anxieties, and later fantasies of rape, as well as reactions to early sexual observations; and finally certain contents and consequences of the anxiety produced in women by masturbation. If I take all the foregoing data together, I can see only one hypothesis which gives a satisfactory answer to all the questions which present themselves, the hypothesis, namely, that *from the very beginning the vagina plays its own proper sexual part.*

Closely connected with this train of thought is the problem of frigidity, which to my mind lies *not* in the question how the quality of libidinal sensibility becomes transmitted to the vagina,[7] but rather, how it comes about that the vagina, in spite of the sensibility which it already possesses, either fails altogether to react or reacts in a disproportionately small degree to the very strong libidinal excitations furnished by all the emotional and local stimuli in coitus? Surely there could be only *one* factor stronger than the will for pleasure, and that factor is anxiety.

We are now immediately confronted by the problem of what

[7] In reply to Freud's assumption that the libido may adhere so closely to the clitoral zone that it becomes difficult or impossible for sensibility to be transferred to the vagina, may I venture to enlist Freud against Freud? For it was he who showed convincingly how ready we are to snatch at fresh possibilities of pleasure and how even processes which have no sexual quality, e.g., movements of the body, speech or thought, may be eroticized and that the same is actually true of tormenting or distressing experiences such as pain or anxiety. Are we then to suppose that in coitus, which furnishes the very fullest opportunities for pleasure, the woman recoils from availing herself of them! Since to my thinking this is a problem which really does not arise, I cannot, moreover, follow H. Deutsch and M. Klein in their conjectures about the transference of the libido from the oral to the genital zone. There can be no doubt that in many cases there is a close connection between the two. The only question is whether we are to regard the libido as being "transferred" or whether it is simply inevitable that when an oral attitude has been early established and persists, it should manifest itself in the genital sphere *also*.

is meant by this vaginal anxiety or rather by its infantile conditioning factors, analysis reveals, first of all, castration impulses against the man and, associated with these, an anxiety whose source is twofold: on the one hand, the subject dreads her own hostile impulses and, on the other, the retribution which she anticipates in accordance with the law of talion, namely, that the contents of her body will be destroyed, stolen or sucked out. Now these impulses in themselves are, as we know, for the most part not of recent origin, but can be traced to old, infantile feelings of rage and impulses of revenge against the father, feelings called forth by the disappointments and frustrations which the little girl has suffered.

Very similar in content to these forms of anxiety is that described by Melanie Klein, which can be traced back to early destructive impulses directed against the body of the mother. Once more it is a question of the dread of retribution, which may take various forms, but the essence of which is broadly that everything which penetrates the body or is already there (food, feces, children) may become dangerous.

Although, at bottom, these forms of anxiety are so far analogous to the genital anxiety of boys, they take on a specific character from that proneness to anxiety which is part of the biological make-up of girls. In this and earlier papers I have already indicated what are these sources of anxiety and here I need only complete and sum up what has been said before:

(1) They proceed first of all from the tremendous difference in size between the father and the little girl, between the genitals of father and child. We need not trouble to decide whether the disparity between penis and vagina is inferred from observation or whether it is instinctively apprehended. The quite comprehensible and indeed inevitable result is that any fantasy of gratifying the tension produced by vaginal sensations (i.e., the craving to take into oneself, to receive) gives rise to anxiety on the part of the ego. As I showed in my paper "The Dread of Woman," I believe that in this biologically determined form of feminine anxiety we have something specifically different from the boy's original genital anxiety in relation to his mother. When he fantasies the fulfillment of genital impulses he is confronted with a fact very wounding to his self-esteem ("my penis is too

small for my mother"); the little girl, on the other hand, is faced with destruction of part of her body. Hence, carried back to its ultimate biological foundations, the man's dread of the woman is genital-narcissistic, while the woman's dread of the man is physical.

(2) A second specific source of anxiety, the universality and significance of which is emphasized by Daly,[8] is the little girl's observation of menstruation in adult relatives. Beyond all (secondary!) interpretations of castration she sees demonstrated for the first time the vulnerability of the female body. Similarly, her anxiety is appreciably increased by observations of a miscarriage or parturition by her mother. Since, in the minds of children and (when repression has been at work) in the unconscious of adults also, there is a close connection between coitus and parturition, this anxiety may take the form of a dread not only of parturition but also of coitus itself.

(3) Finally, we have a third specific source of anxiety in the little girl's reactions (again due to the anatomical structure of her body) to her early attempts at vaginal masturbation. I think that the consequences of these reactions may be more lasting in girls than in boys, and this for the following reasons: In the first place she cannot actually ascertain the effect of masturbation. A boy, when experiencing anxiety about his genital, can always convince himself anew that it does exist and is intact:[9] a little girl has no means of proving to herself that her anxiety has no foundation in reality. On the contrary, her early attempts at vaginal masturbation bring home to her once more the fact of her greater physical vulnerability,[10] for I have found in analysis that it is by no means uncommon for little girls, when attempting masturbation or engaging in sexual play with other

[8] Daly, "Der Menstruationskomplex." *Imago.* Bd. XIV, 1928.

[9] These real circumstances must most certainly be taken into account as well as the strength of unconscious sources of anxiety. For instance, a man's castration anxiety may be intensified as the result of phimosis.

[10] It is perhaps not without interest to recall that the gynecologist Wilhelm Liepmann (whose standpoint is not that of analysis), in his book *Psychologie der Frau,* says that the "vulnerability" of women is one of the specific characteristics of their sex.

children, to incur pain or little injuries, obviously caused by infinitesimal ruptures of the hymen.[11]

Where the general development is favorable, i.e., above all where the object-relations of childhood have not become a fruitful source of conflict, this anxiety is satisfactorily mastered and the way is then open for the subject to assent to her feminine role. That in unfavorable cases the effect of the anxiety is more persistent with girls than with boys, I think, indicated by the fact that, with the former, it is relatively more frequent for direct genital masturbation to be given up altogether, or at least it is confined to the more easily accessible clitoris with its lesser cathexis of anxiety. Not seldom everything connected with the vagina—the knowledge of its existence, vaginal sensations and instinctual impulses—succumbs to a relentless repression: in short, the fiction is conceived and long maintained that the vagina does not exist, a fiction which at the same time determines the little girl's preference for the masculine sexual role.

All these considerations seem to me to be greatly in favor of the hypothesis that *behind the "failure to discover" the vagina is a denial of its existence.*

It remains to consider the question of what importance the existence of early vaginal sensations or the "discovery" of the vagina has for our whole conception of early feminine sexuality. Though Freud does not expressly state it, it is none the less clear that, if the vagina remains originally "undiscovered," this is one of the strongest arguments in favor of the assumption of a biologically determined, primary penis-envy in little girls or of their original phallic organization. For, if no vaginal sensations or cravings existed, but the whole libido were concentrated on the clitoris, phallically conceived of, then and then only could we understand how little girls, for want of any specific source of pleasure of their own or of any specific feminine wishes, must be driven to concentrate their whole attention on the clitoris, to compare it with the boy's penis and then, since they are in fact at a disadvantage in this comparison, to feel themselves definite-

---

[11] Such experiences often come to light in analysis, firstly, in the form of screen-memories of injuries to the genital regions, sustained in later life, possibly through a fall. To these recollections patients react with a terror and shame out of all proportion to the cause. Secondly, there may be an overwhelming dread lest such an injury should possibly occur.

ly slighted.[12] If on the other hand, as I conjecture, a little girl experiences from the very beginning vaginal sensations and the corresponding impulses, she must from the outset have a lively sense of this specific character of her own sexual role, and a primary penis-envy of the strength postulated by Freud would be hard to account for.

In this paper I have showed that the hypothesis of a primary phallic sexuality carries with it momentous consequences for our whole conception of feminine sexuality. If we assume that there is a specifically feminine, primary, vaginal sexuality the former hypothesis, if not altogether excluded, is at least so drastically restricted that those consequences become quite problematical.

[12] Helene Deutsch arrives at this basis for penis-envy by a process of logical argument. Compare Deutsch, "The Significance of Masochism in the Mental Life of Women," *International Journal of Psychoanalysis*, 1930, Vol. XI.

VI

Female Sexuality[1]

By Sigmund Freud

I

In that phase of children's libidinal development which is characterized by the normal Oedipus complex we find that they are tenderly attached to the parent of the opposite sex, while their relation to the other parent is predominantly hostile. In the case of boys the explanation is simple. A boy's mother was his first love-object; she remains so, and, as his feelings for her become more passionate and he understands more of the relation between father and mother, the former inevitably appears as a rival. With little girls it is otherwise. For them, too, the mother was the first love-object; how then does a little girl find her way to her father? How, when and why does she detach herself from her mother? We have long realized that in women the development of sexuality is complicated by the task of renouncing that genital zone which was originally the principal one, namely, the clitoris, in favor of a new zone—the vagina. But there is a second change which appears to us no less characteristic and important for feminine development: the original mother-object has to be exchanged for the father. We cannot as yet see clearly how these two tasks are linked up.

We know that women with a strong father-attachment are numerous and need not by any means be neurotic. In studying

---

[1] ['Über die weibliche Sexualität.' First published *Int. Z. Psychoanal.*, Vol. 17 (1931), 317. Translation, reprinted from *Int. J. Psycho-Anal.*, Vol. 13 (1932), 281, by Joan Riviere.]

this type I have made some observations which I propose to communicate here and which have led me to a certain view of female sexuality. I have been struck, above all, by two facts. First, analysis has shown that where the attachment to the father was peculiarly strong it had been preceded by a phase of equally strong and passionate attachment exclusively to the mother. Except for the change in the object, the love-life had acquired hardly a single new feature in the second phase. The primary mother-relation had developed in a very rich and many-sided way.

Secondly, I learned that the duration of this attachment to the mother had been greatly underestimated. In a number of cases it persisted well into the fourth and, in one, into the fifth year, so that it comprised by far the longer period of the early sexual efflorescence. Indeed, one had to give due weight to the possibility that many a woman may remain arrested at the original mother-attachment and never properly achieve the change-over to men.

These facts show that the pre-Oedipus phase in women is more important than we have hitherto supposed.

Since there is time during this phase for all the fixations and repressions which we regard as the source of the neuroses, it seems that we shall have to retract the universality of the dictum that the Oedipus complex is the nucleus of neurosis. But if any-one feels reluctant to adopt this correction, he need not do so. For, on the one hand, we can extend the content of the Oedipus complex to include all the child's relations to both parents or, on the other, we can give due recognition to our new findings by saying that women reach the normal, positive Oedipus situa-tion only after surmounting a first phase dominated by the nega-tive complex. Actually, during this phase, to a little girl, her father is not very different from a troublesome rival even though her hostility toward him never reaches such a pitch as does the boy's. We have, after all, long given up any expectation of a neat parallelism between male and female sexual development.

Our insight into this early, pre-Oedipus phase in the little girl's development comes to us as a surprise, comparable in an-other field with the effect of the discovery of the Minoan-Mycenaean civilization behind that of Greece.

Everything connected with this first mother-attachment has in analysis seemed to me so elusive, lost in a past so dim and shadowy, so hard to resuscitate, that it seemed as if it had undergone some specially inexorable repression. But possibly I have received this impression because, when I have analyzed women, they have been able to cling to that very father-attachment in which they took refuge from the early phase of which I am speaking. It would in fact appear that women analysts—for instance, Jeanne Lampl-de Groot and Helene Deutsch—had been able to apprehend the facts with greater ease and clearness because they had the advantage of being suitable mother-substitutes in the transference-situation with the patients whom they were studying. I have not indeed succeeded in completely unraveling any of the cases in point and will therefore confine myself to communicating my most general conclusions and giving only a few examples of the new ideas which have suggested themselves to me. Amongst these is my conjecture that this phase of mother-attachment is specially closely connected with the etiology of hysteria (this is indeed by no means surprising when we reflect that both the phase and the neurosis in question are characteristically feminine); further, that in this dependence on the mother we have the germ of later paranoia in women.[2] For it appears that this germ is the surprising, yet regular, dread of being killed (devoured?) by the mother. It would seem plausible to conjecture that this anxiety corresponds to the hostility which the child develops toward her mother because of the manifold restrictions imposed by the latter in the process of training and physical care, and that the immaturity of the child's psychical organization favors the mechanism of projection.

II

I have begun by stating the two facts which have struck me as new: first, that the great dependence on the father in women merely takes over the heritage of an equally great attachment to the mother and, secondly, that this earlier phase lasts longer than we should have anticipated. I must now go back a little in

[2] In the well-known case [of delusional jealousy] reported by Ruth Mack-Brunswick (1928a) the direct source of the disorder was the patient's pre-Oedipus fixation (to her sister).

order to insert these new conclusions in their proper place in the picture of female sexual development with which we are already familiar. A certain amount of repetition is here inevitable. It will help our exposition if, as we go along, we compare the course of female development with that of the male.

First of all, there can be no doubt that the bisexual disposition which we maintain to be characteristic of human beings manifests itself much more plainly in the female than in the male. The latter has only one principal sexual zone—only one sexual organ—whereas the former has two: the vagina, the true female organ, and the clitoris, which is analogous to the male organ. We believe that we may justly assume that for many years the vagina is virtually non-existent and possibly remains without sensation until puberty. It is true, however, that recently an increasing number of observers have been inclined to think that vaginal stirrings are present even in those early years. In any case female genitality must, in childhood, center principally in the clitoris. The sexual life of the woman is regularly split up into two phases, the first of which is of a masculine character, while only the second is specifically feminine. Thus in female development there is a process of transition from the one phase to the other, to which there is nothing analogous in males. A further complication arises from the fact that the clitoris, with its masculine character, continues to function in later female sexual life in a very variable manner, which we certainly do not as yet fully understand. Of course, we do not know what are the biological roots of these specific characteristics of the woman, and we are still less able to assign to them any teleological purpose.

Parallel with this first great difference there is another, which concerns the love-object. The first love-object of the male is the mother, because it is she who feeds and tends him, and she remains his principal love-object until she is replaced by another which resembles her or is derived from her. With the female too the mother must be the first object, for the primary conditions of object-choice are the same for all children. But at the end of the girl's development it is the man—the father—who must come to be the new love-object; i.e., as she changes in sex, so must the sex of her love-object change. What we now have to discover is how this transformation takes place, how radical or how incomplete it is, and all the different things that may happen in this process of development.

We have already observed that there is yet another difference between the sexes in their relation to the Oedipus complex. We have the impression that what we have said about that complex applies in all strictness only to male children, and that we are right in rejecting the term "Electra complex" which seeks to insist that the situation of the two sexes is analogous. It is only in male children that there occurs the fateful simultaneous conjunction of love for the one parent and hatred of the other as rival. It is thereupon the discovery of the possibility of castration, as evidenced by the sight of the female genital which necessitates the transformation of the boy's Oedipus complex, leads to the creation of the superego and thus initiates all the processes that culminate in enrolling the individual in civilized society. After the paternal function has been internalized so as to form the superego, the next task is to detach the latter from those persons of whom it was originally the psychical representative. In this remarkable course of development the agent employed to restrain infantile sexuality is precisely that narcissistic genital interest which centers in the preservation of the penis.

One residue of the castration complex in the man is a measure of disparagement in his attitude toward women, whom he regards as having been castrated. In extreme cases this inhibits his object-choice, and, if reinforced by organic factors, it may result in exclusive homosexuality. Very different is the effect of the castration complex on the girl. She acknowledges the fact of her castration, the consequent superiority of the male and her own inferiority, but she also rebels against these unpleasant facts. So divided in her mind, she may follow one of three lines of development. The first leads to her turning her back on sexuality altogether. The budding woman, frightened by the comparison of herself with boys, becomes dissatisfied with her clitoris and gives up her phallic activity and therewith her sexuality in general and a considerable part of her masculine proclivities in other fields. If she pursues the second line, she clings in obstinate self-assertion to her threatened masculinity; the hope of getting a penis sometime is cherished to an incredibly late age and becomes the aim of her life, while the fantasy of really being a man, in spite of everything, often dominates long periods of her life. This "masculinity complex" may also result in a manifestly homosexual object-choice. Only if her development follows the third, very circuitous path does she arrive at the ultimate normal feminine attitude in which she takes her father as love-object, and thus arrives at the Oedipus complex in its feminine form. Thus, in women, that complex represents the final result of a lengthy process of development; castration does not destroy but rather creates it, and it escapes the strong hostile influences which, in men, tend to its destruction—in fact, only too often a woman never surmounts it at all. Hence, too, the cultural effects of the break-up of this complex are slighter and less important in women than in men. We should probably not err in saying that it is this difference in the interrelation of the Oedipus and the castration-complexes which gives its special stamp to the character of woman as a member of society.[3]

We see then that the phase of exclusive attachment to the mother, which may be called the *pre-Oedipus* phase, is far more important in women than it can claim to be in men. Many phenomena of feminine sexual life which were difficult to understand before can be fully explained by reference to this phase. For example, we had noted long ago that many a woman who takes her father as the model for her choice of a husband, or assigns her father's place to him, yet in her married life repeats with her husband her bad relations with her mother. He should have succeeded to her relation with her father, but in reality he takes over her relation to her mother. This is easily explained as an obvious case of regression. The mother-relation was the original one, upon which the father-relation was built up; in married life the original basis emerges from repression. For her

---

[3] It is to be anticipated that male analysts with feminist sympathies, and our women analysts also, will disagree with what I have said here. They will hardly fail to object that such notions have their origin in the man's "masculinity complex," and are meant to justify theoretically his innate propensity to disparage and suppress women. But this sort of psychoanalytic argument reminds us here, as it so often does, of Dostoevsky's famous "knife that cuts both ways." The opponents of those who reason thus will for their part think it quite comprehensible that members of the female sex should refuse to accept a notion that appears to gainsay their eagerly coveted equality with men. The use of analysis as a weapon of controversy obviously leads to no decision.

development to womanhood consisted mainly in transferring affective ties from the mother to the father-object.

With many women we have the impression that the period of their maturity is entirely taken up with conflicts with their husbands, just as they spent their youth in conflicts with their mothers. In the light of what I have now said we shall conclude that the hostile attitude to the mother is not a consequence of the rivalry implicit in the Oedipus complex, but rather originates in the preceding phase and has simply found in the Oedipus situation reinforcement and an opportunity for asserting itself. Direct analytic investigation confirms this view. Our interest must be directed to the mechanisms at work in the turning away from the mother-object, originally so vehemently and exclusively loved. We are prepared to find not one solitary factor but a whole number of these contributing to the same end.

Amongst these factors are some which are conditioned by the circumstances of infantile sexuality in general and so hold good equally for the love-relations of boys. First and foremost we must mention jealousy of other persons—brothers and sisters and rivals, amongst whom is also the father. Childish love knows no bounds, it demands exclusive possession, is satisfied with nothing less than all. But it has a second characteristic: it has no real aim; it is incapable of complete satisfaction and this is the principal reason why it is doomed to end in disappointment and to give place to a hostile attitude. Later on in life, the lack of ultimate gratification may conduce to a different result. This very factor may ensure the undisturbed continuance of the libidinal cathexis, as is the case in love-relations inhibited in their aim. But in the stress of the processes of development it regularly happens that the libido abandons its unsatisfactory position in order to find a new one.

There is another, far more specific motive for the turning away from the mother, arising out of the effect of the castration-complex on the little creature without a penis. Some time or other the little girl makes the discovery of her organic inferiority, of course earlier and more easily if she has brothers or other boy companions. We have already noted the three paths which diverge from this point: (a) that which leads to the suspension of the whole sexual life, (b) that which leads to the defiant overemphasis of her own masculinity, and (c) the first steps toward definitive femininity. It is not easy to say precisely when these processes occur or to lay down their typical course. Even the point of time when the discovery of castration is made varies and many other factors seem to be inconstant and to depend on chance. The condition of the girl's own phallic activity plays a part, as also whether it is discovered or not, and how far it is hindered after the discovery.

The little girl generally finds out spontaneously her mode of phallic activity—masturbation of the clitoris—and in the first instance it is no doubt unaccompanied by fantasies. The way in which the tending of the child's body influences the awakening of this activity is reflected in the very common fantasy of seduction by her mother, her wet-nurse or nursemaid. Whether little girls practice masturbation more rarely and from the beginning less energetically than little boys is a point which we must leave undecided: quite possibly this is the case. Actual seduction is likewise common enough, either at the hands of other children or of nurses who want to soothe the child, send her to sleep or make her dependent on them. Where seduction intervenes, it invariably disturbs the natural course of development and often has profound and lasting consequences.

The prohibition of masturbation may, as we have seen, act as an incentive for giving the habit up, but it may also operate as a motive for rebellion against the person who forbids, i.e., the mother, or the mother-substitute who later regularly merges into the mother. The defiant persistence in masturbation would appear to open the way to masculinity. Even when the child does not succeed in mastering her habit, the effect of the apparently unavailing prohibition is seen in her later efforts to free herself at all costs from a gratification which has been made distasteful to her. When the girl reaches maturity her object-choice may still be influenced by this firmly maintained purpose. Resentment at being prevented from free sexual activity has much to do with her detachment from her mother. The same motive recurs after puberty when the mother takes up the duty of protecting her daughter's chastity. Of course, we must remember here that the mother opposes masturbation in the boy in the same way, thus providing him also with a powerful motive for rebellion.

When a little girl has sight of a male genital organ and so

discovers her own deficiency, she does not accept the unwelcome knowledge without hesitation and reluctance. As we have seen, she clings obstinately to the expectation of acquiring a similar organ sometime, and the desire for it survives long after the hope is extinguished. Invariably the child regards castration in the first instance as a misfortune peculiar to herself; only later does she realize that it extends to certain other children and at length to certain adults. When the universality of this negative character of her sex dawns upon her, womanhood, and with it also her mother, suffers a heavy loss of credit in her eyes.

Very possibly this account of the little girl's reaction to her impression of castration and the prohibition of masturbation will strike the reader as confused and contradictory. That is not altogether the writer's fault. A description which fits every case is in fact almost impossible. In different individuals we find the most various reactions; even in the same individual contrary attitudes exist side by side. With the first intervention of the prohibition there begins a conflict which from that moment will accompany the development of the sexual function. It is particularly difficult to get a clear insight into what takes place because it is so hard to distinguish the mental processes of this first phase from the later ones by which they become overlaid and distorted in memory. For example, the fact of castration is sometimes construed later as a punishment for masturbation, and its infliction is ascribed to the father; of course, neither of these ideas can be the original one. With boys also it is regularly the father from whom castration is dreaded, although in their case, as in the little girl's it is mostly the mother who utters the threat.

However this may be, at the end of this first phase of attachment to the mother there emerges, as the strongest motive for turning away from her, the child's reproach that her mother has not given her a proper genital, i.e., that she was born a woman. A second reproach, not going quite so far back, comes as rather a surprise: it is that the mother gave the child too little milk and did not suckle her long enough. Under the conditions of modern civilization this may very often be quite true, but certainly not so often as is maintained in analysis. It would seem rather that this complaint expresses the general dissatisfaction of children who under our monogamous civilization are weaned at the age of from six to nine months, whereas the primitive mother devotes herself exclusively to her child for two or three years. It is as if our children remained forever unappeased, as if they had never been suckled long enough. But I am not sure whether, if one analyzed children who had been suckled as long as those of primitive races, one would not encounter the same complaint. So great is the greed of the childish libido! If we survey the whole range of motives brought to light by analysis for turning away from the mother: that she neglected to provide the little girl with the only proper genital organ, that she did not feed her enough, compelled her to share her mother's love with others, never fulfilled all the expectations of the child's love and, finally, that she first excited and then forbade her daughter's own sexual activity—all these seem inadequate as a justification of the hostility finally felt. Some of these reproaches follow inevitably from the nature of infantile sexuality; others look like rationalizations devised later to explain the uncomprehended change in feeling. Perhaps the real fact is that the attachment to the mother must inevitably perish just because it is the first and the most intense, similarly to what we so often find in the first marriages of young women, entered into when they were most passionately in love. In both cases the love-relation probably comes to grief by reason of the unavoidable disappointments and an accumulation of occasions for aggression. As a rule second marriages turn out much better.

We cannot go so far as to assert that the ambivalence of emotional cathexes is a universally valid psychological law, that it is quite impossible to feel great love for a person without the accompaniment of a hatred perhaps as great, and vice versa. Normal adults do, undoubtedly, succeed in separating these two attitudes, and do not find themselves compelled to hate their love-objects and love as well as hate their enemies. But this seems to be the result of later development. In the first phases of the love-life ambivalence is evidently the rule. Many people retain this archaic trait throughout life; it is characteristic of obsessional neurotics that in their object-relations love and hate counterbalance one another. In members of primitive races also we may say that ambivalence predominates. We shall conclude, then, that the little girl's vehement attachment to her mother is strongly ambivalent and that, reinforced as it is by the above other factors, it is precisely this ambivalence which determines the child's turning away from her. That is to say, it is the consequence once more of one of the universal characteristics of infantile sexuality.

An objection immediately presents itself to the explanation I have suggested: How is it that boys succeed in keeping intact their attachment to the mother, which is certainly no less strong than the girl's? An instant answer is: Because boys are able to deal with their ambivalent feelings toward her by transferring all their hostility to the father. But, in the first place, we should be chary of asserting this until we have exhaustively studied the pre-Oedipus phase in boys and, secondly, it would probably be more prudent altogether to admit that we have not yet got to the bottom of processes which, after all, we have only just come to know of.

III

Another question is this: What exactly is it that the little girl demands of her mother? What is the nature of her sexual aims during the period of exclusive attachment to her mother? The answer which we gather from the analytic material is just what we should expect. The little girl's sexual aims in relation to her mother are both active and passive and are determined by the different libidinal phases through which the child passes. Here the relation of activity to passivity is specially interesting. It is easy to observe how, in every field of psychical experience and not merely in that of sexuality, an impression passively received evokes in children a tendency to an active response. They try to do themselves what has just been done to them. This is part of their task of mastering the outside world, and may even lead to their endeavoring to repeat impressions which they would have good reason to avoid because of their disagreeable content. Children's play, too, is made to serve this purpose of completing and thus, as it were, annulling a passive experience by active behavior. When, in spite of resistance, a physician has opened a child's mouth to exmine his throat, the same child will, after he has gone, play at being "the doctor" and will repeat the same forcible procedure on a little brother or sister, as defenseless against him as he was against the physician. We cannot fail to recognize here a revolt against passivity and a preference for the active role. This swing-over from passivity to activity does not take place with the same regularity and vigor in all children: in some it may not occur at all. From their behavior in this respect we can draw some conclusion as to the relative strength of the masculine and the feminine tendencies which will be revealed in their sexual life.

The first sexual or sexually tinged experiences of a child in its relation to the mother are naturally passive in character. It is she who suckles, feeds, cleans and dresses it, and instructs it in the performance of all its physical functions. Part of the child's libido goes on clinging to these experiences and enjoys the various gratifications associated with them, while another part strives to convert them into activity. First, the process of being suckled at the mother's breast gives place to active sucking. In its other relations with its mother the child either contents itself with independence (*i.e.*, with successfully performing itself what was previously done to it) or with actively repeating in play its passive experiences, or else it does really make the mother the object in relation to which it assumes the role of the active subject. This last reaction, which comes into play in the form of real activity, I long held to be incredible, until experience removed all my doubts on the subject.

We seldom hear of a little girl's wanting to wash or dress her mother or tell her to perform her bodily functions. Sometimes she says: "Now let's play that I am mother and you are child"; but generally she fulfills these active wishes indirectly in playing with her doll, she herself representing the mother and the doll the child. The fact that girls are fonder of playing with dolls than are boys is commonly interpreted as an early sign of awakened femininity. That is quite true, only we must not overlook that fact that it is the *active* side of femininity which finds expression here and that the little girl's preference for dolls probably testifies to the exclusiveness of her attachment to her mother, accompanied by total neglect of the father-object.

The very surprising sexual activity of the little girl in relation to her mother manifests itself in chronological succession in oral, sadistic and finally even phallic impulses directed upon her. It is difficult to give a detailed account of these, because often they are dim impulses which it was impossible for the child to grasp psychically at the time and which were only interpreted later, and express themselves in analysis in forms that are certainly not the original ones. Sometimes we find them transferred to the later father-object, where they do not belong and badly interfere with our understanding of the situation. We find aggressive oral and sadistic wishes in a form forced on them by early repression, i.e., in the dread of being killed by the mother—a dread which on its side justifies the death-wish against her, if this enters consciousness. It is impossible to say how often this dread of the mother draws countenance from an unconscious hostility on her part, which the child divines. (The dread of being *eaten* I have so far found only in men; it is referred to the father, but is probably the result of the transformation of oral aggressive tendencies directed upon the mother. The person the child wants to devour is the mother who nourished him: in the case of the father there is no such obvious occasion for the wish.)

The women patients characterized by a strong attachment to the mother, in whom I have been able to study the pre-Oedipus phase, have all told me that when their mother gave them enemas or rectal douches they used to offer the strongest possible resistance and react with fear and screams of rage. This is probably very usual or even universal with children. I only came to understand the reasons for this specially passionate struggle through a remark by Ruth Mack-Brunswick, who was studying these problems at the same time as I was. She said that she would compare the outbreak of fury after an enema with the orgasm following on genital excitation. The accompanying anxiety should be construed as a transformation of the desire for aggression which had been stirred up. I believe that this is actually the case and that, on the anal-sadistic level, the intense passive excitation of the intestinal zone evokes an outbreak of desire for aggression, manifesting itself either directly in the form of rage or, as a consequence of suppression, as anxiety. In later years this reaction seems to die away.

In considering the passive impulses of the phallic phase we are struck by the fact that girls regularly charge their mothers with seducing them, because their first or at any rate strongest genital sensations came to them when they were being cleansed and tended by their mothers (or the nurses representing them). Mothers have often told me that they have observed that their little daughters of two or three years old enjoy these sensations and try to get their mother to heighten them by repeated touching and rubbing of the parts. I believe that the fact that the mother so unavoidably initiates the child into the phallic phase is the reason why in the fantasies of later years the father so regularly appears as the sexual seducer. When the girl turns away from the mother she transfers to the father at the same time the responsibility for having introduced her to sexual life.

Finally in the phallic phase strong active wishes toward the mother also make their appearance. The sexual activity of this period culminates in clitoridal masturbation; probably the child accompanies this with images of her mother, but whether she really imagines a sexual aim and what that aim is my experience does not make clear. It is only when all her interests have received a fresh impetus through the arrival of a baby brother or sister that we can clearly recognize any such aim. The little girl, just like the boy, wants to believe that she has given her mother this new child, and her reaction to the event and her behavior toward the child are the same as his. I know this sounds quite absurd, but perhaps only because the idea is such an unfamiliar one to us.

The turning-away from the mother is a most important step in the little girl's development: it is more than a mere change of object. We have already described what takes place and what a number of motives are alleged for it; we must now add that we observe, hand in hand with it, a marked diminution in the active and an augmentation of the passive sexual impulses. It is true that the active impulses have suffered more severely from frustration: they have proved totally impracticable and therefore the libido has more readily abandoned them. But the passive trends also have not escaped disappointment. Frequently, with the turning-away from the mother there is cessation of clitoridal masturbation, and very often when the little girl represses her previous masculinity a considerable part of her general sexual life is permanently injured. The transition to the father-object is accomplished with the assistance of the passive tendencies so far as these have escaped overthrow. The way to the development of femininity then lies open to the girl, except in so far as she is hampered by remains of the pre-Oedipus mother-attachment which she has passed through.

If we survey the phases of feminine sexual development I have described, there is a definite conclusion about femininity as a whole which we cannot resist: the same libidinal forces, we have found, are at work in female and in male children, and we have been able to convince ourselves that for a certain period these forces take the same course and produce the same results.

Subsequently, biological factors deflect them from their original aims and conduct even active and in every sense masculine strivings into feminine channels. Since we cannot dismiss the notion that sexual excitation is derived from the operation of certain chemical substances, it would at first seem natural to expect that some day biochemistry will reveal two distinct substances, the presence of which produces male and female sexual excitation respectively. But this hope is surely no less naïve than that other one which has happily been abandoned nowadays, namely, that it would be possible to isolate under the microscope the different causative factors of hysteria, obsessional neurosis, melancholia, etc.

In sexual chemistry, too, the processes must be rather more complicated. For psychology, however, it is a matter of indifference whether there is in the body a single sexually stimulating substance, or two, or an endless number. Psychoanalysis teaches us to manage with a single libido, though its aims, i.e., its modes of gratification, are both active and passive. In this antithesis, above all in the existence of libidinal impulses whose aims are passive, the rest of our problem is contained.

IV

A study of the analytical literature on this subject makes evident that it already contains everything that I have said here. This study would be superfluous were it not that in so obscure a field of research every account of any worker's direct experience and the conclusions to which he personally is led may be of value. I have, moreover, I think, defined certain points more precisely and shown them in stricter isolation than has hitherto been done. Some of the other writings on the subject are confusing because they deal at the same time with the problems of the superego and the sense of guilt. This I have avoided, and also, in describing the various outcomes of this phase of development, I have refrained from touching on the complications which arise when a child, disappointed in her relation with her father, returns to the abandoned mother-attachment, or in the course of her life repeatedly shifts over from the one attitude to the other. But just because this article is only one contribution among others I may be dispensed from an exhaustive survey of the literature on the subject and will confine myself to indicating the more important points on which I agree with some or differ from other writers.

Abraham's (1921) description of the manifestations of the female castration complex is still unsurpassed, but one would have liked it to include the factor of the original exclusive attachment to the mother. With the principal points in Jeanne Lampl-de Groot's (1927) important work I am in agreement. She recognizes that the pre-Oedipus phase is completely identical in boys and in girls, and she affirms (and proves from her own observations) that the little girl's attitude toward the mother includes sexual (phallic) activity. The turning-away from the mother is traced by this writer to the influence of the child's perception of castration, which forces her to abandon her sexual object and often at the same time the practice of masturbation. The whole development is described in the following formula: the little girl has to pass through a phase of the "negative" Oedipus complex before arriving at the positive. There is one point in which I find her account inadequate: she represents the turning-away from the mother as merely a change of object and does not show that it is accompanied by the plainest manifestations of hostility. To this factor complete justice is done in Helene Deutsch's latest paper on the subject (1930), in which she also recognizes the little girl's phallic activity and the strength of her attachment to her mother. Helene Deutsch states, further, that in turning to the father the little girl follows her passive tendencies (already awakened in her relation with her mother). In her earlier book (1925) this author was still influenced by the endeavor to apply the Oedipus scheme to the pre-Oedipus phase and for this reason she interpreted the little girl's phallic activity as an identification with the father.

Fenichel (1930) rightly emphasizes the difficulty of recognizing in the material produced in analysis what represents the unchanged content of the pre-Oedipus phase and what has been distorted in the course of regression (or some other process). He does not accept Jeanne Lampl-de Groot's view of the little girl's phallic activity and he protests against Melanie Klein's (1928) "displacement backwards" of the Oedipus complex, whose beginnings she assigns to the commencement of the second year of life. This view of the date of origin of the complex, in addition to its necessitating a modification of our view of all the rest of the child's development, is in fact not in accordance with what we learn from the analyses of adults and is especially incompatible with my findings as to the long duration of the girl's pre-Oedipus attachment to her mother. This contradiction may be softened by the rejection that we are not as yet able to distinguish in this field between what is rigidly fixed by biological laws and what is subject to change or shifting under the influence of accidental experience. We have long recognized that seduction may have the effect of hastening and stimulating to maturity the sexual development of children, and it is quite possible that other factors operate in the same way; such, for instance, as the child's age when brothers or sisters are born or when it discovers the difference between the sexes, or, again, its direct observation of sexual intercourse, its parents' behavior in evoking or repelling its love, and so forth.

Some authors are inclined to disparage the importance of the child's first, most primal libidinal impulses, laying stress rather on later developmental processes, so that—putting this view in its extreme form—all that the former can be said to do is to indicate certain trends, while the amounts of energy [*Intensitäten*] with which these trends are pursued are drawn from later regressions and reaction-formations. Thus, for example, Karen Horney (1926) is of opinion that we greatly overestimate the girl's primary penis-envy and that the strength of her subsequent striving toward masculinity is to be attributed to a *secondary* penis-envy, which is used to ward off her feminine impulses, especially those connected with her attachment to her father. This does not agree with the impressions that I myself have formed. Certain as it is that the earliest libidinal tendencies are reinforced later by regression and reaction-formation and difficult as it is to estimate the relative strength of the various confluent libidinal components, I still think that we must not overlook the fact that those first impulses have an intensity of their own which is greater than anything that comes later and may indeed be said to be incommensurable with any other force. It is certainly true that there is an antithesis between the attachment to the father and the masculinity-complex—this is the universal antithesis between activity and passivity, masculinity and femininity—but we have no right to assume that only the one is primary, while the other owes its strength merely to the process of defense. And if the defense against femininity is so vigorous, from what other source can it derive its strength than from that striving for masculinity which found its earliest expression in the child's penis-envy and might well take its name from this?

A similar objection applies to Jones's view (1927) that the phallic phase in girls represents a secondary, protective reaction rather than a genuine stage of development. This does not correspond to either the dynamic or the chronological conditions.

VII

On Female Homosexuality

By Helene Deutsch

This paper is based on the experience gained from the more or less profound analysis of eleven cases of female homosexuality. I should like, first of all, to stress the fact that none of these eleven women presented physical signs which might indicate that there had been a constitutional deviation, physiologically, in the direction of masculinity. The signs of accentuated bisexual disposition mentioned in this paper refer to forerunners of what, in later development, we usually call masculinity. These preliminary stages, however, appear to have no physical correlates, or at any rate none that can be determined, for the patients showed no physical signs of masculinity. There are, to be sure, certain homosexual types whose personality, mental and physical, including the secondary sexual characteristics, are of the type which is appropriate to the other sex; but none of my patients belonged to this type.

The first of the eleven cases of female homosexuality was analyzed twelve years ago. Although the patient was aware of her sexual inversion, she did not indulge in homosexual practices; she knew that her erotic potentialities and fantasies were directed toward members of her own sex, and she would unequivocally become sexually excited when she embraced and kissed certain women. Toward these women, she was faithful and monogamous; her relations with them were purely platonic and remained platonic even when she knew that the women had a perverse tendency like her own. There was no particular type of woman which especially attracted her. The women were not in any instance of a masculine type, and she herself was blonde and feminine. She felt no hostility toward men, had a number of male friends, and accepted their favors and courtship without protestation. She had married a man of outspoken masculine appearance, and had several children by him to whom she gave a maternal, even if not excessively warm, response.

She was unable to explain why her homosexuality had not developed in a more active and urgent way; she only knew that her inhibitions against it were too strong—inhibitions which she rationalized on the basis of social shyness, family duty, and fear of psychic subjugation. She could trace her love response to women as far back as puberty, when it began in a typically adolescent way, directed toward teachers and other individuals more or less in authority. I cannot remember whether she characterized these individuals as particularly strict; in any event she was dominated by two feelings: a feeling of being sheltered, and, on the other hand, a feeling of fear of the individual in question. She was never really in love with a man. She had been attracted to her husband originally because she saw in him an exceptionally active and masculine personality. She was disappointed in marriage from the outset because, as she says, in this very relationship her husband failed to come up to her expectations. He lacked passion and was unaggressive particularly in sexual matters, and in other situations as well he failed her when she was most counting on his activity.

The patient came into analysis on account of neurotic difficulties. She had suffered for years from depressions and feelings of anxiety with a particular ideational content: she could not find the courage to assume the fitting authoritative attitude toward women in her employ. As a matter of fact, she expected a great deal of her servants and was upset when they failed to meet her demands, but she was quite unable to give them orders, much less to reprimand them. In situations which required this of her, she was overcome with timidity and anxiety in the presence of the person to be reproved. With every change in the personnel, and the consequent anticipation of a new woman in the household, her anxiety and conflict were greatly intensified. In these situations, moreover, she quite consciously reproached her husband for his lack of zeal in protecting and supporting her.

In recent years, her depressions had become more and more frequent and were intimately associated with the danger of suicide. The patient had already made a number of unsuccessful suicidal attempts; the last one had brought her to the verge of death. It happened that the physician called to her rescue was a close friend of mine, and he assured me that her intention to commit suicide had been genuine.

The patient's analysis for months revolved about the castration complex. At the time of this analysis—twelve years ago—the assumption of a castration complex in women was not such a matter of course as it is today. During the analysis I was so fascinated by the material dealing with this theme, that I was tempted to consider the castration complex the nucleus of her neurosis as well as of her perversion. She was so full of penis envy that it appeared even in her relation to her little boys whose penis she cut off in dreams and fantasies. Even though the patient was dominated by marked sadistic tendencies, her conscious personality was more reactive in character. That is to say, she was kind and gentle and showed unmistakable obsessional neurotic traits, such as exaggerated decorum and propriety. Her transference to me was very pronounced and was characteristic of that type whose actions as well as conscious responses over a long period of time reveal nothing except tenderness, respect and a feeling of safety. The patient was very happy and felt as if she had at last found a kind, understanding mother, who was making up to her all that her own mother had denied her. Her mother had been a stern and distant individual whom the patient had quite consciously hated all her life. After her mother's death (which occurred several years before the analysis began) the patient had a severe depression, during which she made one of her attempts at suicide.

The patient had several attacks of depression during the course of the analysis, following one another at short intervals. They were always accompanied by characteristic dreams and brought to light definite material. I discussed these dreams at the time—twelve years ago—at a meeting of the Vienna Psychoanalytic Society in a brief communication, under the title of *Mutterleibsträume und Selbstmordideen* (Uterus Dreams and

Suicidal Ideas). Without presenting these dreams in detail, I may state that they contained practically everything we know about uterine symbolism; they were dreams of dark holes and crevices in which the patient crawled, dreams of comfortable dark places in which the dreamer felt at home and in which she lingered with a feeling of peace and redemption. These dreams appeared at a time when the patient was weighted down by conscious urges to kill herself, and was insisting that if it were not for her relation to me and her confidence in me, no power in the world could restrain her from committing suicide. One special dream-picture kept reappearing in the dreams: the patient saw herself as an infant swaddled with strips of tape or bandages. Her associations to this dream-picture made it clear that two hazy memories were emerging in these dreams. One referred to her last suicidal attempt (with poison): she awoke from a deep loss of consciousness while still strapped to the stretcher; she saw the doctor with a kind smile on his face, leaning over her, realized that he had saved her life (which was quite true) and thought, "This time you saved me, but after all you can't give me any real help."

Another set of associations led to the memory of a dangerous operation which her mother had undergone. The patient remembered seeing her mother, wrapped up as she herself was to be later, transported to the operating-room on a stretcher.

Starting from this memory the analysis led to an aggressive, murderous hate against the mother, which up to this point had been repressed, but which now became the central theme of the analysis. After eight months' analysis, childhood memories began to appear, and these turned out to be the nucleus of her neurosis as well as the nucleus of her perversion. The memories went back to the time between the patient's fourth and sixth years when she was masturbating to an alarming extent—at least from the mother's point of view. It was impossible to decide whether this masturbation really exceeded the normal amount, nor could we determine the content of the fantasies which, presumably, had accompanied the masturbation. But it is a fact, according to the patient's statement, that the mother resorted to the following method of checking the patient's masturbation: she bound the patient's hands and feet, strapped them to the crib, and said, as she stood looking on, "Now play if you can!"

This aroused two reactions in the little girl. One was ungovernable rage against her mother, which was prevented by the fetters from discharge in motor activity. The other was intense sexual excitement, which she tried to satisfy by rubbing her buttocks against the bedding regardless of her mother's presence, or perhaps to vent her spite on her mother.

The most dreadful thing in this scene, for her, was the fact that her father, summoned by the mother, was a passive witness and did not offer to help his little girl despite his tender affection for her.

This memory was recovered in the analysis while the patient was associating to the following dream:

> She saw herself behind the bars in a police station, accused of some sort of sexual offense—apparently brought in from the street on suspicion of being a prostitute. The police sergeant, a kindly man, stood on the other side of the railing and did nothing to help her.

This is an almost direct repetition of the childhood situation. The patient stopped masturbating after this childhood scene, and with this renunciation for a long while repressed her sexuality. At the same time, she repressed her hatred for her mother, to which she had in reality never given full expression.

I do not believe that the scene with her mother, which occurred in the patient's childhood, was traumatic in the sense of causing the patient's later attitude. But concentrated in it were all of the tendencies which had a determining influence on her whole sexual life. Her reproach—that her mother had forbidden her to masturbate—would certainly have been present even without this scene. The hate reaction against her mother, in accordance with the patient's sadistic constitution, was also to be seen in other childhood situations, as well as the reproach that her father did not protect her from her mother. But this scene brought all of these tendencies to the boiling point, as is were, and so became the prototype for later events.

From this time on, all sexual excitement was bound up with the maternal prohibition and with the most intense aggressive impulses toward the mother. Her whole psychic personality resisted these hate impulses, and as a reaction to them there awakened in her an intense sense of guilt toward her mother, which led to a transformation of the hate into a masochistic libidinal attitude. It is, therefore, comprehensible that the patient should reply to the direct question, why she had never yielded to a homosexual attachment, with the answer that she was afraid of becoming subjugated to the sexual partner. She was, indeed, afraid of being masochistically attached to her mother. It will also become clear why she was afraid of the women in her employ and why she chided her husband for not adequately protecting her.

Even though, during her analysis, the patient manifested an exaggerated penis envy, it did not stand in the center of her personality, either characterologically or in her behavior toward men. She was not a woman with a "masculinity complex." However, it seems that this had not always been the case, for in her childhood before the eventful experience and also during puberty, there had been periods in which infallible signs of strongly developed masculine activity could be demonstrated. Especially at puberty many of her interests were quite unusual for a young girl in her social class at the time. This streak of masculinity was splendidly sublimated at the time, and indeed throughout her life. Yet a not inconsiderable part persisted and burdened her psychic economy, as dreams and certain inferiority feelings, etc., clearly showed.

I was very much tempted to assume that the patient was living out her masculinity in her homosexuality. But in this very point she failed to fulfill my analytic expectations, and presented me with a problem at the time which I could understand only years later. In order to adhere to a somewhat chronological order and present the facts as I learned them, I shall, for the time being, discontinue theoretical formulations.

After the above-mentioned part of the analysis had been worked through (after eight months) the father made his first real appearance as a topic of analytic material, and at the same time all of the impulses belonging to the Oedipus complex were revived, starting with the chief, unremitting, reproach against the father that he had been too inactive to love his daughter. I should like to emphasize the fact that even at that time it was clear to me that the hate against her mother and libidinal desire for her were much older than the Oedipus complex.

I hoped that the patient's libidinal future would shape up more satisfactorily with a revival of the father relationship, especially when this relationship had been retouched and corrected. I referred her to an analyst of the fatherly type. Unfortunately, the transference did not advance beyond respect and sympathy, and the analysis was interrupted after a short time. About a year later I met the patient and saw that she had become a vivid, radiant person. She told me that her depressions had entirely disappeared. The wish to die which had been almost continuously present and her nostalgia had apparently receded completely. At last she had found happiness in a particularly congenial and uninhibited sexual relationship with a woman. The patient, who was intelligent and conversant with analysis, informed me that their homosexual relationship was quite consciously acted out as if it were a mother-child situation, in which sometimes one, sometimes the other played the mother —a play with a double cast, so to speak. Moreover, the satisfactions sought in this homosexual love play involved chiefly the mouth and the external genitalia. No "male-female" contrast appeared in this relationship; the essential contrast was that of activity and passivity. The impression gained was that the feeling of happiness lay in the possibility of being able to play *both* roles.

The result of her analysis was evident. Everything that had come to the surface so clearly in the analytic transference was now detached from the person of the analyst and transferred to other women. The gratifications denied her in the analytic situation could now be found in the relationship with the new objects. It was evident that the overcoming of her hostility toward the analyst had brought with it the overcoming of her anxiety and, consequently, a positive libidinal relationship to women could appear in place of the anxiety and hostility which had caused the neurotic symptoms—only, of course, after the mother-substitute object had paid off the infantile grievances by granting her sexual satisfactions. The analytic treatment had not brought about the further and more favorable solution of the mother attachment, that is, a renunciation of her homosexuality and an inclination toward men. Here I should like to interrupt my discussion and present some of the other analyzed cases before continuing with the theoretical considerations. For the sake of completeness, it may be added that after the analysis the patient made no more suicidal attempts; but I have heard that the old difficulties with women in her employ have recently begun again. I suppose that some disturbances in the love relationship occurred, which probably resulted in a neurotic reaction. But in any case there has been no suggestion of the depressions as they were before the analysis.

In the course of the last three years I have analyzed several cases of female homosexuality—cases in which the perversion was more manifest than in the one just described. Analysis with them began, so to speak, where this patient's analysis left off. All of them were in a more or less consciously recognized mother-child relationship with their love object. Sexual satisfaction was obtained in all these cases from the following practices: close embrace, mutual sucking at the nipples, genital and (more prominently) anal masturbatory stimulation, and intense mutual cunnilingus. Of special interest is the prominence given to the double role in these cases also.

One of these patients had divided the double role between two type of objects: one type, represented by an insignificant, needy young girl, who would take the part of the child; the other by an older, very active and very authoritative woman with whom the patient herself played the part of the child. The latter type of relationship usually began when the patient, who was very active and professionally ambitious, entered into a sublimated relationship with the woman, remained for a short time in a scarcely noticeable attitude of competition (of which she became conscious only through analysis), and then began to fail in her work in a clearly neurotic way, so that she would be in a subordinate position to the particular woman in question. For example, the end-result of writing a technical article, which had been undertaken jointly, was that the patient—perhaps the more gifted of the two—would play the part of a secretary in editing the work. If sexual approaches were made during work of this kind, the role of active seducer was always conceded to the other woman.

From the life history and the analysis, I shall select only the material needed for the theoretical considerations to be presented later.

The patient belonged to a very large family; she had many

sisters and two brothers, of whom only one, four years her senior, played a part in her life story. When she was only nine months old, a new sister arrived, a competitor who disputed her right to the mother's breast. She suffered, in early childhood, from all sorts of oral symptoms, from which it was possible to reconstruct a situation which might be described as "oral envy." She remained for a long time in a competitive relation to this sister, to whom, even in childhood, she gave precedence—an evident overcompensation. For instance, she recounted in the analysis that very early in childhood, she had heard that when there is such a slight difference in age and such a striking resemblance between two sisters as there was between her and her sister, only one of them could marry and have children. She thus retired from the feminine role in favor of her sister; and in adolescence, when her parents were divorced after the birth of the last child, she waived her claim to the father to the advantage of the other children and remained with her mother.

Very early in childhood, the patient developed reaction formations to aggressive tendencies which, before the birth of the next sister (when she was six), were suggestive of obsessional neurosis; they did not, however, develop to any great degree. At any rate, during her mother's pregnancy at that time, she reproached herself bitterly because she did not feel as kindly disposed toward her mother and the expected baby as her younger sister Erna did; she was convinced that the latter prayed every morning for the well-being of the mother and child.

The analysis uncovered strong aggression against the mother,[1] especially against the *pregnant* mother, and against the newborn child. The life of the patient and her whole character had developed, as it turned out, under the pressure of an attempt to dispel thoughts of killing her mother and the child.

The reaction recurred afresh at the two following pregnancies of her mother—the children again were both girls; and only after the birth of her youngest sister, when the patient was twelve years old, did her psychical situation change. When she was

[1] Melanie Klein's observations show very clearly how bloodthirsty and aggressive a child's relations to its mother are, especially when an actual event (e.g., the birth of a younger child) mobilizes the aggression. The great value of these observations lies in the fact that they were made directly on children.

very young, the patient always thought of her father as a mysterious, strange and powerful man, in whose presence one could not help feeling timid and anxious; but her attitude gradually changed, for the father had acquired a heart debility which finally incapacitated him for work. The family was thus involved in material difficulties, and with this stimulus, the patient took over the father's role herself, and gave free play to fantasies in which she held good positions and supported the family. As a matter of fact, by dint of hard work she later realized these fantasies.

In spite of the identification with her father, and in spite of the fact that she envied her brother's masculinity, she did not take the competitive attitude toward her youngest sister that she had taken to the other sisters when they were born. She was, on the contrary, highly pleased with the role of being a "little mother" and claimed the child entirely for herself. In this situation, she was behaving quite normally as far as the Oedipus complex was concerned. The analysis showed that this positive Oedipus attitude was reached only because she had dethroned her father from his position of supreme and unapproachable power, and that only then could she overcome the intense fear of the masochistic, sexual experience which she desired.

My experience substantiates my assumption that this change of object—the libidinal turning away from the mother to the father—is accomplished with more difficulty, the more aggressive and sadistic are the predominating dispositions in the little girl, not only because the change of object is hindered by the active strivings, but also because the change into the passive attitude must, in cases of this type, assume a marked masochistic character and be repudiated by the ego as dangerous.

Our patient had certainly attained the normal Oedipus situation, as her puberty clearly showed, but the ensuing rivalry with her mother provided fresh fuel for the old pre-Oedipal aggression. This intensified her sense of guilt, which could be relieved only by means of a new overcompensation—renunciation of her father and definite persistence in her mother attachment.

To reduce the psychological basis of this relationship to a formula, we might say: "I do not hate you; I love you. It is not true that you have refused me the breast and given it to my youngest (so to speak, pre-Oedipal) sister; you gave it to me, and, therefore, I do not need to kill you and the child. It is not true that I have killed the child, for I myself am the child whom you love and suckle." This fundamental attitude toward the mother is reflected not only in the form of the direct oral satisfaction in homosexual intercourse with the young girl (see above), but also in the above-mentioned submissive, passive attitude to the elder love-partner.

It must be noted that homosexuality as stated in the above formula as yet does not involve the Oedipus situation, and is a continuation of and a reaction to the pre-Oedipal situation.

However, the type of relationship which the patient had with the young girl corresponds not only to the active part of the original mother-child relationship—in which she makes a typical identification with the nourishing mother—but quite clearly makes use of new elements taken from the Oedipus situation. The young girl is always a surrogate for her youngest sister—toward whom she actually had assumed a maternal role as a lifelong sublimation—but she is unsublimatedly homosexual with her love object, a relatively unknown young girl. In this relationship, she is at times the mother who suckles her child (or the father's child), and at times the suckled child herself. In this sexual experience she is able to transform the hate of her mother into love, for she is given the mother's breast; at the same time, she can be the active, suckling mother and thereby transform the aggression against her mother into activity.

At this point I should like to report some of the dreams which occurred in this patient's analysis, and from abundant material I shall select those which offer confirmation for the above statements even in the *manifest* dream content. One dream ran as follows:

> The patient sees herself on the street with her younger sister. She is pregnant. She is in a hurry to reach a house which she sees in front of her. In the middle of the front of this house is a large projecting bay-window with one of the windows open. This is her mother's room; she wants to get there to give birth to her child. She is very much afraid that she will lose the child on the street, that is, that she will miscarry before she reaches the house. She expresses this fear to her sister, and then really does miscarry in the street.

The dream was readily explained by the patient's actual situation at the time. The day before the dream, she had been visited by a young friend, living in another city, whom she had not seen since the beginning of the analysis. This friend was really a homosexual object after the pattern of her youngest sister. They slept together, and the patient held her in her arms, pressed closely against her. But before there was any sexual release, she was upset by an uneasy feeling that the gratification of her homosexual wishes might possibly interfere with the analysis. She therefore made the friend leave the bed—lost her, as it were, out of her arms—in order not to disturb her relationship with me. It is clear that the pregnancy in the dream—the condition in which she has the child with her (within her)—is equated with her experience of the sexual embrace. The longing for her pregnant mother in the dream, which appears as a uterine fantasy in terms of a projecting bay window, and her simultaneous identification with her mother and with the child *in utero* is unusually clear. Furthermore, in the same analytic hour the patient remembered, for the first time, that when she was about three and a half years old, her mother had had a miscarriage. It was in this period of her childhood that she had been deeply attached to her mother and had reacted with such extraordinary aggression to the pregnancy.

The other fragment of the dream: "I am walking with my youngest sister"—likewise expresses the situation before she fell asleep and means: "I have my beloved one beside me." This dream situation betrays the analytically established fact that the sexual relationship with her friend also includes a fulfillment of the Oedipal wish, since the new little daughter belongs to her and not to her mother. The dream situation—to reach the mother and bear the child, or, on the contrary, not to reach the mother and to lose the child—portrays with unusual clarity the identity mother-child; that is, "to bear" equals "to be born," relates to the pre-Oedipal situation at the time of the mother's miscarriage. The fusing of this situation with Oedipal wishes and its screening by the wishes of the Oedipus attitude also seem to be clear in this case. I shall report only a fragment of a second dream:

> The patient lies dreaming on a couch, a figure approaches her and tries to expose her. She tries to shriek and wakes up with the exclamation. "My God, doctor!"

She notices on awakening that she had her hands between her legs.

A series of associations to the dream led to a theme with which her analysis was dealing at this particular time—namely, masturbation. For quite a long time during the analysis the patient had refrained from masturbation because of the embarrassment she might feel in telling me of it. Shortly before, however, she had begun to allow herself to do it—with inhibitions—under the impression that I had nothing against it. Her exclamation, "My God!" referred to me and meant that I should save her from the danger of punishment—that is, protect her or give her my sanction. This interpretation was clear from the associations, some of which led to the memory of a childhood experience. She had once touched an electric switch with a wet hand, so that the current had run through her, and she could not take her hand away. In response to her outcry ("My God") her mother had hurried to her, and also became a part of the circuit; with this, the current was weakened and the patient was able to release her hand. She had been rescued by her mother's interference. Like her mother, then, in the dream, I was to save her from "touching"—from the consequences of trespassing and doing a forbidden thing, by coming into the circuit of her excitement myself, by embracing her and gratifying her.

This excerpt from the dream serves to illustrate the other important feature of her homosexuality; her conflict over masturbation is brought to this apparently favorable solution by maternal intervention—that is, by the mother's expressed sanction. In another dream:

A tall, heavy-set woman she takes to be her mother, although she is taller and heavier than the latter, is in deep mourning because Erna (her next younger sister) has died. The father is standing nearby. She herself is in a cheerful mood because she is about to go away with her father on a spree. A glance at her mother warns her that this will not do, and that she must stay with her grieving mother.

This dream interprets itself. The patient is unable to satisfy her Oedipal wishes and cannot be gay and happy with a man, because her feelings of guilt, which refer to the mother whose child she has killed, bind her to her mother and force her into homosexuality. From another long and informative dream, I cite here only a fragment.

> She sees herself in analysis with Miss Anna Freud who is wearing men's clothes. This was explained in the dream by the fact that it was necessary for her to change analysis. With me it had been a question of producing free associations, with Miss Anna Freud it was a question of experiences.

On the evening before this dream, the patient was taken by her friends to a lecture held in the rooms of the Vienna Psychoanalytic Society, at which both Miss Freud and I were present. She told me in connection with this dream, that originally Miss Freud and I had been recommended to her as analysts. From the descriptions of us which she had heard, she had made up her mind what we were like; in her imagination Miss Freud represented a maternal ideal, a person who was motherly to all children, and ready to give them succor whenever they turned to her for help; my motherliness, she imagined, was directed especially toward my own children (that is to say, sexualized). Furthermore, it occurred to her at this point that before making her final decision, she had intended to write to us both, but, as a matter of fact, and as she now remembered for the first time, she had asked only for my address.

The evening before the dream, she had had a chance to compare us. She thought to herself, how true her idea about us had been, and how happy she was to be in analysis with me. This protestation seemed somewhat dubious to me, and I called her attention to the fact that the dream appeared to contradict it. It had struck me that the patient, who had gone to the lecture to see a certain analyst there, had not said a word about him, although he was sitting next to Miss Freud. Furthermore, she had not explained why, in the dream, Miss Freud appeared in men's clothing. A few days later she dreamed:

> I am sitting facing her instead of behind her (as I always do) and am holding a cigar in my hand. She thinks, "The ashes are so long on the cigar that they will drop off any second."

She says, as her first association to the cigar, "Only men smoke cigars."

The masculinity, attributed to me, reminded me of the corresponding detail in regard to Miss Freud in the preceding dream. I then remembered that as the patient sat facing Miss Freud at the lecture, she must at the same time have seen on the wall the picture of Professor Freud, in which he holds a cigar in his hand. A similar picture is on my office desk. I showed this to her, and she agreed that the position of the hand holding the cigar was the same as mine in the dream.

Further analysis showed that she had dearly wished to be analyzed by Professor Freud, but that this wish, springing as it did from her deep longing for the great man—the father—had been repressed, and that along with it, Miss Freud had been included in the repression. In addition, as already stated, she repressed the fact that she had met the analyst referred to above, and her impression of Professor Freud's picture. The repressed then asserted itself in the masculinity attributed to Miss Freud and me.

The way the father reappears in the dreams testifies to the fact that the patient's turning to the woman corresponds also to a flight from the man. The analysis revealed the source from which this tendency to flight originated: feelings of guilt toward the mother, fear of disappointment and of rejection.

To survey the case again briefly, we see that the first period of the patient's life was passed under somewhat unusual conditions. For a while she was nursed together with a younger sister, and when, finally, she had in her sister's interest to give up suckling, she developed (somewhat justifiably) a marked oral envy. When she was three years old, her mother became pregnant again, and she reacted to the anticipation of the child with great hostility and jealousy. The dream of the miscarriage illustrated the psychic condition of the little girl at the time, and her intense wish that she herself should be the child in the mother's womb.

This dream however was screened by reminiscences from a later period of her life (her twelfth year), and in the identification with her mother she betrayed her wish to have the child herself. This wish already is part of the Oedipal attitude, which developed apparently late and slowly, but none the less *powerfully*, as we could see in the analysis.

It is hard to say whether her infantile and never relinquished longing to possess her mother for herself alone and be fed and cared for by her, tended to have an inhibitory effect on normal libidinal development, or whether the difficulties of the Oedipus complex, as we know them in other cases, were the decisive factors in determining the later fate of the little girl's sexuality. I tried to show, above, in interpreting the dreams, that her return to her mother had not made her relinquish her longing for her father, but that she was constantly and anxiously fleeing from him, and consequently repressing her feminine attitude to men.

From the reported material, I should now like to deduce certain theoretical conclusions, which seem to me to represent important additions to our understanding of female sexuality in general, and of female homosexuality in particular.

It is repeatedly stated that our knowledge of *female* sexuality reaches no further than its correspondence with *male* sexuality in *childhood*. Only in *puberty*, when women really become feminine in the biological sense, are the conditions clearer and more comprehensible. Some of the important processes of the early stages of development were clarified by Freud's paper, *Einige psychische Folgen des anatomischen Geschlechtsunterschiedes.* In this paper he demonstrates the fact that the Oedipus complex is not established in girls until after the phallic phase. I had already discussed[2] the stage in a girl's development which follows the phallic phase, and in which there is a thrust into passivity *(Passivitätsschub).* The central feature of this phase is the wish to be given an anal child by the father. I pointed out, in this discussion, that the thrust into passivity is really a regressive process, and represents a regression to a phase preceding the phallic organization which is identical in boys and girls. We are too readily fascinated, I think, by the events which take place in the phallic phase and by its manifestations and latent potentialities, so that we have emphasized the phallic phase to the neglect of the succeeding stage of passivity, which has been treated more like a stepchild. We rest content with the fact that the wish to have a penis has been yielded in *exchange* for the wish to have a child, and that then it is up to the normal psychical powers inherent in the child to cope with the next frustration and to solve the new problem without harming itself.

[2] Helene Deutsch, *Psychoanalyse der weiblichen Sexualfunktionen.* Int. Psa. Verlag, 1925.

There is, I believe, no clinical observation to confute the idea that the intensity with which a child is desired is entirely dependent on the intensity of the preceding wish for a penis; therefore, one may say that the stronger the wish to have a penis, the stronger will be the subsequent wish to have a child; and the more difficult it is to bear being denied a penis, the more aggression will there be in the reaction to the thwarting of the wish for a child. Thus arises a vicious circle which often obscures the state of affairs for analysts; we find repeatedly that the very women whose violent psychic conflict was occasioned by the castration complex (i.e., by penis envy) are the ones who also have an ardent feminine wish for a child.

A girl may have had a fairly normal sexual development up to the beginning of the Oedipus complex and given up all hope of having a penis, so that she is ready for the transition from phallic activity into passivity—that is to say, she is ready to conceive the anal child by her father. This, however, is not sufficient to enable her to withstand the next bitter disappointment, which appears when she is denied a child. Keeping in mind the scheme of libidinal development we must not forget that along with this thrust into passivity a number of active forces are revived and raise their heads again because of the renewed cathexis of pregenital tendencies. They find their place without difficulty in the normal mental economy. For the role of the mother with the child, as the little girl playing with her dolls well illustrates, is an active one.

But what happens when the girl recoils in fright from the masochistic danger of the thrust into passivity? And when she cannot bear the actual disappointment of being denied a child, yet is convinced of the futility of her wish to have a penis? Let us get the situation clearly in mind: the child is no longer narcissistically stimulated by the wish for a penis which she recognizes cannot be fulfilled; she feels rejected by her father, because of denial, disappointment or anxiety; she is left with libido which has little opportunity for sublimation. What will she do? She will do what all living creatures do in situations of danger. She will flee for refuge to the shelter where she once enjoyed protection and peace, to her mother. To be sure, she had been disappointed by her mother too, but preceding all her denials there had been a time of satisfaction, for the refusing, hated mother had been at one time the source of all gratifications.

There is no doubt that even in the phallic phase the sexual instincts derive some satisfaction from the mother's routine care of the child. But apparently the claims at this time are more intense and they cannot, because of their dependence on the functions which are helping to build the ego, be satisfied to the same far-reaching extent as they were in preceding phases. Let us consider also that the phallic sexual aims were undisguised, that they were voiced easily, and that the mother's horror on her discovery of the wishes betrayed by the child was evident. We know from the analyses of mothers that their horror at the masturbatory actions of the child is the greater, the more their own unconscious memories of their own childhood masturbation are mobilized by direct observation of their children's behavior. The restrictions to which the child is now subjected will cause a stronger reaction the more the mother herself has excited the child, in her unconscious role of seducer. Subsequent *direct* prohibition of masturbation and forcible interference with masturbatory activity rouses the hostility against the disciplinary mother to a high pitch. Moreover, with phallic masturbation comes the *affective* discovery of the anatomical "defect."

We already know that the girl blames her mother for depriving her of a penis. The sadistic impulses of the phallic phase are, accordingly, directed against the mother, and they are probably the impetus for the change of object. The change to a sadistic attitude toward the mother facilitates the passive masochistic attitude toward the father; all of this results from the phase that I have called the "thrust into passivity." It is certain, however, that the aggression is not entirely conducted into the masochistic passive attitude. Much of the aggressive impulse is turned against the disappointing father, and much remains attached to the mother who is now regarded as a rival. The intensity in any case is dependent upon the strength of the phallic activity. Furthermore, the change to masochism will occur with greater intensity, the more it is nurtured from the sources of aggression. Analysis of patients who have a very strong castration complex shows unequivocally how full of danger the passive attitude is as regards the development of masochism, and how bloodthirsty and murderous are the ideas of revenge on the mother, especially on the mother who in fact or fantasy is pregnant, or who already has another child. This attitude supplies the masochism with its moral component in addition, and the strength of the moral component is directly proportionate to the strength of the aggression.

We are thus aware of the dangers with which the little girl is beset in this phase:

1. Libidinal masochistic danger because of the expectation that her father may fulfill her wishes.

2. The danger of losing the newly chosen object as a result of refusal on her father's part.

3. Dangers of narcissistic injury of the ego libido, incident to the realization of the permanent lack of a penis.

In the midst of these great dangers, the libido, as we have said, turns to the earlier object again, and obviously more easily and more ardently the stronger the earlier attachments had been. It is a reversion to previously enjoyed experiences, as it were. I mean by this, that the aggression due to rivalry arising from the Oedipus complex, and the more highly organized sense of guilt, are now combined with the early infantile ambivalence conflicts.

The economic advantage of this new turning to the mother lies in the release from a feeling of guilt. But it seems to me that its most important accomplishment lies in the protection from the threatened loss of object: "If my father won't have me, and my self-respect is so undermined, who will love me, if not my mother?"

Analytic experience offers abundant evidence of this bisexual oscillation between father and mother, which may eventuate in neurosis, heterosexuality or inversion. We see the libido swinging between the poles of two magnets, attracted and repelled. Prospects of wish-fulfillment represent the *attraction* by one pole, frustration, fear, and mobilization of guilt feelings the *repulsion* from the other; and we see the same thing happening in the case of other magnets; and as one of the most serious results of this oscillation, an obstinate narcissistic standstill appears somewhere in between. There are cases of blocking of affect, and especially clinical pictures of narcissistic disorders, which do not fit into any of the recognized forms of neurosis, but which do correspond to a standstill in the pendulum swing of libido as just described. If the oscillation is set in motion again in the analytic transference, the obsessional neurosis, whose oscillating ambivalence had been concealed by the emotional block, becomes apparent.

There was in these cases of female homosexuality a longer or shorter phase of indecision, which offers proof that it was not a question of a simple fixation on the mother as the first love object, but rather a complicated process of returning. The decision in favor of the mother as the attracting magnet lies naturally in the old powers of attraction, but also in the repelling forces from other magnets—denial, anxiety, and guilt reactions.

The return to the mother, when once started, needs the completion of still another process before it attains the character of a genuine inversion. First of all, the motives which once really induced the little girl to respond to the biological urge toward the father must be made retroactive. Accordingly, the sexual satisfaction of masturbation, which has been forbidden by the mother, must not only no longer be prohibited, but must be consented to by the mother by an active participation. The denial of the past must be made good by subsequent permissions, and indeed quite as much in reference to the original passive experience as to the subsequent active experience. One might say that the interruption of the phallic activity is made up for by this consent to activity which had been impossible in the past. The form which this active behavior of the girl toward the maternal object takes depends on the developmental stage at which the homosexual object relationship is taking place; that is, to speak more correctly, it depends on which is the most predominant stage, for, on closer observation, we see in the re-activation *all* phases in which the mother played a role, which is equivalent to saying, all the stages of the preceding infantile development. Usually the most urgent tendencies are the phallic ones, and they cause the relationship of one female to another to assume a male character, whereby the absence of a penis is denied. These tendencies can indeed dominate the general picture of homosexuality, and may give rise to a definite, and as a matter of fact, the most outstanding, homosexual type.[3] This type denies the absence of a penis, expects that her feminine object will grant her her masculinity, and accepts phallic masturbation as a confirmation in the above-mentioned sense. It is then not very important whether the femininity of the object is to be emphasized, or whether both the subject and object are simultaneously affirming possession of a penis, so that the object may also take her turn in playing the masculine role. These are two sub-types of the same species. The extent of the old competitive attitude, especially in cases where an early displacement from the mother on to a sister took place, the quantum of masochistic or sadistic component, that is to say, the preponderance of aggressive tendencies or of reactions of guilt, a more passive or a more active casting of the role—these are all merely details in the total problem of female homosexuality.

I said that the phallic masculine form of homosexuality was the most outstanding one. But there are always many deeper currents hiding behind it. It is my impression, indeed, that this masculine form is sometimes brought into evidence for the very purpose of hiding the more infantile, but none the less predominating tendencies. The majority of the cases which I have analyzed were forced to an honest and extensive relinquishment of their masculine behavior by the strength of their pregenital urges. The mother-child relationship at pregenital levels, in the deeply entrenched fixation of the pre-phallic phases (whether consciously or unconsciously), dominated the perversion. The wish for activity belonging to the phallic phase is carried along in the regression, and reaches its most satisfactory fulfillment in the homosexual relationship. The frequent expression of the small child, "when you are little and I am big," finds its realization

[3] The case of female homosexuality published by Freud would also be classified under this "masculine" type, even though the original attitude of the patient was thoroughly feminine, and the masculine wish corresponded only to a subsequent identification with the once loved father. (Freud: *Über die Psychogenese eines Falles von weiblicher Homosexualität*. Ges. Schr. V. Trans. in *Coll. Papers*, II.)

The two cases of female homosexuality described by Fenichel in *Perversionen Psychosen, Charakterstörungen*, Int. Psa. Verlag, Wien, 1932, illustrate the same mental mechanisms as Freud's case. These cases also represent a "masculine" identification with the father as a reaction to being disappointed by him.

here in this double role which is always played in this relationship, in which the child does everything with her mother that the mother had at one time done with her. Such freedom of activity, and the giving of free rein to masturbation are motives held in common by all forms of homosexuality. If in the phallic situation the mother compensates for the child's hurt by some sort of assent to the child's belief in the presence of a penis, then, in this new edition of the mother-child relationship, the pregenital frustrations and denials must also be compensated, and this indeed happens often enough in the satisfaction which homosexual persons derive from their activities. Freud laid special emphasis on the marked preference of the oral mucous membrane in the activities of female inverts in the *Three Contributions to the Theory of Sex*[4] and Jones[5] has found the disposition to female homosexuality in the oral sadistic phase. I feel that all my cases offer thorough confirmation of this dispositional element. I can state, furthermore, with complete security that not one of my cases failed to have a very strong reaction to the castration complex; a complete Oedipus complex with exceedingly powerful aggressive reactions could be demonstrated in every case.

The return to the mother-child attitude was always introduced by the wish for the child which had been expected long since in place of a penis, but which had continued to be withheld. One of the sources from which the inversion is nourished is the reaction to the fact: "It is my mother who gets the child, not I." Not until later when the child herself has become a mother does the disposition for cruelty indicated in this reaction find adjustment, and then in a complicated manner in her own mother-child relationship. The above-mentioned patient produced unequivocal evidence for this in her dreams.

Considering the great complexity of the mother-child relationship, it is not surprising that the longing for the mother assumes the character of womb fantasies. We were able to observe this tremendous combination of longing for the mother with a wish to die in our first patient, as a contribution to the subject of mother attachment and fear of death.

[4] Ges. Schr. V. English trans. by A. A. Brill.
[5] Ernest Jones, *The Early Development of Female Sexuality*. Int. J. Ps-A. VIII, 1927.

I cannot leave this subject without a few remarks on a question which has a bearing in this connection. Is it really necessary to explain the little girl's attachment to a maternal object in such a roundabout way? Would it not be much simpler, for instance, to speak of an original fixation and to look for the causes in constitutional factors? I have considered the material without prejudice, and yet in every one of my cases of analyzed homosexual women, the light or the shadow cast on the original relationship by the father's presence has played an important and necessary part.

As a matter of fact, in recent years, I think I have occasionally observed a state of affairs in certain cases in which the Oedipus complex had apparently played no role at all, or almost none, and in which the libido had never known but *one* object—the mother. But these were very special cases, whose whole neurosis had the character of general psychic infantilism with diffuse anxieties and perversions, and whose transference could not be released from an obstinate incorrigible, anxious attachment.

Under the stimulus of Freud's latest paper,[6] it would be an undertaking well worth while to collect some of the obscure clinical cases, since they might possibly find their explanation in the primary mother attachment. In this group, in addition to the above-mentioned cases of infantilism, there would surely belong certain forms of hysteria whose "secondary gain" proves so incorrigible because it is a clear repetition of the early infantile situation, when the child was taken care of by the mother.

Returning to my theme, there still remains the question as to when the girl's final decision in favor of homosexuality occurs. It is known that the girl's infantile period of sexual development does not come to such a sudden and radical conclusion as the boy's. The change of object takes place gradually and it would seem that only with puberty comes the final decision both as to the choice of object and the readiness for the passive attitude.

Girls show a much stronger dependence on the mother during the latency period than boys. This may be related to the girl's fear of losing her object, as I have tried to explain above, and also to the type of sublimation, which in girls tends rather to

[6] Sigmund Freud, *Über die weibliche Sexualität*, Int. Ztschr. f. Psa. XVII, 1931.

establish affectionate object relationships, and in boys is expressed in an active response to the outer world. On the other hand, it appears that during puberty the girl shows a more definite sublimation in the direction of the outer world in the "thrust of activity" *(Aktivitätscchub)*, which I have described.[7] This would indicate that the feminine passive attitude is not completely formed during the infantile phase. The tomboyish period during the girl's puberty is widespread and normal. The girl derives from it the best energies for sublimations and for the formation of her personality, and I think I make no mistake in allowing myself this variation of a statement by Richard Wagner: "The girl who had nothing of the boy in her during her youth will turn out to be a *vacca domestica* in later life." Of course, we are aware of the great dangers which this period of activity conceals with respect to the "masculinity complex" and its neurotic consequences. If it is true that the final change of object takes place in puberty, then this shift to activity must add dangers for the heterosexual attitude, and the masculine tendencies of puberty will also contribute their share to homosexuality.

In conclusion, we have still to mention the final struggles in *overcoming* the Oedipus complex during puberty. We have a classical example of this in a case of female homosexuality (to which we were introduced in the above-mentioned publication of Freud), which developed in puberty as a result of difficulties with the Oedipus complex. However, I must repeat that in all of the cases under my observation the cornerstone for later inversion had already been laid in the first infantile period.

[7] Deutsch, *op. cit.*

VIII

Passivity, Masochism and Femininity*

By Marie Bonaparte

I. *The pain inherent in the female reproductive functions.*
II. *Erotic pleasure in women.*
III. *The infantile sadistic conception of coitus.*
IV. *The necessary fundamental distinction between masochism and passivity.*
V. *The female cloaca and the male phallus in women.*

I. *The pain inherent in the female reproductive functions.* The most superficial observer cannot help noting that in the sphere of reproduction the lot of men and of women, in respect of pain suffered, is an unequal one. The man's share in the reproductive functions is confined to a single act—that of coitus—which he necessarily experiences as pleasurable, since, for him, the function of reproduction coincides with the erotic function. The woman, on the other hand, periodically undergoes the suffering of menstruation, the severity of which varies with the individual; for her, sexual intercourse itself is initiated by a process which involves in some degree the shedding of her blood, namely, the act of defloration; finally, gestation is accompanied by discomfort and parturition by pain, while even lactation is frequently subject to painful disturbances.

* Based on a paper read before the Thirteenth International Psycho-Analytical Congress, Lucerne, August, 1934. The original paper, the contents of which are here reproduced in a revised form, was entitled "Du masochisme féminin essentiel."

Already in the Bible[1] woman is marked out for the pain of child-bearing, the punishment for original sin. Michelet[2] describes her as "*l'éternelle blessée*" ("the everlastingly wounded one"). And, in psychoanalytical literature, Freud,[3] discussing the problem of masochism, that bewildering product of human psychosexuality, characterizes it, in its erotogenic form, as "feminine," while Helene Deutsch[4] regards it as a constant factor in female development and as an indispensable constituent in woman's acceptance of the whole of her sexuality, intermingled, as it is, with so much pain.

II. *Erotic pleasure in women.* There is, however, another fact no less striking even to a superficial observer. In sexual relations women are often capable of a high degree of erotic pleasure; they crave for caresses, it may be of the whole body or of some particular zone, and in these caresses the element of suffering, of masochism, is entirely and essentially absent. Moreover, in actual copulation the woman can experience pleasurable orgasm analogous to that of the man.

Of course, in this connection we must bear in mind the biological fact of which, for that matter, many biologists appear to be ignorant, though Freud has accurately appraised its importance: in women, as contrasted with men, there are two adjacent erotogenic zones—the clitoris and the vagina—and these reflect and confirm the bisexuality inherent in every woman. In some instances there is an open outbreak of antagonism between the two zones, with the result that the woman's genital erotism becomes centered exclusively either in the vagina or in the clitoris, with, in the latter case, vaginal anesthesia. In other instances, and I think these are the more common, the two zones settle into harmonious collaboration, enabling her to perform her erotic function in the normal act of copulation.

Nevertheless, woman's share in sexual pleasure seems to be derived from whatever virility the female organism contains. The

[1] Genesis iii. 16.

[2] *L'Amour,* Vol. I, ch. ii, p. 57, Calmann Lévy, 1910.

[3] "The Economic Problem in Masochism" (1924), *Collected Papers,* Vol. II.

[4] *Psychoanalyse der weiblichen Sexualfunktionen,* 1925; "The Significance of Masochism in the Mental Life of Women," *International Journal of Psychoanalysis,* Vol. XI, 1930.

great biologist Marañon[5] was in the right when he compared woman to a male organism arrested in its development, half-way between the child and the man—arrested, that is to say, precisely by the inhibitory influence exercised by the apparatus of maternity, which is subjoined to and exists in a kind of symbiosis side by side with the rest of her delicate organism.

The residue of virility in the woman's organism, is utilized by nature in order to eroticize her: otherwise the functioning of the maternal apparatus would wholly submerge her in the painful tasks of reproduction and motherhood.

On the one hand, then, in the reproductive functions proper—menstruation, defloration, pregnancy and parturition—woman is biologically doomed to suffer. Nature seems to have no hesitation in administering to her strong doses of pain, and she can do nothing but submit passively to the regimen prescribed. On the other hand, as regards sexual attraction, which is necessary for the act of impregnation, and as regards the erotic pleasure experienced during the act itself, the woman may be on equal footing with the man. It must be added, however, that the feminine erotic function is often imperfectly and tardily established and that, owing to the woman's passive role in copulation, it always depends—and this is a point which we must not forget —upon the potency of her partner and especially upon the time which he allows for her gratification, which is usually achieved more slowly than his own.

III. *The infantile sadistic conception of coitus.* Let us now go back to the childhood situation.

Psychoanalytical observations have proved beyond any doubt that when, as often happens, a child observes the coitus of adults, he invariably perceives the sexual act as an act of sadistic aggression perpetrated by the male upon the female—an act not merely of an oral character, though little children do so conceive of it, because the only relations between one human being and another of which they have at first any knowledge are of an oral nature. But, seeing how early the cannibalistic phase occurs, it seems certain that this *oral* relation is itself conceived of as

[5] *La Evolucion de la Sexualidad y los Estados Intersexuals,* Madrid, Morata, 1930. French translation by Sanjurjo D'Arellano, Paris, Gallimard, 1931.

aggressive. Nevertheless, it so frequently happens that the child is in the anal-sadistic phase when he makes these observations that his predominating impression is that of an attack made by the male upon the female, in which she is wounded and her body penetrated. Having regard to the primitive fusion of instincts we may perhaps say that the earlier these observations occur the more marked is the sadistic tinge which they assume in the child's mind. In his perception of the acts of adults the degree of his own aggressiveness, which varies with the individual child, must also play a decisive part, being projected on to what he sees.

In the mind of a child who has witnessed the sexual act the impressions received form, as it were, a stereotyped picture which persists in the infantile unconscious. As he develops and his ego becomes more firmly established, this picture is modified and worked over, and doubtless there are added to it all the sado-masochistic fantasies[6] which analysis has brought to light in children of both sexes.

The very early observations of coitus, made when the child was still in the midst of the sadistic-cloacal and sadistic-phallic phases (which, indeed, often overlap), were effected in the first instance with partial object-cathexes relating to the *organs* which children covet to gratify their libidinal and sadistic impulses. Little by little, however, the whole being of the man and of the woman becomes more clearly defined as male or female, and the difference between the sexes is at last recognized.

Thereafter, the destiny and influence of the infantile sadistic fantasies will differ with the sex of the child. The sadistic conception of coitus in boys, the actual possessors of the penetrating penis, will evade the centripetal, cloacal danger and tend to take a form which is centrifugal and vital and which involves no immediate danger to their own organism. Of course it will subsequently come into collision with the *moral* barriers erected by civilization against human aggressiveness, with the castration complex especially; but the Oedipal defusion of instincts through which the boy's aggression is diverted to his father, while the greater part of his love goes to his mother, is of considerable

---

[6] Compare especially Melanie Klein, *The Psycho-Analysis of Children,* 1932.

assistance to him in distinguishing sadism from activity and subsequently orientating his penis—active but no longer sadistic—in the direction of women.

In girls, the sadistic conception of coitus, when strongly emphasized, is much more likely to disturb ideal erotic development. The time comes when the little girl compares her own genitals with the large penis of the adult male, and inevitably she draws the conclusion that she has been castrated. The consequence is that not only is her narcissism mortified by her castration but also, in her sexual relations with men, the possessors of the penis which henceforth her eroticism covets, she is haunted by the dread that her body will undergo some fearful penetration.

Now every living organism dreads invasion from without, and this is a dread bound up with life itself and governed by the biological law of self-preservation.

Moreover, not only do little girls hear talk or whispers about the sufferings of childbirth and catch sight, somehow or other, of menstrual blood: they also bear imprinted on their minds from earliest childhood the terrifying vision of a sexual attack by a man upon a woman, which they believe to be the cause of the bleeding. It follows therefore that, in spite of the instinct which urges them forward, they draw back from the feminine erotic function itself, although of all the reproductive functions of woman this is the only one which should really be free from suffering and purely pleasurable.[7]

[7] In my opinion this primitive drawing back is a motion of the *vital ego* and not primarily, as Melanie Klein holds, that of a precocious *moral superego*. In this connection my view agrees more nearly with that of Karen Horney, though I differ from her on another point, namely, the constitutional phallic element—what I should term the bisexuality—in the nature of women. Compare Melanie Klein, *The Psycho-Analysis of Children*, quoted earlier in this paper, and Karen Horney, "The Flight from Womanhood," *International Journal of Psychoanalysis*, Vol. VII, 1926, and "The Denial of the Vagina," *International Journal of Psychoanalysis*, Vol. XIV, 1933. The outbreak of rage to be observed in so many children, when an attempt is made to give them an enema, is, I believe, to be explained as the defense set up by this same instinct of self-preservation against penetration of their bodies. This seems to me much more probable than that it is the expression of a kind of orgasm, as Freud holds (no doubt with some justice in certain cases), following Ruth Mack-Brunswick. (Freud, "Female Sexuality," *International Journal of Psychoanalysis*, Vol. XIII, 1932.)

IV. *The necessary fundamental distinction between masochism and passivity.* As the little girl grows up, her reactions to the primal scene become more pronounced in one direction or another, according to the individual case, the determining factors being, on the one hand, her childhood experiences and, on the other, her constitutional disposition.

In the first place, there is bound to be a distinct difference between the reactions of a little girl who has actually witnessed the coitus of adults and those of a little girl who has fallen back upon phylogenetic fantasies, based on her inevitable observations of the copulation of animals. It seems that the severity of the traumatic shock is in proportion to the earliness of the period in which the child observes human coitus and to the actuality of what she observes.

Above all, however, the violence of the little girl's recoil from the sexual aggression of the male will depend on the degree of her constitutional bisexuality and the extent of the biological bases of her masculinity complex. Where both these factors are marked, she will react in very much the same way as a little boy, whose reaction, since he also is bisexual, will be likewise of the cloacal type, though very soon his vital phallic rejection of the passive, cloacal attitude will turn his libido into the convex, centrifugal track of masculinity.

For there are only two main modes of reaction to the sadistic conception of coitus harbored by the little girl's unconscious mind throughout childhood and right up to adult life. Either she must accept it and, in this case, in order to bind masochistically her passive aggression there must be an admixture of eros equivalent to the danger which, she feels, threatens her very existence. Or else, as the years pass and her knowledge of reality increases, she must recognize that the penetrating penis is neither a whip nor an awl nor a knife nor a cartridge (as in her sadistic, infantile fantasies) and must dissociate passive coitus from the other feminine reproductive functions (menstruation, pregnancy, parturition); she must accept it as the only act which is really purely pleasurable, in sharp contrast to the dark background of feminine suffering, an act in which libido—that biological force of masculine extraction—is deflected to feminine aims, always passive but here not normally masochistic.

It is true that in woman's acceptance of her role there may be a slight tincture—a homeopathic dose, so to speak—of masochism, and this, combining with her passivity in coitus, impels her to welcome and to value some measure of brutality on the man's part. Martine declared that she wished "to be beaten." But a real distinction between masochism and passivity must be established in the feminine psyche if her passive erotic function is to be normally accepted upon a firm basis. Actually, normal vaginal coitus does not hurt a woman: quite the contrary.

If, however, in childhood, when she is brought up against the sadistic conception of coitus, she has, if I may so put it, voted for the first solution, namely, a masochism which includes within its scope passivity in copulation, it by no means follows that she will accept the masochistic erotization of the vagina in coitus. Often the dose of masochism is in that case too strong for the vital ego, and it is a fact that even those women in whom the masochistic perversion is very pronounced often shun penetration and content themselves with being beaten on the buttocks, regarding this as a more harmless mode of aggression since only the outer surface of the body is concerned.

The vital, biological ego protests against and takes flight from masochism in general and may establish very powerful hypercathexes of the libido's defensive positions.

V. *The cloaca and the phallus in women.* At this point we must remind ourselves that in females there are two erotogenic zones and that woman is bisexual in a far higher degree than man.

Earlier in this paper I quoted the views of the Spanish biologist, Marañon, who holds that a woman is a man whose development has been arrested, a sort of adolescent to whose organism is subjoined, in a kind of symbiosis, the apparatus of maternity, which is responsible for the check in development.

In woman the external sexual organs, or, more correctly, the erotogenic organs, appear to reflect her twofold nature. A woman, in fact, possesses a cloaca, divided by the recto-vaginal septum into the anus and the specifically feminine vagina, the gateway to the additional structure of the maternal apparatus, and a phallus, atrophied in comparison with the male penis—the little clitoris.

How do these two zones react, on the one hand to the little girl's constitution and, on the other, to the experiences which exercise a formative influence upon her psychosexuality?

There are various stages and phases[8] in libidinal development. The oral phase is succeeded by the sadistic-anal phase which, in view of the anatomical fact of the existence of the vagina in little girls, I should prefer to call the sadistic-cloacal phase.

There is, therefore, a cavity (as yet, no doubt, imperfectly differentiated in the child's mind) which in the little girl's sadistic conception of coitus is penetrated in a manner highly dangerous. (The little boy, for his part, arguing from his own physical structure, often recognizes the existence of the anus only.) Consequently, when coitus is observed at this early age, the result is the mobilization, firstly, of the erotic wish for the penis, coveted by the oral and cloacal libidinal components, and, secondly, of the dread of penetration which wounds and is to be feared.

Before long, however, the phallic phase, which is a regular stage in the biological development of both sexes, is reached by little girls, as by little boys, being accompanied in the former by clitoridal masturbation. Doubtless, at this period, masturbation is not confined exclusively to the clitoris but is extended in a greater or lesser degree to the vulva and the entrance to the adjacent vagina. How far this is so depends on the individual and on the amount of her constitutional femininity (her prefeminine, erotogenic cloacality).

At this point, however, through a confusion of passivity with masochism, the little girl may take fright and reject her passive role. The dread of male aggression may be too strong, the admixture of masochism already present too great, or too potent a dose of it may be required to bind and accept the dread. When this is the case, her ego draws back and her eroticism will cling, so to speak, to the clitoris. The process is something like that of fixing a lightning-conductor to a house in order to prevent its being struck: the electricity (in this case, the child's eroticism) is diverted into a channel in which it does not endanger life.

[8] Freud, *Drei Abhandlungen zur Sexualtheorie*, 1905; Abraham, "A Short Study of the Development of the Libido," *Selected Papers*, (1924), Chap. XXVI.

Thus a sort of *convex erotic engram,* upon which her erotic function as a woman will be modeled, is set up in opposition to the *concave erotic engram* which is properly that of the female in coitus.

Now the convex orientation of libido is the very direction taken by the eroticism of the male, as he develops anatomically, and, further, the erotogenic, centrifugal orientation of the penis. Consequently, such an orientation of libido in a woman is highly suggestive of a considerable degree of constitutional masculinity. Here, passivity being more or less inextricably confused with erotogenic masochism, its *vital* (self-preservative) rejection and its *masculine* rejection coincide. *Moral* repression, on the other hand, which has its source in educational influences and is maintained by the superego, tends to attack feminine sexuality as a whole, without discrimination of its specifically vaginal or clitoridal character, and, when carried to its extreme, tends to result in total frigidity.

Nevertheless the phallus itself, an organ essentially male even when it goes by the name of the clitoris, can be used for ends which are, at bottom, feminine.

It is true that the clitoris, the rudimentary phallus, is never destined to achieve, even in its owner's imagination, the degree of activity to which the penis can lay claim, for in this respect the male organ is far better endowed by nature. The clitoris, like the little boy's penis, is first aroused when the mother is attending to the child's toilet, the experience being a passive one. Normally the clitoris, after passing through an active phase, should have a stronger tendency than the penis to revert to passivity: the little girl's biological castration complex paves the way for her regression. Next, when her positive Oedipus complex is established, with its orientation to the father, the clitoris readily becomes the instrument of those libidinal desires whose aim is passive. And this prepares the way for the clitoridal-vaginal erotic function by means of which, in so many women, the two zones fulfill harmoniously their passive role in coitus and which is opposed to the functional maladjustment of women of the clitoridal type, in whom the phallus is too highly charged with active impulses.

From the biological standpoint, nevertheless, the ideal adaptation of woman to her erotic function involves the functional suppression of the active, and even of the passive, clitoris in favor of the vagina, whose role is that of purely passive reception. But in order that the vital ego may accept this erotic passivity, which is specifically and essentially feminine, a woman, when she reaches full maturity, must as far as possible have rid herself of the infantile fear which has its origin in the sadistic conception of coitus and from the defensive reactions against the possibility of masochism which are to be traced to the same source.

IX

Special Problems of Early Female Sexual Development

By Phyllis Greenacre, M.D.*

The sexual development of women is complicated by the presence of two main zones of erotogenic pleasure—the clitoris and the vagina. The most generally accepted theory of development of sexuality in women, as stated by Freud is substantially as follows: the two sexes develop in much the same way until the onset of the phallic phase. At this time the girl behaves like a little boy in discovering the pleasurable sensations from her clitoris and associates its excitation with ideas of intercourse. At this stage the clitoris is the center of the girl's masturbatory activity, the vagina remaining undiscovered to both sexes. It would thus seem that the children of both sexes are at this point little boys—the girl being the littler boy, considered from the angle of body sensations. With the change to a feminine orientation under the influence of the penis envy, the girl repudiates her mother and renounces clitoris masturbation, becomes more passive and turns to the father with the Oedipal wish for a child, a state which may persist well into adult life or be only partially dissipated. Freud believed that the failure to make this feminine identification and the development of the masculinity complex in its place was largely due to constitutional factors: the possession of a greater degree of activity, such as is usually characteristic of the male. He believed further that there was,

* From the New York Hospital, and the Department of Psychiatry, Cornell University Medical College, New York.

strictly speaking, no feminine libido, in so far as the female function was essentially passive from a teleological point of view and that Nature's aims (of reproduction) being possibly achieved through the aggressiveness of the male with little or no co-operation from the female, the masculine function is, from a teleological angle, more important and the female function correspondingly less differentiated (3). In his chapter on the psychology of women in the *New Introductory Lectures on Psychoanalysis* (1933) from which I have summarily quoted, he left the mechanism by which transferral of erotic sensation to the vagina was accomplished pretty much undiscussed. That it might be anticipated by the wish for a child from the father, with a clearer idea of the child from within, and a clearer conception of intercourse seemed possible—only to be accomplished in many instances, if at all, by the actual experiences of intercourse is implied rather than expressed. That such a course of development occurs with relative frequency and that often no transferral of sensation of the vagina is accomplished is also the experience of all those who deal with the intimate problems of women. Freud considered that what he said about the psychology of women was incomplete and fragmentary. This paper is based on the closing admonition of his chapter. "If you want to know more about femininity, you must interrogate your own experience, or turn to the poets, or else wait until Science can give you more profound and more coherent information." From all three sources, I would proceed.

The material of this paper is drawn predominantly from cases of pathological sexual development and as such may be open to criticism as the basis of deductions regarding normal female sexual development. Only in a few instances has it been possible to supplement it by observations on girl babies and children, and from the experiments and observations of other investigators. It is necessary at the very outset to establish these limitations, and present the material as problems of female sexual development rather than attempting any consistent theory. It seems, however, that pathological conditions often are the source of much stimulation for deductions and observations regarding normal conditions, and it is hoped that this presentation of problems may serve ultimately therefore to extend our knowledge of the normal as well as of the disturbed sexuality of women.

As has been repeatedly indicated in previous papers, it is my belief that genital stimulation may occur much earlier than the phallic stage, and that it occurs in situations of extreme or general stress to the organism where there is a diffuse surcharging of the neuromuscular equipment and a consequent utilization of all mechanisms of discharge. That such discharge tends to be mediated first through the organs whose functions have already matured is evident, but under conditions where relief in this way is insufficient it appears that there may be a diffusing into systems not yet quite matured, and a premature functioning which might conceivably then promote their anatomical and physiological maturing in the way indicated by Langworthy (13) in his investigations, if the strain is not too great. That such a forced premature functioning may occur and become established at a moderately stable but vulnerable level is quite apparent in the common experience of bowel and urinary training which is accomplished before the neuromuscular development has reached its optimum state.

In the investigation of the development of female sexuality the relation between two main erogenous zones, the clitoris and the vagina, must always be considered. It may be, however, that the progressive development does not always follow so regularly the sequence outlined already as we have thought. In this same chapter on the psychology of women (p. 161) Freud states, "It is true, that here and there, reports have been made that tell us of early vaginal sensations as well; but it cannot be easy to discriminate between these and anal sensations or from sensations of the vaginal vestibule; in any case, they cannot play a very important role." It is only with this last conclusion in regard to the importance of the observations that this paper would wish to bring further evidence; i.e., in regard to the question of the significance of such early sensations—and as a part of this problem, their peculiar relationship in time and in meaning whether in contrast to or in amalgamation with clitoral sensations.

The material of this paper will be discussed under the following headings: (A) Indications and conditions of early vaginal sensations; (B) Evidences and frequency of prephallic clitoral sensations; (C) Clitoral stimulation during the phallic phase; (D) Early situations in which a bipolarity between clitoris and vagina occurs; (E) Later results of bipolarity of clitoris and vagina; (F) Conditions of vaginal dominance; (1) through special accentuation of vaginal stimulation; (2) through by-passing of clitoral stimulation and (3) through repression of clitoral sensations; (G) A special elaboration of the penis envy and castration complex in which the struggle is reflected on to the breast-testicles—"the Medea complex"; and finally (H) A review of the literature.

INDICATIONS AND CONDITIONS OF EARLY VAGINAL SENSATIONS

For many years I have had the impression, based wholly on clinical observations, that vaginal sensation does not develop by any means uniformly secondarily to that of the clitoris, and certainly does not always await actual intercourse for its establishment, but may be concurrent with or even precede clitoral sensation. In deeply regressed psychotic women patients it is noted that autoerotic sensations are of a vaginal type in an unusually high proportion of patients. This was obvious to me during my years in psychiatric hospitals in the direct observation of masturbatory practices as well as in the bizarre hypochondriacal complaints and delusions of such patients. Thus the genital orgastic explosions complained of by some schizophrenics as annoyingly produced by others seem more often located in the vagina than in the clitoris, even in women who have been vaginally frigid in their prepsychotic conscious sexual lives. The automatic orgasm of latent psychotic patients or those in a state of prolonged panic is more often vaginal than clitoral. Here the orgasm occurs spontaneously without manipulation or conscious fantasy, and literally overtakes and bewilders the patient who is sometimes unaware of what stimulus in the environment has set off the discharge. According to whatever clinical investigations I have been able to make, this particular type of vaginal orgasm seems to occur in patients who have suffered long, severe and early anxiety and who show other autoerotic discharges as well. I have thought that it occurred then as part of the revival of an intense polymorphous perverse period in which the incapacity of the weak infant to endure the overstimulation to which it was subjected caused a diffuse and disorganized general response with discharges through many channels, including the genitals even before genitalization had become a well-focused phase, as already mentioned.

Fitting in with this is the fact that such spontaneous vaginal orgasms rarely give adequate relief and are felt by the patient as being shallow, and not so sharp as the clitoral orgasm nor so full as the more regularly aroused vaginal response.

It has appeared, however, that there are also vaginal sensations derived from early rectal and anal stimulation—a fact clearly recognized by Freud, in the quotation already cited. It is to be remembered that in the girl the lower rectum and the vagina have actually been fused into a common opening, the cloaca, until relatively late in fetal life, and even at birth it may be that this differentiation is incomplete in the central nervous system localizations—in other words that the fetal central registration, or body image, weak as it probably is, may still persist. The fact that in many infants a stimulation of the mouth through feeding produces a readily observed lower bowel stimulation (which may in the girl communicate itself to the vagina as well) gives us an additional understandable factor in the mouth-vagina equation universally present in women. That this is not on an intellectual visually symbolic basis was amply evident to me in the analysis of several women patients. One patient, at a time when she suffered from a severe paroxysmal cough, awoke in a coughing fit to find herself in a simultaneous vaginal orgasm, associated with a dream which showed quite clearly the mouth with entrance to lungs and esophagus equated with the genital groove with anal and vaginal openings. I have also recovered evidences of similar states in childhood in patients who had then suffered from severe whooping cough.

In some instances there is a special linking of the activity of the musculature of the vaginal introitus with anal sphincter activity and with the acts of suckling and swallowing. This seemed possibly the situation in the case of the patient with the audible vaginal tic, mentioned in my second paper on the "Predisposition to Anxiety" (6). It may not be a mere figure of speech to refer to this condition as a kind of smacking of the vaginal lips associated with air swallowing. In cases where there has been much oral stimulation in infancy associated with strong anal sphincter arousal, or where this latter has been accentuated by early constipation and the use of enemas and suppositories, the vaginal introitus itself may become involved in the anal sphincter sensitization and vaginal sensations from this area become well marked and strong. Such rhythmic vaginal contractions, clearly felt as comparable to swallowing, are described occasionally by women patients and may be observed directly in the course of gynecological examinations. They are associated with subjectively felt erotic sensations in varying degrees, sometimes being quite detached. This especially strong sphincter responsiveness favors the development of vaginismus, which further promotes and is in turn determined by the development of severe castrating desires as part of the penis envy problem.

Just as oral stimulation may produce lower bowel (and vaginal) activity in the infant, so oral frustration may produce a special form of active response, evident in the erection of the male infant—in Halverson's experiments (7)—but not readily visible in the female infant. This may produce sufficient stimulation to set up a masturbation by thigh pressure and/or a vaginal discharge. It should be noted, however, that such a local response, even if not apparent grossly, would promote genital (and if I am correct, generally vaginal) sensation which would be registered somewhat in the central body image of the infant. Here again I must differ slightly from Freud's idea that children of both sexes know nothing of the vagina early. I am impressed in the course of analyses that in some female patients there has been some kind of vaginal awareness very early, hazy and unverified though it is. This may occur quite definitely even in patients who have not had extreme early stress. This has also been noted by a number of other analysts whose observations will be discussed later in this paper. Vaginal awareness is further increased in those female patients who in infancy have been subjected to repeated stimuli of the rectum and anus, and when this stimulation has occurred before the phallic phase, a strong oral-vaginal response occurs in reaction to primal scene observations.

EVIDENCES AND FREQUENCY OF PREPHALLIC CLITORAL SENSATIONS

Clitoral sensations do occur in some children earlier than their regular appearance with the phallic phase, but, in my experience with analytic patients, are much less frequent than vaginal sensations. At first thought this might seem peculiar inasmuch as erections in the male infant occur quite frequently and are especially noted under conditions of stress. Further consideration and comparison of the anatomical relations in the two sexes presents a reasonable basis for the clinical observations. In the female the greater connection between the vagina and the rectum may mean that the vagina is readily stimulated by anal discharges and, since this mechanism matures earlier than that of the clitoris, the vagina thus regularly borrows stimulation earlier, and the clitoris would only receive such stimulus as could not be discharged at the earlier level. In the girl child, bladder distension seems to merge in sensation and stimulus with the rectum and vagina while irritability of the urethra may sometimes combine with clitoral sensations but more often with sensations from the vaginal introitus. The urethra is actually closer to the vaginal opening than to the clitoris. Examination of a sagittal section of the pelvis shows quite clearly how distension of the excretory organs, bladder or bowel, would produce mechanical pressure stimulation on the vagina more readily than on the clitoris, which is rather surprisingly isolated from the other organs. In the male, on the other hand, urinary functioning causes a direct stimulation to the penis, and since there is only the one organ of genital pleasure discharge, this alone can be available also for channeling diffusion responses from central stimulation.

In those patients in whom clear clitoral sensations seemed to have occurred in the prephallic phase, I have suspected and in some instances had definite evidence that there had been direct manipulation of the clitoris by the mother or nurse in repeated overanxious cleansing activities, in the effort "to break up adhesions" around the clitoris—one form of the so-called female circumcision which used to be advised by doctors as a cure for or a prophylactic against masturbation, which it actually promoted. Since the clitoris is extremely variable in size and in degree of exposure—although commonly it is fairly effectively embedded—these facts alone must influence the amount of casual stimulation to which it is subjected, and the latter vary accordingly much more than in the analogous stimulation of the penis.

CLITORAL STIMULATION IN THE PHALLIC PHASE

That the maturation of the clitoral sensitivity to stimulation in the phallic phase causes it to be the site of spontaneous masturbation in the girl is probably the usual but by no means the universal story, in this way differing somewhat from the boy where the constant inevitable stimulation of the penis by bedding and clothing and the permissiveness to handle the organ in urination cause a uniformity of response to the heightened sensitivity initiated by the phallic phase. In the girl, however, the masturbatory clitoral stimulation undoubtedly becomes fixated when the little girl at this particular time and under the influence of awareness of the pleasure of her organ, sees a contemporary boy either urinate or masturbate. The very focused quality of pleasure to the girl then becomes the occasion for intense jealousy of the boy and envy of his organ. This susceptibility to penis envy remains heightened, I believe, until and throughout the Oedipal period because of the inevitable frustration in the wish for the child and the relatively recent phallic discovering in herself. Under the influence of the disappointment about this, the regression to the wish to have a larger pleasure organ is obviously easy and increases the masculinity complex. All this may be very much heightened if a younger brother is born at this time, in which case the girl's masculinity takes the form of a particularly heightened masculine maternity or of a frank identification with the masculine sex through the adoption of the illusory penis—the assumption that she has a penis which is not directly visible.

Thus the castration guilt so typical of the girl may be quite short-lived, and very quickly surmounted by the establishment of the illusory penis on the very basis of the clitoral awareness and the peculiar reinforcement of the penis envy under these special circumstances.

EARLY SITUATIONS IN WHICH BIPOLARITY BETWEEN CLITORIS AND VAGINA DEVELOP

Some degree of bisexual identification probably occurs in most girls at some times during the latency period, unless the girl remains almost exclusively under the domination of prolonged

Oedipal striving. However strong the masculine identification may be in conscious or unconscious fantasy, still there is a reality knowledge supported by body image from reality sensations which does not permit the girl to abandon completely her feminine identification (except in those rare and extreme states of psychotic development where fantasy takes over). Quite occasionally in the course of analyzing women, however, symptoms may be encountered which have arisen from an unusual balancing of the masculine and feminine identifications with a continued localization of genital sensations in the clitoris and in the vagina, the two never being harmonized—resulting in a confusion which has affected the sense of reality, especially the sense of identity, and interfered with the thinking. This clearly may contribute to states of depersonalization. Such a marked degree of polarization of feeling between clitoris and vagina occurs, in my experience, when there has been (a) very early vaginal stimulation in any of the ways already mentioned followed by (b) a strong phallic phase, reinforced by observation of masturbation in a contemporaneous boy, this combination of affairs resulting in an especially strong penis envy and establishment of very intense fantasy of having a penis. It is noted from clinical study that situations of early anxiety which have contributed to the overflow of stimulation to produce an increase in vaginal reactivity, produce also an incomplete development of the sense of reality, with a prolongation of the tendency to primitive identification with others in the environment (in other words, an incomplete separation of the self from the environment) and an increase in the tendency to magic thinking and fantasy. These very concomitants of the predisposition to anxiety would tend, therefore, to strengthen the intensity of the illusory penis with its primary locus on the clitoris if exposure to comparison with a boy has occurred during the stage of clitoral masturbation, to circumvent castration guilt. The displacement of the illusory penis to the "inside" certainly occurs in many girl children, utilizing the vaginal and upper rectal sensations. But under other conditions, especially if reality exposure to penis rivalry continues and clitoral masturbation is prolonged and is followed in the Oedipal period by an especially poor resolution of the Oedipal conflict with resultant identification with the father, the clitoral illusory penis persists with great intensity. It is also noted that if a strong oral-anal-vaginal stimulation has occurred before the phallic phase, the girl under the influence of the Oedipal disappointment regresses not only to the clitoral pleasure, but in just those cases of the birth of younger brother at this time there is not only the increase of penis envy, but a further regressive tendency increased by the breast and oral envy from the sight of the baby nursing. Under these conditions an extreme polarity of oral-vaginal and phallic clitoral sensitivity may develop. Looked at from another angle, it might be said that both pressures are so great that there is a real conflict between the body image based on the actual experiences and the fantasy phallic image which has its nucleus of reality in the clitoral sensations.

Later Sequelae of Bipolarity between Vagina and Clitoris

When both vagina and clitoris excitability have been established in an early, strong and mutually antagonistic way, the clitoris may be the site of a persistent and practically hallucinatory penis, and this is maintained generally throughout the latency period; i.e., the masculinity complex is particularly strong and this element plays a part in the overwhelmingly severe reaction to puberty. Such girls are frequently unusually aggressive during the latency period and may participate actively in all sorts of investigations, sexual and otherwise, but at the same time carry on secret fantasies of great elaborateness concerning passive and masochistic activities. The condition of phallic hallucination involves not only a visual hallucinatory state but a combination of this with hallucinated tactile and tumescent sensations, derived not only from clitoral tumescence but especially from the overplastic body responses and "body suggestibility" of children whose first stage of ego development in infancy has been impaired. It does not preclude the girl hanging on to the father with an oral-vaginal babyish grasp which alternates with her phallic strivings. There is then actual conflict between the hallucinated phallic genital image and the actual body image arising from the endogenous vaginal sensations which may not be as sharp but have a longer history and the greater force of reality than the phallic ones.

This conflict between the two images of the genital self sometimes results in constant pendulum shifts from clitoral to vaginal orientation or may give rise to a state of unreality with the abandonment of the problem and a flight into thought of a characteristically vague and airy kind. This is most frequently seen in a well-developed form under the influence of further anxiety generated by the onset of puberty, especially the appearance of the menses. Such girls may then frankly "founder on the rock of puberty" and break down, or retreat into unproductive intellectuality and philosophizing.

Sometimes, however, one zone is disowned or suppressed in favor of the other. Probably the clitoris wins out more often, partly by virtue of its special capacity for sharpness of sensation; the repression of vaginal awareness being furthered by the female castration problems at puberty, which have previously been repressed or successfully defended against in the infantile period, especially when associated with actual experiences causing a fear of pregnancy and childbirth. A strong (latent) homosexuality develops with particularly stubborn vaginal frigidity. These patients may present superficially the appearance of the beginning of a sexual development resembling the ordinary sequence described by Freud, but transferral of sensation to the vagina does not occur under the influence of real experience with intercourse.

Conditions of Vaginal Dominance

The condition in which the vagina, whether in its upper segment or in its introitus, appears as the leading or practically the only source of genital pleasure to the girl comes about (1) through an accentuation of vaginal awareness not balanced by the development of a strong illusory penis; (2) through situations causing either a bypassing of interest in the clitoris or the repression of clitoral interest and pleasures after its development.

The general conditions promoting premature awareness of the vagina, viz., conditions early in life, in the prephallic eras, which cause an overstimulation of the infant and the need for total discharge reactions have already been discussed. Such conditions, especially when combined with prolonged oral stimulation, with or without states of urinary or bowel retention but without marked anal sphincter stimulus—and especially in those infants in which there is not any definite synchronization of the responses in the entire gastrointestinal tract (5)—may promote a strong vaginal stimulation in the prephallic period. Stated in another way, the receptive-distensive elements of the early disturbance are increased but in the absence of strong anal sadism. This is presumably due not only to the special vicissitudes of the infantile life but to differences in body constitution, involving proportionately different peripheral muscle and visceral reactivities. If, on this basis, penis envy is especially delayed due to the girl child being totally surrounded by females as occasionally happens when all the siblings are girls, or for other reasons girls are in the dominant role in the environment, then the vagina may take over and remain the leading erotic zone. The late competition with boys which follows lacks the keen personal rivalry so apparent in girls who have had an earlier penis envy with strong castrative desires or with definite illusory penis formation. No true masculinity complex seems to develop, and the competition is either genuinely lacking or takes the form of a withdrawal from boys' activities and a singular disregard of them. Such girls may be somewhat competitive with other girls, but even there the competition is not characterized by the sharp pressure which so regularly occurs among girls, in whom it is derived essentially from an earlier penis envy. It is my belief, based, however, on a very limited experience with this type of woman, that other functions may become patterned after this essential genital one, and that such women may appear vague, lack force in social and intellectual pursuits, but are not necessarily unproductive. In the one case that I worked with most thoroughly, there was a kind of withdrawnness which was not primarily a reactive introversion, but which gave a superficial impression of a princess complex, though without haughtiness.

In this case there had been a practical ignoring of the clitoris, probably due in part to its being small and deeply embedded, as well as to other conditions which did not induce its being especially favored as it was discovered by the child under humiliating circumstances when she was not yet at the phallic stage. Clitoral interest was then inhibited, and this became chronic—promoted by the actual anatomical smallness and protection of the organ. It should be noted, however, that clitoral sensation was not repressed; i.e., there was no clitoral frigidity, only its participation in erotic pleasure was never demanded.

It is conceivable that there may be a real failure of development of clitoral sensation due to a bypassing of the organ and a failure of stimulation. Such a case has, however, never come under my observation and it seems more probable that there is regularly some degree of clitoral sensitivity which develops by the spontaneous masturbation of the phallic phase, and that this subsequently meets with repression. In those patients who presented a history of no clitoral sensations, deeper psychoanalytic investigation generally revealed that there had actually been a very intense clitoral phallic phase, which had occurred simultaneously with exposure to penis envy together with open threats from parents or nurses who observed the girl's clitoral masturbation. The latter may be so completely repressed that the clitoris remains frigid thereafter and is eliminated as the site of phallic strivings, the girl then either develops an especially severe castration complex with resultant masochism, or reallocates the phallic desire to other parts of the body, determined by special narcissistic and/or erotized foci, of which the vagina may be one. In such cases vaginal dominance takes over, the penis envy struggle sometimes resulting in a complete frigidity.

THE MEDEA COMPLEX[1]

There is a form of deformation in the sexual development of some women in which there may be an exaggerated semblance of femininity coupled with great narcissism and a desire for extreme revenge when the woman loses her mate through death,

[1] According to the Greek myth Medea was a resourceful woman who helped Jason to seize the golden fleece by giving the dragon knock-out drops. She had fallen in love with Jason and quickly eloped with him, delaying her father in his pursuit by slaying her younger brother and depositing his bones where the father would find them and be distracted by his grief. Returning thus with Jason to the court of Pelleas, his usurping uncle, she bore Jason two sons and succeeded in poisoning Pelleas. Jason, still unable to seize power for himself, fled with his wife and two sons to Corinth. The tragedy of Euripides begins with the period in Corinth. Jason, the weak and boastful husband, resented his guilty indebtedness to

or especially if she suffers rejection at his hands. The analytic experience I have had with this type of woman leads me to believe that there is a rather special constellation of breast and penis envy with the severest form of castration, reflected in a breast-testicle comparison which allows the girl a specious expectation of superiority after puberty.

The basic situation which seems to favor this is the birth of a younger sibling before the fifteenth to sixteenth month, that is, in the preverbal era. The envy and jealousy of the baby, especially the baby at the breast, is felt by the little girl with an extreme oral intensity, and possibly can be compared to the terrible jealousy evident in some animal pets when a baby is born. If the baby is a boy or if a boy sibling is born within the next two to three years this original oral and visual envy is augmented by or converted into penis envy at the third to fifth year. The castration complex is extremely severe and the child may retreat to an oral craving for the mother or have especially pronounced oral components in the attitude toward the father. The primitive sense of deprivation and of being an outcast is very tenacious and forms a more than ordinary basis for the typical feminine guilt feelings of the developing castration complex. The image of the breast seems especially strong back of that of the penis, and the compensation "I will have better and bigger ones when I grow up" may finally be achieved in the post-Oedipal period of superego building.

Such children often clearly eliminate or disregard the penis and fixate rather on the testicles, while the breast is exalted over *any* male genitals. They delay any adequate solution of the Oedipal disappointment or the penis envy problem until puberty. Until then they feel deprived but hopeful. One patient of this type told me of an early memory from the fifth to sixth year period when the chauffeur's son had "shown her his testicles." When I asked what had happened to his penis she at

his wife. He decided to marry the Corinthian princess, excusing this on the basis that this marriage would consolidate his position at Corinth and he could then pass on the protection to Medea and the children. Medea's possessive and single-minded love for Jason turned to hate and revenge. She poisoned the Corinthian king and princess with poisoned gifts; and completed her revenge on Jason by killing the two sons who were dear to him.

first said that she simply could not remember his having had one, and then quickly brought another memory of another boy, also considered inferior but socially of her class, who in school stood in front of the blackboard beside her "holding his penis in his hand, because he was probably ashamed of it." What a neat way of dealing with her envy of the boy's masturbation!

The oral visual incorporative drives toward the male genitals are especially strong where several younger siblings are born in the patient's early childhood—sometimes with a phase of hope of growing male genitals in this way, the hope being apparently abandoned but actually sustained in the reinstated idea of the breast as already mentioned. A considerable intensity of various drives may permeate the latency period, but become consolidated at or just before puberty, in the expectation of breast development, under impact again with the castration complex and the onset of menstruation.

Such women are extremely fastidious in their dress and body form. This is a somewhat specious femininity, however, both male and female genitals being represented in the breast. These young women often have an appearance of maturity and may be very beautiful, but do not ever achieve a healthy integration and individuation. They are narcissistically lost without a man even for a brief time; but they often marry childlike or weak men. Their attitude toward their children conspicuously lacks tenderness. They may be very proud of them, are generally conscientious toward the children but not infrequently show a hostile type of anxious worrying. If the marriage is disrupted the attitude toward the children may be uncovered in all its rawness, from spiteful possessiveness to revengeful abandonment. The increase in tenderness and appreciation of the individuality of the child is lacking. In the sexual response such women show sometimes a vaginal response (probably based on the extreme orality, with or without clitoral participation). It is possible they may be frigid, depending on other vicissitudes of development.

REVIEW OF THE LITERATURE

One is impressed with the general awareness of complexity of the subject of female sexuality in the minds of most writers, and with the relatively few theories advanced, together with the large number of clinical reports indicating variations from or exceptions to the recognized theories. I have, in my present paper, added to this impression of complexity and variability in sexual development in women. I do not feel sure, by any means, of the frequency of the occurrence of the different types of feminine sexual organization which I have presented in this paper in the development of the more ordinary neuroses of women, having to recognize that my own practice has included a rather disproportionately large number of cases of severe neuroses and latent psychoses and that my earlier psychiatric experience of nearly fifteen years was predominantly with psychotic patients.

I shall make no attempt to make a systematic review of *all* of the literature or to present the historical development of different points of view regarding female sexual development, but attempt to stress rather that which has special pertinence to the points which I have raised in this paper; viz. (a) the possible early vague awareness of the vagina, which however is not subjectively adequately differentiated from the rectum; (b) the influence on vaginal awareness and reactivity by states of oral stimulation or frustration (which may be registered at the lower end of the gastrointestinal tract as well), by direct stimulation of the rectum and anus, and by a surcharging of the organism by massive stimulations greater than can be cared for through appropriate channels of discharge, so that immature discharge mechanisms may be prematurely stimulated. As a corollary to this, there is the implication that there may be distortions of the regular sequence of pre-Oedipal development, or in the extreme, different types of pre-Oedipal organization. This leads to (c), the consideration that clitoris and vagina may have varying relationships to each other, with a patterning which has a far-reaching influence on the sexual response of the woman and a deep, sometimes decisive effect on her character and even sometimes on her intellectual functioning.

I am inclined to question whether these differences in organization may not be the bases of some of the opposing points of view expressed by theorists, where the observations of some one type of organization may have been quite impressive and diverting and yet not really worthy of a complete controversion of the basic theory.

Freud's basic theory regarding female sexual development as stated in his *New Introductory Lectures* (1932) has been summarized at the beginning of this paper. In his paper the previous year (4) he gave a somewhat more explicit account and raised more clear-cut questions on which my own presentation has bearing. In this paper he was greatly concerned with the pre-Oedipal developments in the girl, emphasizing that the early attachment to the mother both in intensity and form lent much to the subsequent Oedipal attachment to the father, that this attachment to the mother did not terminate as early or as decisively as had been thought, but continued on into the phallic phase when it might be found as part of the girl's phallic strivings toward the mother—and that in some cases was never relinquished, the woman treating her husband as she had previously felt toward her mother (rather than her father). While he commented here as in other papers on the number of investigators who believed little girls did have early vaginal sensations, yet he seemed rather to dismiss this again and stated categorically that "we may justly assume that for many years the vagina is virtually non-existent and possibly remains without sensation until puberty." Again in the same paper, however, he commented on his own difficulty in exploring adequately the early development of female patients because (with him) such patients "have been able to cling on to that father attachment in which they took refuge from the early phase" and he believed that women analysts were "better able to apprehend the facts with greater ease and clearness because they had the advantage of being suitable mother-substitutes in the transference-situation with patients whom they were studying." In a paragraph in which he discussed the girl's phallic wishes toward the mother, and the way in which children react with passionate rage toward the giving of an enema by the mother and then reverse the proceeding with the wish to attack her, he stated that he had understood their peculiarly passionate fury when Dr. Ruth Brunswick had interpreted this as comparable to the orgasm following genital excitation; and that the accompanying anxiety should be construed as a transformation of the desire for aggression stirred up, "and that on the anal sadistic level the intense passive excitation of the intestinal zone evokes an outbreak of desire for aggression, manifesting itself either directly in the form of rage or, as a consequence of suppression, as anxiety."

It has seemed to me, although I am by no means completely sure of the situation, that in these severe enema situations of early childhood the reaction is even more complex, dependent on the amount of actual pain involved and on the attitude of the mother, and that the fury represents indeed a phallic attack sometimes associated with clitoris stimulation, but consists much more in the excitement which cannot attain full orgasm—it leaves the child exhausted rather than relaxed. One encounters this, I believe, even more intensely in boys than in girls. In girls, as I have previously indicated, it seems that the clitoral stimulation is associated most with the extreme sphincter stimulation, whereas the rectal stimulation itself may cause a reaction in the vagina which reaches an orgastic-like climax and relief with the discharge of the bowel contents. In such situations both vagina and clitoris may be stimulated and do not act in harmony. Certainly the situation is by no means entirely simple or clear, and deserves further study.

It is noteworthy that a number of analysts, Lampl-de Groot (12), Jacobson (9), Sachs (16), Müller-Braunschweig (14), Paynel (15), Brierley (1), have all noted the primary appearance of vaginal sensations, but this has been studied largely as part of a situation involving castration anxiety and beginning super-ego formation, earlier in the girl than in the boy. Freud's own comment concerning Melanie Klein's (11) displacement backwards of the Oedipus complex to the beginning of the second year, and Fenichel's objection to it, is an extraordinarily valuable one. Although stating that Klein's deductions are not compatible with his own reconstructive findings in analysis and especially with his observations regarding the long duration of the girl's pre-Oedipal attachment to the mother, still the apparent incompatibility might be softened by the realization that what is demanded rigidly by biological laws and what is subject to shifting under the influence of accidental experience is by no means easily distinguishable. It is exactly in the varying developmental speeds and combinations which may be promoted by accidental or forced premature functioning and/or by the linking of different systems in stimulus and discharge situations that I believe there may be varying pre-Oedipal configurations established, of particular import to the girl because of the two zones of genital reactivity.

The observations of Ernest Jones, expressed in his "Early Development of Female Sexuality"(10) have considerable significance in regard to the content of my present paper.[2] At this early time (1927), Jones had already noted that in women with an extreme attachment to the father this had generally been preceded by an equally extreme fixation in regard to the mother, definitely with the oral stage. He indicated further that following the oral stage there tends to be a bifurcation into clitoris and fellatio directions—"with digital plucking at the clitoris and fellatio phantasies respectively: the proportion between the two naturally differing in different cases; and this may be expected to have fateful consequences for the later development." He believed that in the normal heterosexual development the sadistic phase set in late, neither oral nor clitoral stage receiving any strong sadistic cathexis, and that therefore the clitoris did not become associated with a particularly active masculine attitude, nor on the other hand was the oral sadistic fantasy of biting the penis at all highly developed, that rather in the normal heterosexual development, the oral attitude is largely a receptive sucking one and passes into the anal stage. The two alimentary orifices thus constitute the receptive female organ. According to Jones, *The anus is evidently identified with the vagina to begin with, and the differentiation of the two is an extremely obscure process, more so perhaps than any other in female development. I surmise, however, that it takes place in part at an earlier age than is generally supposed.*—"This mouth-anus-vagina represents an identification with the mother."

Although I have found evidence of the degree of oral sadism described by Klein and Jones, occurring only in adults and exceptionally impaired infancy (mostly in latent psychotic in-

---

[2] Jones's remark "There is a healthy suspicion growing that men analysts have been led to adopt an unduly phallo-centric view of the problems in question, the importance of the female organs being correspondingly underestimated. Women have on their side contributed to the general mystification by their secretive attitude towards their own genitals and by displaying a hardly disguised preference for interest in the male organ" reminds us that anatomical structure promotes these attitudes: the man's organs are central and visible, whereas the woman's are mysteriously secreted.

dividuals), the emphasis on the early oral-anal-vaginal antic-ipates very much the findings which I have described and believe to be relatively frequent. Ruth Brunswick in her paper on the pre-Oedipal phase of libido development (2) called definite attention to vaginal sensitivity arising early, associated with anal stimulation but considered it probably minor. Hendrick (8) reported a direct observation in which a three-year-old girl was obviously aware of pleasurable sensation from both clitoris and vagina, and in which the behavior suggested an association of vagina with anus, yet a definite differentiation from it. It is possible that a careful scanning of the experience of pediatricians would bring much more evidence of this kind to light.

CONCLUSION

The importance of the present paper, incomplete and sketchy as it is, may lie in its indicating not only the probability of vary-ing configurations in the bi-zonal female sexual development in the pre-Oedipal phases rather than merely by the different de-grees and routes of the resolution of the castration and the Oedipal complexes, but especially in the further indications of the existence of different types of interorganization of the pre-Oedipal phases in general, whether male or female.

REFERENCES

1. Brierly, M. "Specific Determinants in Feminine Development," *Internat. J. Psa.*, XVII, 1936.

2. Brunswick, R. M. "The Pre-Oedipal Phase of Libido Develop-ment," *Psa. Quart.*, IX, 1940.

3. Freud, S. *New Introductory Lectures on Psychoanalysis*, Chap. 5, Norton, New York, 1933.

4. Freud, S. "Female Sexuality," *Coll. Papers*, V.

5. Gesell, A. and Ilg, F. *Infant and Child in the Culture of Today*, Harper, New York, 1943.

6. Greenacre, P. "Predisposition to Anxiety. Part II," *Psa. Quart.*, X, 1941.

7. Halverson, H. M. "Infant Sucking and Tensional Behavior," *J. Genet. Psychol.*, LIII, 1938.

8. Hendrick, I. "Instinct and the Ego During Infancy," *Psa. Quart.*, XI, 1942.

9. Jacobson, E. "Development of the Feminine Superego," *Internat. Ztsch. f. Psa.*, XXIII, 1937.

10. Jones, E. "Early Female Sexuality," *Papers on Psychoanalysis*, Bailliere, Tindall and Cox, London, 1938.

11. Klein, M. "Early Stages in the Oedipus Conflict," *Internat. J. Psa.*, IX, 1928.

12. Lampl-de Groot, J. "The Evolution of the Oedipus Complex in Women," *Internat. J. Psa.*, IX, 1928.

13. Langworthy, O. R. "Development of Behavior Patterns and Myelinization of the Nervous System in the Human Fetus and Infant," *Contributions to Embryology*, Carnegie Institute of Washington, D.C., Vol. XXIV, No. 139, 1933.

14. Müller-Braunschweig, C. "The Genesis of the Feminine Superego," *Internat. J. Psa.*, VII, 1926.

15. Payne, S. M. "A Conception of Femininity," *Brit. J. Med. Psychol.*, 1936.

16. Sachs, H. "One of the Motive Factors in the Formation of the Superego in Women," *Internat. J. Psa.*, X, 1929.

X

Self-Esteem (Dominance-Feeling) and Sexuality in Women[1]

BY A. H. MASLOW

A. INTRODUCTION

This paper is one of a series presenting the results of a broadly comparative investigation of the dominance or self-esteem syndrome in animals and in humans, studied simultaneously from a biological and a cultural point of view. It was found, in the preliminary studies with monkeys and apes, that there was a remarkably close relationship between dominance and sexuality, so close indeed that we are now inclined to consider sexuality as a sub-pattern in the total dominance syndrome in these animals.

In view of the evidence presented in this paper, we can fairly say that the same conclusions hold true for the dominance syndrome in humans (within the restrictions set by our methods and by our type of subject).[2] The present paper tends to indicate

[1] This research was supported in part by funds from the Carnegie Corporation, administered by E. L. Thorndike at the Institute of Educational Research, Teachers College, June, 1935, to February, 1937.
[2] It is well to express at once some of the theoretical qualms that the writer has about the data and conclusions presented in this paper. The whole field of human personality and sexuality is one in which direct experimental or observational data are practically impossible to obtain. All data presented in this paper have been gathered by questioning people and trusting their answers. Sometimes questioning takes more complex

(continued on following page)

that sexual attitudes and behavior are as much or more truly and closely functions of personality and social and cultural relationships than of sheer biological endowment. This demonstration in no sense minimizes biological influence, for we have also demonstrated with our findings that sheer sexual drive has definite determinative value. But this paper is biological in an even more important sense, namely, it demonstrates that these same personality-sexuality relationships are themselves a biological fact since they hold across species lines; there is also some evidence that they hold across cultural lines. This is then both a biological and a cultural study.

For a discussion of the general concepts and other results of this investigation the reader is referred to other papers by the writer listed in the bibliography but especially to (13, 14). We shall here indicate only in brief outline what has been already presented in these papers.

B. Definitions

Dominance-feeling (or self-esteem), is an evaluation of the self; operationally defined, it is what the subject says about herself in an intensive interview after a good rapport has been established. High dominance-feeling empirically involves good self-confidence, self-assurance, high evaluation of the self, feelings of general capability or superiority, and lack of shyness, timidity, self-consciousness, or embarrassment. Low dominance-feeling is seen as lack of self-confidence, self-assurance, and self-esteem; instead there are extensive feelings of general and specific inferiority, shyness, timidity, fearfulness, self-consciousness. Such people are easily embarrassed, blush frequently, are generally silent and tend to be incapable of normal, easy, outgoing social relationships or forward behavior.

Dominance status is a social relationship; it is an expression of

forms as in hypnosis, dream interpretation, free association, or as in the check questions asked of the subjects' husbands or relatives; sometimes the validity of the writer's trust in the answers of the subjects could be more firmly established by various ad hoc methods. But in the last analysis we are still dealing with questions and answers, however complex they may be. This means that an element of faith in the truthfulness of the subjects is necessarily involved in the consideration of the data and conclusions.

social position with respect to another person, and is always relative to this other person. A person is in dominance-status with respect to another when he feels stronger, more adequate, superior or dominates this other person either overtly in behavior or implicitly in feeling. The dominated or less adequate person is said to be in subordinate status.

TABLE 1

Some Personality Variables That Make Up One Aspect of the Dominance-Feeling Syndrome

High dominance-feeling	*Low dominance-feeling*
Self-confident	Timid
Socially poised	Shy
Relaxed	Embarrassable
Extroverted	Self-conscious
High self-esteem	More inhibited
Self-assured	Modest
Feeling of general capability	Neat
Unconventional	Reliable
Less respect for rules	More honest
Tendency to "use" people	Prompt
Freer personality expression	Faithful
Somewhat more secure	Quiet
Autonomous code of ethics	Introverted
More independent	More inferiority feelings
Less religious	Low self-estimate
More masculine	Somewhat less secure
Less polite	Retiring
Love of adventure, novelty, new experience	More feminine
	More conventional
	More conservative

Variables Relatively Uncorrelated with Dominance-Feeling

Brooding, worrying, moodiness
Weeping
Nervousness and "nervous" habits
Jealousy
Anxiety
Happiness
Neurosis and maladjustment
Intelligence

Dominance behavior is sharply differentiated from dominance-feeling since there is rarely a one-to-one relationship between them. Dominance-feeling is only one of the determiners of dominance behavior. Other determiners are dominance status, compensatory efforts, specific training, the specific situation, and cultural pressures, both local and general. Diagnosis of dominance-feeling from dominance-behavior alone is apt to be inexact. Examples of dominance behavior are bursts of temper, aggressive behavior, insistence on one's rights, free expression of resentment or hostility, openly overriding rules or conventions, arguing freely, etc.

C. METHOD

The main method used for gathering of data was the intensive, semi-psychiatric interview. Since the term "interview" ordinarily means a procedure very different from the one used in this research, we must go into some detail to explain our procedure more fully.

In the first place, questioning was started only after a satisfactory rapport had been established between the interviewer and the subject. This means mostly a frank, friendly, trusting relationship of an equalitarian rather than dominance-subordination type.

In the second place, the investigator subordinated objectivity and routinized procedure to the necessities of the separate situations presented by each different subject. Each one was treated as a unique individuality to be understood and interacted with in a different way. The investigator attempted always to be sensitive and adaptable to these widely varying situations. He conceived his first business to be to understand the person before him *as an individual,* and only then to try to follow through the more specific demands of the research. Our method is, then, a fusion of the clinical and experimental approaches.

Another difference was the extreme flexibility of the interview itself. In the beginning stages of the research, all questioning was purely exploratory. The only cues available were those obtained from the previous work with infra-human primates, from general clinical experience and from study of the writings of Adler, Freud and others. With each subject more was learned and lists of questions could be made. These lists expanded as time went on, even though questions found useless were dropped from time to time. These questions were, in any case, no more than a list of cues. For instance, the word "self-conscious" served as a reminder to find out all that was possible about this topic. The particular questions were determined by the particular situation and subject, her general level of self-esteem, her security, her loquacity, her co-operation, etc.

As a result, our data are not quite comparable for all our subjects, not in the sense that they do not mean the same thing when we do have data, but rather that we do not have complete data for all subjects.

In addition, some of our knowledge of people with low self-esteem was obtained in a rather incomplete form. That is, one person would be willing to talk about her personality but not about her family; another might be willing to speak about certain aspects of her sexual history but not about others. Such people have been only partially useful for our statistical tables but have nevertheless been valuable in furnishing us with a more adequate appreciation of the personality and sexual outlook of such women. General clinical experience also contributed to this backlog of general information about women with low self-esteem.

1. Variables Studied; Rating Scales

The list of variables which were correlated is:

1. Rating for dominance-feeling (or self-esteem).
2. Rating for sex drive.
3. Rating for sex attitude.
4. Presence or absence of technical virginity (if married, whether or not virgin at time of marriage).
5. Promiscuity (number of men with whom sex relations were had).
6. Presence or absence of any history of masturbation since puberty, no matter how infrequent.
7. Score in the Maslow "Social Personality Inventory," a paper and pencil test of dominance-feeling (self-esteem).

We used for our guidance roughly constructed 9-point scales of sexual drive and sexual attitude. These are not reproduced here for fear that they would give a spurious impression of exactness and objectivity. In actuality these variables were rated not only by objective scales but also by a careful judgment about what they would be theoretically if there were no other factors in the picture. That is, the attempt was made to discount the influence of other determiners of sexuality, e.g., whether husband was loved or not, opportunity, fatigue, compensatory efforts, etc. Such ratings are objective only in a very broad sense, i.e., another judge would probably assign the same rating only if he knew *all* the relevant information, rather than just the reports of sexual behavior and feelings in isolation.

In making the rating of sex drive we proceeded from no fixed principle or single definition of sex drive. Our rating is a compound of many elements reported by the subject in response to direct questions after rapport had been established.

1. Frequency and intensity of logical genital reactions, and of conscious sexual relations or masturbation, actual or desired.

2. Percentage frequency of climax in heterosexual acts, the ease or difficulty of achieving the climax, the kinds and amount of stimulation needed to come to it, and its intensity (in terms of overt loss of control, sounds, etc., and in terms of introspective description).

3. Subject's estimate of ease of excitability.

4. Number and extent of erotogenic zones of the body reported by subject.

5. Number of everyday stimuli consciously regarded as sexual stimuli.

It is possible to quarrel about any single one of the questions asked to elicit this information, and one must admit that any sexual response whatsoever is of course a resultant of many factors aside from sex drive itself. For instance, the frequency of conscious sex desire probably is as much a function of inhibition or repression as of sex drive. It was in making this rating that the weakness of the question-answer method revealed itself clearly.

Taking the list as a whole, however, with its close emphasis on physiological reaction, we must say, that in spite of our many theoretical qualms, we have found it useful. It is especially so when we are comparing people at the same level of dominance-feeling and sexual experience. At such times, the fact is brought forcefully home that people vary in their physiological endowment.

Generally it must be remembered that such mistakes as were made in this sex drive rating would in any case tend to make it correlate too highly with self-esteem, sex attitude, and sex behavior.

2. Unconscious vs. Conscious

The possibility of unconscious falsification or repression has been neglected, advisedly (in the writing of this paper, *not* in the investigation itself). There are many reasons for this: (*a*) any other procedure would have created tremendous experimental difficulties; (*b*) on general grounds of scientific parsimony, it was thought wisest to see what could be done with the simplest concepts available; (*c*) our subjects were relatively "normal" (as distinguished from "neurotic") and a good many experimental psychologists feel that extensive and important unconscious influences and sexual repressions are less frequent or less crucial in normal people than in neurotic individuals; (*d*) our search was for heuristic concepts that would be useful in further researches.

In general, the feeling of the writer is that this non-use of the concept of unconscious repression and falsification has been justified by the results. It should be mentioned here that we feel our data on personality and sex to be quite compatible with those obtained by the group of sociologically oriented psychoanalysts—Horney, Fromm, Kardiner, etc. The concepts of character structure elaborated by them are different from those indicated by our data, but it is the writer's feeling that they lead in the same direction of considering conscious self-confidence or self-esteem or a similar concept to be a fundamental and important determining force in a descriptive dynamic analysis of the normal adult personality, and particularly in the sexual life.

The writer must admit, however, that for more complex cases, e.g., neurotics, his simple methods are quite inadequate to reveal the unconscious motivations which undoubtedly exist and are an important factor in the personality. All the questioning in the world will then be useless (unless interpretations are also made) since the subject herself does not know the whys and wherefores

of her feelings and behavior. In such people, a rating of dominance-feeling is often (not always) meaningless. Accordingly,
such people have not been used as subjects in our criterion group.

3. Sampling Errors

When this research was about half completed, certain very
important facts became apparent, that seemed to limit not only
the usefulness of the research, but also to cast a definite shadow
of doubt on previous sexological studies.

At this point about 90 per cent of our subjects were in the
middle and high dominance groups and only about 10 per cent
were low dominance women. It is necessary to examine carefully
the method of getting subjects for our research to understand
this fact. A good many of these people were volunteers, people
who had heard of the research and were interested in helping it.
Thus a large percentage were graduate students. These tried to
get their friends to submit to interviewing also. Many other
people were approached with a request to be subjects but the
writer never insisted or urged his case. People who showed any
signs of distaste or withdrawal or hesitancy were not bothered
further. At this point the only low-dominance subjects we had
were graduate students in psychology who felt it to be their
scientific duty to submit to interviewing.

A survey of the data at this point revealed the startling fact
that *all* our low-dominance subjects were virgin, were non-
masturbators, were low in sexual attitude, etc., so that in spite
of the fact that at this point in the research only about 30 per
cent of the total group of subjects were virgin, 100 per cent of
the low-dominance group were virgin.

At this point special efforts were made to inveigle low-
dominance women into the research. The writer devoted himself
to the hasty construction of a crude paper and pencil test for
dominance-feeling with which large populations could be tested
and subjects selected. [The unexpected success of this test led
to the final construction of the *Social Personality Inventory*
(16).] From the large groups of people tested in various college
classes, the writer selected out enough low dominance subjects
to make the distribution more balanced, always also selecting
out an almost equal number of high dominance subjects to con-

trol out the various special factors bound up with attendance at a particular school, etc. These people were actively approached, the whole research was carefully explained, the difficulties presented and a personal plea for co-operation was then made. Of all these people, the writer remembers only one or two that refused. The others, in spite of their obvious reluctance, usually decided to submit to interview. The interviews with these subjects were particularly long, careful, and thorough.

As we continued working with these subjects, our percentage of virginity went higher and higher, while the percentages of masturbation and promiscuity went lower and lower.

This history becomes very important when we examine the various sexological researches in the literature, and realize that most of the data obtained, e.g., by Hamilton (5), are probably from high-dominance men and women and that therefore they must be considered to some extent unrepresentative and a product of bad sampling. Any study in which data are obtained from volunteers will always have a preponderance of high-dominance people and therefore will show a falsely high percentage of non-virginity, masturbation, promiscuity, homosexuality, etc., in the population. This criticism must be directed to some extent against even such figures as Dickinson's (2, 3) for we know that the low-dominance woman shuns pelvic examination whenever possible, and will not volunteer comments about her sexual history. Any study, also, which relies for its data on anonymous questionnaires must meet the same criticism, especially if partial mail returns are obtained, for it is probable that a far higher percentage of low-dominance individuals will not return their questionnaires, e.g., Davis' studies (1).

Our device for controlling this factor of selection is, in addition to the deliberate selection of low-dominance cases, the use of a statistic which obtains its final figures by averaging the sum of the averages for each of the deciles of dominance-feeling. Thus the raw percentage of virginity in our total number of subjects is 59 per cent, but by the aforementioned technique the figure is 71 per cent. For our criterion group the raw percentage of virgin subjects is 52 per cent but by controlling the factor of dominance-feeling, the percentage obtained is 66.5 per cent. These differences exist even after we have succeeded to some extent in obtaining a more equable distribution of cases with low and high dominance-feeling. These "prediction tables" are presented in Tables 3 and 4.

4. Some Theoretical Difficulties

There are numerous theoretical difficulties to be met with in this type of research.

The most difficult to handle has been a methodological one, namely, the study of parts of an inter-related whole with analytic or atomistic techniques. For instance, every effort has been made to treat sex drive as a variable separate from and independent of self-esteem or sexual attitude, when it is obvious that it is *not* separate or independent. In a certain sense, then, we have isolated artificially, unisolable variables in the effort to prove in the end that they are after all related to each other. Sex drive, let it be said then, is an artificial, heuristic concept and not an empirical, directly observable fact. In part this difficulty has been surmounted by what the writer considers a valid synthetic-analytic technique. This, briefly, consists of studying a particular aspect of personality against the background of a previously acquired knowledge of the total personality. This means a certain loss of objectivity in the conventional sense, but a tremendous increase of validity.

Another difficulty is obvious. What relation do these data bear to the Freudian and Adlerian theories? In a certain sense our data have no bearing whatsoever upon these theories, for we have worked only with conscious, reportable data in the writing of this paper (although as might be expected, other data have also been obtained). And still we feel constrained to record our opinion that these data do have a wider validity and do to some extent bear on the depth theories, particularly on the libido theory as presented, let us say, by such writers as Abraham. The writer himself cannot claim ever to have been able to understand just what *the* libido theory was. For that matter it is very doubtful whether there ever was any single "libido theory" that could either be accepted or rejected. Today even many orthodox Freudians have watered it down to a mere insistence on the potency of drives or to a stress on somatic causation, which the writer is of course completely willing to accept (as who is not?).

It is interesting that some analysts who have seen our data feel that they do not contradict "the" libido theory; others just as firmly feel that they do. Obviously they have different theories in mind.

Another theoretical difficulty which by now is certainly apparent is that of drawing a line between the "normal" and the "neurotic" individual. Our so-called criterion group of 70 individuals, it was stated, were relatively normal people. What this means to the writer has been fully presented elsewhere (17) and we need do no more than express the beliefs underlying this research. These are (a) that a differentiation between normal and neurotic must be made if the words are to mean anything. These are relative words of course but it is a disservice both to semantic principles and to psychology to say therefore that everybody is neurotic; (b) this line, though it must be drawn is certainly not a clear one. Normality is a matter of degree. (c) A concept of neurosis very largely acceptable to the writer is that presented in Horney's writings. (d) We feel that there are remarkable qualitative as well as quantitative differences between normal and neurotic people, and it seems certain that these are not merely operational, methodological differences.

5. *Security and Self-Esteem*

In general our results hold for average, normal members of our society. Since our society tends to general insecurity, the average citizen may be expected to be fairly insecure. Wertheimer has pointed out that any discussion of dominance must be a discussion of insecure people, that is, of slightly sick people. Our data show this to be true. Study of carefully selected psychologically secure individuals indicates clearly that their sexual lives are little determined by dominance-feeling. In fact, in such people, the phrase, dominance-feeling, is a misnomer. High self-esteem in secure individuals results in strength rather than power-seeking, in co-operation rather than competition. High self-esteem in insecure individuals eventuates in domination, urge for power over other people and self-seeking. Since these researches were started with the use of the concept of dominance-feeling, we have retained it, using it, however, interchangeably with the term self-esteem throughout this paper.

D.   QUANTITATIVE RESULTS

The specific results are presented in Tables 2 to 6. The results are presented in two forms always, one for the total group of subjects, and one for the criterion group. The criterion group was selected by excluding people over 28 years of age, Catholic and Jewish women, married women, and severely maladjusted women. The exceptions to these rules were a few women who had been married only a year or two and also a few women of Catholic background who were not now practicing Catholicism. The total group numbered 139, the criterion group about 70. As has already been explained, we do not have complete data for all subjects. The number of subjects involved in each correlation therefore will vary.

Generally it will be noticed that correlations for the criterion group are higher than for the total group in spite of the fact that the number of cases is considerably smaller. This supports our contention that in this type of investigation homogeneous groups are necessary for the best results. Our experience has shown us that differences in religion, cultural background, socioeconomic

TABLE 2

Intercorrelations of Various Scores and Ratings

	Dominance test score	Sex drive	Sex attitude	Virginity	Mastur- bation
		Criterion group			
Dominance rating from interviews	.90	.20	.85	−.81	.53
Dominance test score		.17	.71	−.66	.41
Sex drive			.43	−.36	.51
Sex attitude				−.89	.68
		Total group			
Dominance rating from interviews	.89	.14	.83	−.73	.42
Dominance test score		.10	.72	−.60	.30
Sex drive			.34	−.24	.25
Sex attitude				−.82	.55

TABLE 3

Percentage of Masturbators in Each Decile of Dominance-Feeling as Measured by the Social Personality Inventory with a Corrected Prediction of Masturbators in the Theoretical Population at Large

(See text for explanation of this corrected prediction.)

Dominance scores arranged in deciles (highest scores at top)		Criterion group %	N	Total group %	N
61 -	182	64	25	70	44
32 -	60	50	6	54	13
16 -	31	75	4	71	7
1 -	15	33	6	50	8
0 -	−12	25	4	57	7
−13 -	−28	40	5	62	8
−29 -	−40	33	3	20	5
−41 -	−58	50	2	20	5
−59 -	−81	0	3	29	7
−81 -	−145	17	6	30	10
Predicted estimate of percentage of masturbators in a general population comparable to ours (obtained by averaging the percentages for all the deciles).		38.7%		46.3%	

status, marital condition, and geographic differences all have attenuating effects on correlations between self-esteem and sex behavior. We shall, then, henceforth discuss only the correlations obtained in the criterion group in spite of the fact that because of smaller number of cases they are less reliable statistically than those obtained with the total group.

We may say here at once that we have little faith in the absolute value of these correlations as true expressions of the quantitative relationships involved. We shall place much more emphasis on the generalized qualitative relationships as they impressed the experimenter, that is, on clinical rather than statistical correlations. We have used these statistical correlations almost solely for the sake of comparisons between dominance-feeling and sex drive, as they relate to sexual behavior and attitude.

An inspection of Tables 2-6 shows that closer correlations exist between promiscuity, masturbation, sexual attitude, and dominance-feeling (measured both by rating and by test score) than between these sexual variables and sex drive. Masturbation correlates about equally with sex drive and with dominance-feeling, but we must not neglect the fact of self-correlation, that is, the rating for sex drive depended to some extent on the presence or absence of masturbation. This factor of self-correlation also shows its influence in the slight discrepancies between the correlations with dominance-feeling rating and dominance-feeling score. It must be remembered that the rating was made after an exploration of the whole personality *including sexual attitudes and behavior*. This is not true for test score, which is based entirely upon non-sexual questions. Incidentally, the writer feels that the remarkably close correspondence (in spite of the

TABLE 4

Average Promiscuity Index and Percentage of Virginity in each Decile of Dominance-Feeling, as Measured by the Social Personality Inventory, with a Corrected Prediction of Virginity in the Theoretical Population at Large

Dominance scores arranged in deciles (highest scores at top)		CRITERION GROUP			TOTAL GROUP	
		% of virgins	Prom-iscuity	N	% of virgins	Average prom-iscuity	N
61 -	182	35	6.5	26	41	4.4	51
32 -	60	29	2.6	7	33	3.5	15
16 -	31	25	3.5	4	50	1.9	8
1 -	15	33	2.0	6	40	1.8	11
0 -	-12	80	2.4	5	75	1.6	8
-13 -	-28	80	1.4	5	80	1.0	10
-29 -	-40	100	0.0	3	100	0.0	6
-41 -	-58	100	0.0	4	100	0.0	9
-59 -	-81	100	0.0	4	100	0.0	8
-82 -	-145	83	0.2	6	85	0.2	13

Predicted estimate of percentage of virgins in a general population comparable to ours (obtained by averaging the percentages for all the deciles).

66.5%   70.4%

TABLE 5

Relation of Promiscuity to Presence or Absence of Masturbation;
Promiscuity Index Equals Number of Men with Whom Sexual
Relations Have Been Had

Criterion group ($N = 71$)

Average promiscuity index of masturbators	7.8	($N = 37$)
Average promiscuity index of non-masturbators	0.3	($N = 34$)

Total Group ($N = 124$)

Average promiscuity index of masturbators	5.3	($N = 73$)
Average promiscuity index of non-masturbators	0.5	($N = 51$)

above factor of self-correlation) between the correlations obtained with test score and with rating is a convincing proof of the validity and objectivity of the interview procedure and of the data obtained in these interviews.

The highest correlations obtained, as might be expected, are between sexual attitude and sexual behavior. The correlations between sex drive and sex behavior and attitude are probably too high, first because of self-correlation, and second because it was very difficult to get this rating disentangled from personality and cultural factors. The writer feels that if ever some perfectly physiological basis for sex drive is found that is measurable, say, by sheer blood level of the oestrin hormone, the correlations with sexual behavior would be lower than those we have obtained.

We are not stressing in this paper the relations between sexual behavior and attitude and ego-security. These will probably be

TABLE 6

Relation of Virginity to Presence or Absence of Masturbation

	MASTURBATION	NON-MASTURBATION	
	Criterion group ($N = 71$)		
Virgin	24%	76%	$N = 37$
Non-virgin	82%	18%	$N = 34$
	Total group ($N = 127$)		
Virgin	42%	58%	$N = 69$
Non-virgin	78%	22%	$N = 58$

presented in future papers. We may, for the moment, however, point to the differences in correlations between sex drive and masturbation in the Criterion Group and in the Total Group. In the latter group, the factor of ego-security was not as well controlled as in the Criterion Group. We attribute this drop in correlation from .51 to .25 to the intrusion into this picture of the factor of ego-insecurity. It will be observed that no other correlation is as much affected as this one.

Table 6 shows that masturbation and non-virginity go together more than do masturbation and virginity. This indicates that masturbation in normal people need not be thought of only as a method of compensating for lack of love or heterosexual experience, nor that it is solely a product of fear of heterosexuality.

It will be noticed that the correlations between sex drive and dominance-feeling are low ($r = .10 - .20$). Clinically we found almost no predictability at all.

1.   *Validity and Reliability of the Statistical Results*

It is necessary to indicate here what we believe to be the shortcomings of our statistical data.

1. The subjects that we had available are not evenly distributed, nor are there enough cases at some levels of self-esteem.

2. The bi-serial correlations may not be used as absolute quantitative measures since they are valid only when used for normal distributions and for greater number of cases than we had available.

3. Our quantitative ratings are in any case subject to a large number of criticisms which have already been discussed; the most important being that they are too subjective.

4. The question of truthfulness of certain answers in the interview must be considered as a possible attenuating factor. The writer believes that he was able to get frank, truthful answers, but it is difficult to prove this.

5. Self-correlation is present to some extent in correlation between ratings, e.g., the rating for dominance-feeling was made partially on the basis of sexual data. This factor turned out to be quite negligible, for correlations with dominance test scores are just about the same as with dominance rating.

E. QUALITATIVE RESULTS

1. *Cultural, Religious, Background Differences*

Sexual behavior, and to a lesser degree, sexual attitude, is a very sensitive resultant of many diverse influences, of which self-esteem and sex drive are only two. For instance, Jewish women, who have been found in general to be higher in dominance-feeling, and even more so in dominance behavior, than either Catholics or Protestants, nevertheless show higher percentages of virginity than either of the other groups. This has nothing to do with religion as such because very few of our Jewish subjects had ever been religious. When subjects *were* religious, whether Jewish, Catholic, or Protestant, they were much more apt to be virgin, not to masturbate, and to have lower ratings for sex attitude.

The Jewish women as a group were found to be markedly ambivalent toward sex, being attracted and frightened by it simultaneously. We have elsewhere (13) propounded the tentative hypothesis that their compensatory dominance behavior is partly a function of cultural insecurity; i.e., belonging to a cultural sub-group that is somewhat rejected and segregated by the larger group. The sexual findings for these women may also be a function or result of this same cultural position.

We have too few Catholic subjects for any final conclusions.

Certainly our data seem to indicate differences as a result of different religious or sub-cultural backgrounds. In dealing with individuals (rather than groups), this is even more apparent. So also are differences in educational background, differences in kind of parents, etc.

Geographical or sectional differences also seem to be possibly important. Subjects originally from the South carried with them a tradition or emphasis on purity, virginity, etc. "Being a lady" and "being common" were two sharply distinct things for them.

Certain kinds of progressive education or the influence of sophisticated parents seem also to instill a freer attitude toward sex, although it does not seem to affect actual sex behavior very much. On the other hand, being brought up by grandparents gave two subjects, both high in dominance, a more Puritan, antagonistic attitude toward sex.

2. Homosexual Behavior

Five of our subjects had had active homosexual experiences. Only one of these could be called "really" homosexual, preferring it to contact with men. Three of these were rated 9 in dominance-feeling (highest possible rating in our nine-point scale), one 8, and the "real" homosexual, 7. Of our total group of subjects six were rated 9 in dominance-feeling. In this group of six, of the three who had *not* had homosexual experiences, two consciously desired it and the last was not averse to it. The only other two subjects who admitted homosexual desires were rated 8.

Two of our subjects had had passive homosexual experience. One was rated 5.5 in dominance-feeling, the other 4.5 (5 is the median rating).

The implications are obvious even if our numbers are not great. In women with *very* high dominance-feeling, the probability is much higher than it is in the general population, that investigation will find either active homosexual episodes in the history or else conscious tendencies, desires, or curiosity.

In only one of these people was the homosexuality preferred or long continued. It came usually either from intense curiosity or from the inability to find a man suitably high in dominance-feeling as a mate. In these cases when a suitable man came along, the homosexuality was dropped at once.

In our two cases with passive homosexual episodes in the history, both were well-sexed, and at the time somewhat afraid of men and sex in general. Both were virgins. Conscious guilt feelings were present in both of these, but in *none* of the high dominance women. Both eventually turned to heterosexual interests.

Our one homosexual by preference (of course not included in our criterion group of "normal" women) did not look masculine but behaved so in many ways, preferring men's clothes, occupations, sports, etc. Sexual relations with men were reported but with no pleasure. They were indulged in "only to keep up a front" (the girl was terribly afraid of discovery).

Her history consists of the seduction of one girl after another in a very systematic fashion, always selecting women who "challenge" her. They are always taller than she is, always beautiful and feminine, and she is initially attracted because they dislike her, are antagonized by her, or are aloof and stand-offish. She is not attracted to those who obviously like her. She systematically, over a long period of time, gets them to tolerate holding hands, embracing, kissing, etc. The climax comes at the moment when she first induces orgasm in her partner: "At such times I get a feeling of smug power, and of great satisfaction." Her own orgasms come much later in the history of the relationship and are definitely not the primary goal in the seduction.

It is obvious that these findings (in the normal women) suggest an interpretation of homosexual behavior in terms of dominance which appears to be far more valid and useful than a purely physiological interpretation. The reader should compare these data and interpretations with our data on infra-human primates (12). An identical conclusion was reached therein.[3]

3. *The Influence of Sexual Position*

The facts upon which any theorizing must be based are as follows: Many of the women very high in dominance-feeling get a tremendous thrill out of occasionally assuming the above position in the sexual act; such behavior is unthinkable for women low in dominance-feeling; in those couples in which the wife has dominance-status over the husband, these women to some extent, regardless of level of dominance-feeling, are impelled to assume this position as the only or the best means of obtaining erotic pleasure. It will be remembered that certain relevant data are available in monkeys also, with respect to the dominance meaning of "above-ness" and "below-ness" in sexual behavior. In these animals we came to the conclusion that the face-to-face sexual position also had dominance meaning. This position was observed only in pairs in which the animal in subordinate status had, at the same time, high dominance-feeling. Our interpretation was that such a position signified greater equality than the ordinary dorso-ventral sexual position. This conclusion was further supported by the observation of the frequency of this face-to-face position in chimpanzees, in which dominance-subordination is of the friendly, more equal type. It is also found

---

[3] These comments of course do not purport to be a general theory of human homosexuality.

frequently in marriages of secure people for whom dominance-subordination usually is not a factor (in which status is equal).

These data clearly indicate the possible psychological and even biological importance and meaning of sexual position. The above position often has a deep connection with dominance, both feeling and status, and the below position seems often to be connected with subordinate status and feeling, although this latter connection is more influenced by other variables than is the former. For instance, we are forced to the conclusion that, in certain women whose high self-esteem is of the "ego-secure" type, the below position seems to carry with it no implication of submissiveness nor the above position any implication of dominance (the sexual act is not for them a "dominance act"). Also, religious dogma has standarized the below position as "normal" for women. It is interesting to notice in this connection that in our couples in which the women assumed dominant status and the above position, they all reported feeling "forced to do it," and that they felt that somehow they were not "normal." We have also two subjects who felt dominant to their husbands but nevertheless submitted to sexual relationships. Both were psychologically frigid with their husbands and both preferred the position in which, lying side by side, the man made entrance from behind. The statements of both women indicated that any other position would have indicated participation and neither felt that she was participating. This was a way then of saying, "I am outside of this affair."

The almost universal prevalence of the ventro-ventral position in most of the cultures of the world indicates closer, more friendly, more equal relationships between the sexes with mutual participation than is the case in animals. It is the writer's impression, although he is not at all certain of this, that in those cultures in which the dorso-ventral position is the more common one the men are completely dominant over the women and do not value them as individuals. The converse seems not to be true, however, for there are cultures of this latter type in which the ventro-ventral sexual position is the rule.

Possibly, more data on the sexual behavior of the primitives would yield us easy answers to many of our questions. For instance, such behavior as the following seems to the writer to be of great value in any general consideration of relationships between dominance and sexual behavior. In the Trobriand Islands (11) a commoner man married to a noble woman is not allowed to be physically above her in the sexual act. Among the Arunta of Australia (18) some women, known as "Alknerintja," refuse to submit to men. Men are afraid of them and at the same time very much attracted to them. To have had sexual relations with such a woman is a matter for boasting. An interesting folk-belief is that if a man dreams of an "Alknerintja" woman he must get up at once and run away or else she will put him on his back, sit on his erect penis and force him to the female role. In the few reports the writer remembers of groups in which women raped men, the procedure is to place him on his back and sit on the erect penis, thus assuming the above position.

4. Dominance in Sex and Marriage

In general our main conclusions are as follows. The best marriages in our society (unless both husband and wife are definitely secure individuals) seem to be those in which the husband and wife are at about the same level of dominance-feeling or in which the husband is *somewhat* higher in dominance-feeling than the wife. In terms of status this means that marriages with equality status or "split-dominance" status, or the husband in dominant status (but not markedly so) are most conducive to happiness and good adjustment for both husband and wife. In those marriages in which the wife is definitely dominant over her husband, trouble is very likely to ensue in the form of both social and sexual maladjustment unless they are both very secure individuals. This seems to be true also, but to a lesser extent, in those marriages in which the husband is *very* markedly dominant over his wife.

It follows from these statements that we should expect a greater incidence of divorce among such couples. A group of about 20 divorced women given our test for dominance-feeling scored significantly higher, on the average, than a comparable group of married women. It is interesting to notice that all of these cases but one fell at the middle of the range for dominance-feeling or above. The one exception was just as definitely below the median. No information could be elicited from her about the situation leading up to the divorce. However, the study of several marriages in which the husband was very much more dominant than the wife indicated that the marriages were in all cases not as happy as the equal ones. The husband was apt to feel conscious or unconscious contempt for the wife, to look down upon her and to lack respect for her. She was apt to become very insecure, to develop anxiety and jealousy and to be generally unhappy.

A confirmation of our finding about divorced women is found in an article by Johnson and Terman (9). The picture that they have derived of divorced women with personality tests is almost exactly like the one we have drawn of the high-dominance woman. For instance, to select only a few of the items, they found divorced women to be, on the average, high in volitional strength, tolerance, self-assertiveness, initiative, decisiveness, self-reliance, independence, ambition. They were more accustomed to take the lead in activities, more willing to be different or unconventional, and more able and willing to take jeers and criticism when they knew they were right. They were less docile and compliant, preferred working for themselves to taking orders. They blushed rarely. In general they lacked the element of sweet femininity but commanded respect for rugged strength, self-sufficiency, and detached tolerance.

Another very interesting finding in our investigation throws some light on an essential mechanism underlying promiscuity, one that we have seen often mentioned in the literature. Married men and women who were also promiscuous, very frequently were quite sure that sheer sexual pleasure and satisfaction was for them confined to the relations with the spouse. Other emotional needs were satisfied in their extra-marital affairs, namely, the desire to be sure they were still attractive, the thrill of novelty, unconscious hostility for the spouse, and often, frankly and consciously, the desire to conquer, to "collect scalps." Most subjects of all kinds admitted that a long-continued permanent relationship seemed to be necessary for the fullest sexual (physiological) pleasure and happiness. In promiscuity this was most often not the aim, nor could it be attained easily even when it was the aim, since it was displaced by the desire to impress, the desire to shine by comparison with other sexual partners, the wish to break down aloofness, coldness, snobbishness, etc. In a word, such hasty copulations are most often best viewed, not as sexual affairs, but as what might be called "dominance affairs" or "insecurity affairs."

The Don Juan (and the Doña Juana) has often been described in the literature as a person who bolsters up an insecure ego by convincing himself and others that he is a strong, conquering and desirable man (or woman). Our data supports such interpretation in a good many cases.[4] From such individuals we get reports that the greatest thrill comes not at the moment of the subject's climax, but at the moment of the partner's climax, for such seems to be the moment of conquering.

In such men, it is interesting to see the continued recurrence, in conversation about a snobbish or aloof woman, of the phrase, "She ought to be raped" as if this were the ultimate humiliation that would bring her to her (psychological) knees and allow the man to feel superior. Such aloof men and women are continual challenges and seem highly attractive sexually to the high-dominance person who is also somewhat insecure. So long as they hold off and fail to make love, they remain attractive, challenging, and superior. As soon as the succumb they have lost their value and are cast aside once the first thrill of conquest is gone. These findings are not true of the secure person and they become untrue for insecure high-dominance people who eventually attain psychological security.

We can say that monogamy, in our culture, if the pair are well matched psychologically (and, consequently, sexually) seems to be far preferable to promiscuity as a channel for sheer sexual satisfaction but does not satisfy the emotional needs of people with ego-insecurity of some sort.

5. *The Meaning of the Sexual Climax*

Attention was called to the possible psychological meaning of orgasm when our most highly sexed subject, a nymphomaniac (also in the highest dominance bracket)[5] reported that she had

[4] Not in all, however. This is too easy an explanation of promiscuity. Other factors are also part of this picture; e.g., a strong sex drive, high sex attitude, high dominance-feeling with its lack of inhibition, etc.

[5] A nymphomaniac is ordinarily defined as one who cannot control her sex urge, and who is insatiable. Usually, however, it is reported that such women do not have orgasm. This was not true in this case even though

(continued on following page)

not had orgasm with two particular men. This was quite un-expected in view of the fact that she could have orgasm merely by looking at a man. Her statement was, "I just couldn't give in to them. They were too weak." She had felt completely dominant over these men.

Another of our insecure subjects in the highest dominance group who had a strong sex drive and who felt dominant to most of the many men with whom she had sexual relations, reported lack of orgasm with most of them and went to extreme lengths to "show them I didn't give a hoot," such as chewing gum and smoking cigarettes during the sexual act.

Another subject, divorced from her husband, reported that she had tried desperately not to have orgasm with him because she hated and scorned him so. When she could not help herself, be-cause of her high sexuality, she inhibited completely any overt indication of what was happening to her. "I wouldn't give him the satisfaction." She despised herself for not being able to prevent the climax.

In cases of middle dominance-feeling and average sexuality, the presence of the orgasm is a fairly good sign of a feeling of love of the husband. If she does not feel loved or secure, the orgasm will be inhibited unless she is strongly sexed. This will also be true very frequently when a wife is dominant over her husband. In two of the subjects whose husbands were instructed concerning suitable dominance behavior, the orgasm was even-tually induced.

In the homosexual subject reported above, it will be re-membered that inducing the climax in her partner was the high spot and the goal toward which all her activity was pointed. In the men that we have interviewed this also seemed often to be the case, at least in those with higher dominance-feeling. One (rather insecure) man reported that he always had a feeling of exultation at such a moment. Also it appears fairly frequently that such men will not be satisfied with wives who do not have

she conformed to the requirements of the usual definition. See Hamilton (p. 223) who says, "Compulsive promiscuity, including those extreme cases . . . labelled 'nymphomania,' is probably never found among women who can have the climax." Most of our subjects who could be called "compulsively promiscuous" were capable of having the climax. Hamilton's statement may or may not be true of neurotic women; it certainly is not true of "normal" women (6).

orgasm, and to the researcher, there seemed to be some under-mining of their dominance-feeling when they "failed," as they so often put it. One wife reported faking the orgasm when it did not come spontaneously "in order not to make him feel that he isn't good enough."

It would seem then that the orgasm has psychological values for the woman. With it she may "give in," make herself vulner-able, and to a certain extent, put herself into subordinate status. For a man to induce the orgasm in a woman supports his dominance-feeling and also, for the moment at least, gives him dominance status, especially if the sexual position is psycho-logically suitable. We may make the finer distinction between what we may call dominant and subordinate orgasms. Women may achieve the first by assuming the above position, by being active homosexuals, or by being in charge of the whole sexual situation, as with a much younger man. The first type carries with it feelings of triumph, of exultation and of bigness, strength and masculinity.

Such feelings and distinctions are strikingly absent in the "equal" or "secure" marriage, in which also the various sexual positions seem to lose some or all of their dominance meaning. In this type of marriage, we may say in general that the concept of dominance is of little direct use. (This is generally true for secure people.)

6. *Personality and Love-making*

Practically all the books on sexual and love technique make the stupid mistake of assuming that all women are alike in their love demands. And so we find that general instructions are given to apply to all love-making as if one woman were equal to any other woman. That this is completely absurd must already be self-evident from our previous discussions. They are even more absurd when they speak as if the sexual act were merely a problem in mechanics, a purely physical act rather than an emotional, psychological act.

Our data are best presented if we make three general group-ings: low, middle, and high dominance. For these groups the concept of the ideal man, of the ideal love act, and of love-making in general vary widely.

a. The ideal man. For the woman who is high in dominance-feeling, only a high-dominance man will be attractive. He must be highly masculine (psychologically at least), he must be self-confident, fairly aggressive, and even "cocky," sure of what he wants and able to get it, generally superior in most things. Strength and forcefulness of personality are stressed. As we go down in the dominance scale, we find our subjects beginning to stress more and more such qualities as kindness, amiability, love for children, sympathy, gentleness, consideration, romanticism, sentimentality, faithfulness, and honesty. Our middle subjects were somewhat repelled by and afraid of the kind of man attractive to the high-dominance woman. Such men, they feel, are not soft enough, are "too highly sexed," and apt to be too brutal and animal. Generally we might say that the tendency in high-dominance women is to seek a good lover, while middle-dominance and low-dominance women tend rather to seek a good husband and father, an adequate man rather than an outstanding man, a comfortable and "homey" man rather than a man who might inspire slight fear and feelings of inferiority.

We know much less about the ideal man for the low-dominance woman. At times it appears as if there weren't any, at least for those who are also insecure; they are afraid of all men and distrust them. However, children are usually desired and therefore men and sex are unfortunate, even disgusting necessities. Here too we find that the principle of homogamy holds, of like marrying like. It is the low-dominance man who is acceptable, the gentle, timid, shy man who will adore at a distance for years before daring to speak, who also is afraid of sex as such. It is the writer's impression (with inadequate data) that certainly the low- and often the middle-dominance woman chooses a man to whom she can feel maternal at times.

Looked at from another angle, we see amazingly good adaptations in this sphere. For instance, there are roughly about equal percentages of high-dominance men and women, and so on down the scale of dominance-feeling. It seems possible to say, psychologically, that with respect to the one characteristic we have studied, there is a man for every woman. Also we find in men and women at various levels of dominance-feeling almost perfectly complemental characteristics. The high-dominance woman demands only a high-dominance man, but also the high-dominance man prefers the high-dominance woman. The low-dominance woman dislikes or is afraid of sex; so also is the low-dominance man. The middle- and low-dominance woman wishes romance, flowers, dim lights, illusions, sentimental gestures and poetry. These are just what the middle- and low-dominance man is inclined to give.

b. Ideal love-making. The average high-dominance woman in our insecure society prefers straightforward, unsentimental, rather violent, animal, pagan, passionate, even sometimes brutal love-making. It must come quickly, rather than after a long period of wooing. She wishes to be suddenly swept off her feet, not courted. She wishes her favors to be taken rather than asked for. In other words she must be dominated, must be forced into subordinate status.

For the middle-dominance woman gentler, long-prolonged wooing is considered ideal. In love-making, sex as such must be hidden, swathed about with veils of love words, gently and carefully led up to. It must be preceded by a general atmosphere of the type supplied by soft music, flowers, and love-letters. There must usually be a process of habituation and adaptation to the man and to the situation.

So marked are these differences that we may say, with some inaccuracy but with illumination, that the high-dominance woman unconsciously wishes to be raped; the middle-dominance woman to be seduced.

As for the low-dominance woman, it is difficult to know what she wishes. Perhaps it may be fair to say that any commerce with sex will be for the purpose of reproduction or to "satisfy her husband" (except when there is a very high sex drive). In one subject (dominance rating, 4; sex drive rating, 9) divorce came after she had a child. In another (dominance rating, 2; sex drive rating, 5) where there is no possiblity of a child, sexual relations are entirely refused to the husband. In the first of these two subjects the high sex drive has led to some promiscuity, attended by terrific guilt feelings. In some others, regardless of their fears before marriage, some degree of reconciliation and sometimes even liking for it is achieved after marriage if they are not too insecure.

c. Concept of marriage. As might be expected, the different types of women have different philosophies of marriage. A good deal of what might be said here can be directly deduced from the observations reported above. In addition, however, we can point out here that there is also variation in monogamous ideal. Most women insist on monogamy for themselves and their husbands. As we go higher in the scale of dominance, we are told that some promiscuity is expected in the husband and that there is nothing to do about it but adjust to it. Still higher in the scale, overt wishes are expressed by the subjects with relation to extra-marital activity. And, finally, in our highest dominance brackets, we find that the double standard has disappeared; that if the husband is to have extra-marital relations, so also will the wife. Of these subjects, those that are more highly sexed frequently do have extra-marital relations. The monogamous ideal and the acceptance of the double standard are thus seen also to vary with personality position in the dominance scale.

7. *Sexual Attitudes, Tastes, and Behavior*

The concept of sexual attitude as we have used it is not too well defined. What does it mean in terms of specific behavior and tastes?

Ratings were made on a nine-point scale. One extreme is a highly pagan, positive, uninhibited acceptance of anything sexual. The other extreme is a highly "Puritan," inhibited, negative and rejecting attitude toward sex. People who rate high can be said to love sex as such and for its own sake, to regard it as one of the world's best "goods," to approve of all aspects of it, and to regard everything connected with it as good. People who rate low are afraid of it, disgusted and revolted, and feel it must be controlled or justified by babies. For them it is justifiable only as a necessary preliminary to having children, or a necessary concession to the husband. These are the people who cry out and complain that God or nature could have done things in a better way. "Why is it necessary to be an animal before I can have a baby?" If a low sex attitude goes with an average or high sex drive then there is trouble indeed. Horrible guilt feelings, continual self-castigation, disgust and horror, repression and conflicts of all kinds are the lot of such a person. The following is a characteristic statement by a low-dominance woman (dominance rating, 3; sex attitude, 3).

When I think about sex, I feel Nature could have fixed up a better method—it's rather stupid. It seems so similar to animals, it reminds us we haven't evolved very far. In looking forward to sex, I think I'd be ashamed. I can never understand how people can do it. The sexual organs are the ugliest part of the body.

This subject with a low sex drive is fairly well adjusted and has no trouble in maintaining her attitude. In another and similar subject, who, however, had a strong sex drive and had been driven into some promiscuity, there were violent reactions against herself—weeping, self-punishment, and some suicidal thoughts. Such people, when they marry, live highly restricted sex lives.

At the other extreme, however, we find a tremendous flowering out of all kinds of sex behavior—cunnilingus, fellatio, unusual sexual positions, much experimentation even homosexuality or group sexual activities in a few instances.

For instance, cunnilingus is liked very much and indulged in as frequently as possible by a large proportion of the subjects who rate in sex attitude from seven and up, and by practically none who rate five and below. (Because of the very high correlation $[r = .85]$ between dominance rating and sex attitude, these remarks hold true for either dominance or sex attitude.) To a somewhat lesser extent the same is true for fellatio. Generally the higher the dominance (with ego-security held constant), the greater attractiveness the penis has for handling, looking at, and thinking about. High dominance women ordinarily think it to be a very beautiful object in a truly aesthetic sense. Through most of the rest of the population it is considered to be either ugly or neutral in appearance. Incidentally, it is beginning to appear as if exactly the same were true in male attitudes toward the vagina and external pudenda.

This is only a sample of the general attitude of high-dominance people toward sex and sensuality in any of its aspects. Every aspect of it is eagerly, enthusiastically accepted and warmly thought of (where ego-insecurity is not too great), experiments of all kinds are made, all sexual acts are thought of as "fun," rather than as a serious business. Very frequently, in a marriage between high-dominance people, it is found that there has been experience, if only a single experiment, with practically every form of sexual behavior known to the psychopathologist as well as the sexologist, many involved and curious positions or combinations of positions in this sexual act, sodomy, homosexuality, cunnilingus, fellatio, sadism-masochism, exhibitionism, and even coprophilia, sexuality in a larger group, etc. These acts have no pathological tinge nor are they pathogenic in any way. It would appear that no single sexual act can per se be called abnormal or perverted. It is only abnormal or perverted individuals who can commit abnormal or perverted acts. That is, the dynamic meaning of the act is far more important than the act itself.

The strong tendencies to promiscuity found in higher-dominance people also illustrate the point, as does the widespread incidence of masturbation in these people, both before and after marriage (after marriage only when there is deprivation of opportunity for the sexual act). In such people, masturbation is often (not always) found to be a highly sensual affair, protracted and making use of all sorts of titillating and stimulating thoughts, objects and acts. In both masturbation and sexual intercourse the whole body rather than just the restricted genital area, is apt to be involved. Every spot or area that is erotically stimulable is apt to be enlisted in the game that the act has become, and in building up to a tremendous orgiastic climax.

The dreams and fantasies of high-dominance women are of great interest in this connection. In the first place, open dreams of the sexual act are practically restricted to the upper half of the distribution of dominance-feeling in the population. In the lower half of the distribution the "sexual" dreams are always, except in highly sexed women, of the romantic sort, or else are anxious, distorted, symbolized, and concealed. The sex dreams of the high-dominance woman are open, promiscuous, and reflect the same sensuality and desire for wide sexual experience found in the daily life. Thus they dream of intercourse with practically any attractive man met recently, or less often, of a "man" with no particular identity, often with a tremendously enlarged penis. Rape dreams or prostitution dreams are fairly often reported in which the dreamer is forced to submit sexually to a large number of brutal men. These dreams are highly excitable and enjoyable to the high-dominance woman, and of course to the low-dominance woman, completely horrifying. Dreams and fantasies of sexual relations with negro men, large, husky, and beautifully built, are reported by women in the highest brackets of dominance (except women from the South). A few reports of sexual dreams about animals, chiefly horses and dogs, have been made by women in the highest bracket who were also highly sexed. It must be emphasized that all these dreams reflect desires consciously felt in the waking life also. The same subjects are reported in the masturbation fantasies of high-dominance women.

We have previously pointed out (14) that there is a high correlation between dominance-feeling and liking for nudity. This correlation is just as high of course between sexual attitude and nudism. High-dominance people (if not too insecure) have little or no fear of the body or of any of its functions. Thus the sexual organs are not feared, are even especially attractive. This holds true even in like sex groups. Low-dominance men or women hide their sexual organs even in those situations, e.g., gymnasium, swimming pool, etc., where it is more inconvenient to hide than to reveal. In high-dominance marriages urination and sometimes even defecation is not considered a private matter particularly. Nor in such marriages is menstruation hidden from the husband.

Another characteristic of high sexual attitude and high dominance-feeling is the free use of words and phrases ordinarily considered to be obscene or "dirty," words that are apparently completely tabooed by low-dominance men and women.

Generally the sexual act is apt to be taken not as a serious rite, with fearful aspects, and differing in fundamental quality from all other acts, but as a game, as fun, as a highly pleasurable animal act. Such couples speak about it freely to each other, smacking their lips over anticipated or remembered pleasures, and becoming excited all over again in the process.

All these characteristics of high-dominance people (high self-esteem) must inevitably remind us of our previous interpretation of the dominance-feeling as a degree of repression or inhibition. Thus we may characterize high-dominance people as uninhibited or unrepressed, as people whose fundamental impulses, animal or otherwise, are more apt to come out freely into behavior, within limits set by the society. Low-dominance people (low self-esteem) are far more strongly socialized or inhibited.

8. *Sadism-Masochism*

Our data on this subject are somewhat confusing, probably because of our inability to disentangle clearly direct cultural effects from effects of sex drive and dominance-feeling. Generally our data must be discussed against the background of the standardized cultural formulation that women in love and sex relations are supposed to be yielding, submissive, and even to some extent masochistic. Such tendencies, sometimes stronger, sometimes weaker, can be seen in practically all our subjects. Peculiarly enough, it is just those few women who show no signs of this culturally expected attitude of deference to men in whom we find what seems to be a much more truly masochistic attitude (in a psychological rather than a cultural-conventional sense).

What we may call cultural-conventional submissiveness or masochism is the sort of attitude that expresses itself in preferring to be hugged tightly rather than gently and to be slightly hurt in love-making, that delights in the superior physical strength, height, hardness, and initiative of the male, and that generally regards men as superior to women.

On the other hand, in the high-dominance woman *who is also definitely insecure,* we find often the more classical sexual-pathological picture of close relationship between pain and sexual pleasure. For instance, in one case, a rather promiscuous negress had finally fixed on one man, had lived with him for several years with only one or two lapses from faithfulness. She clung to this man because of his tremendously large penis. She reported dreadful pain in the sexual act, but it seemed that just when the pain was greatest so also was the pleasure greatest. The highest dominance women reported rather regularly in their fantasies and in their consciously drawn picture of the ideal sexual partner, men with enormously large sexual organs, large enough to cause pain. It will be remembered that these women reported that the idea of being raped, if not actually attractive, at least was sexually exciting. They definitely prefer rough to gentle love-making (except when the sex drive is low).

It was to be expected from the findings of various of the psychoanalytic psychiatrists that we should find in just these "masochistic" women, an equal amount of sadism. Wherever one was found, so was the other and usually in just about equal proportions.

Perhaps the best way to describe the situation is to say that in these few women, they strive incessantly to dominate all with whom they come in contact and tend to be sadistic in their dominance in so far as they are allowed to by cultural formulations. They do seem to get a sexual thrill of a certain kind from this behavior. But when a man comes along who cannot be dominated, who proves himself stronger, then these women tend to become definitely masochistic, and to glory in being dominated. Apparently the sexual pleasure so derived is strongly preferred over the other kind of thrill derived from dominating.

One such subject described her sexual life as a continual hunt for a man who was stronger than she was. After a long career of promiscuity, she found such a man and married him (and is still as much in love with him as when she married him some years ago). However, she describes her married life in the same way, as a continual testing of his strength. She actually picks fights in which he becomes violent and which usually end in virtual rape. These incidents provide her with her most exciting sexual experiences.

While this case is the most extreme and the most neurotic recorded in our case histories, the same thing seems to be true in other high-dominance women, if in a more diluted form. The insecure high-dominance woman in our society is usually looking for a man who can dominate her. In order to do this, he must of course have extremely high self-esteem.

We can probably extend this rule to almost all insecure women in our society, however high or low their self-esteem may be. As they describe their ideal men they describe men who are somewhat more dominant than they, men who are superior and stronger. Some even describe men who are *much* more dominant than they. However, in reality the good matches that are made are of the type in which the man is *somewhat* more dominant. For one thing, the man who is much more dominant than a particular woman is usually not interested in her or attracted to her. For another thing, she, when she meets him, realizes that she is somewhat afraid of him, disapproves of him and his way of life, and even is apt to dislike him.

We do not wish to give the impression that this power philosophy of sex is universal. The extreme picture that we have given is characteristic of only a small per cent of the population, those that are very high in dominance-feeling and are also very definitely insecure. People who are secure show no sadism-masochism at all, nor do they seek to dominate or be dominated, no matter at what level their self-esteem may be. Here again we have a beautiful example of the sexual selection mechanism that draws to each other just those who are similar and can therefore satisfy each other's needs. Such a woman as we have described above usually finds and selects just that man who can give her what she wants, and who will find in her just what he desires in a wife. As a matter of fact, the man that she married was also extremely high in dominance, high in dominance-feeling and definitely insecure. From a man who was just as high in dominance but was secure, she could not have received the domination, vigor, and aggressive strength that she needed. Such a man is more apt to be kind and co-operative, desiring a wife who is his equal, not one whom he has to beat into line. It is our very strong impression that the principle of homogamy holds strongly in the sphere of self-esteem.

We may now draw the general rule from the data we have presented above. This is, that for relatively insecure people sex is a power weapon, that it is in myriad ways related to dominance-feeling and dominance-status, and indeed may be considered itself simply as a kind of dominance or subordination behavior or at least as a channel through which dominance-subordination may be expressed. In general it has far more intimate relationships with dominance-feeling than it has with physiological drive. This may be interpreted as a definite corroboration of the Adlerian theory of sexuality, at least in its most fundamental emphasis, in so far as it applies to our society taken in general as a relatively insecure society. The Adlerian theory definitely does not hold for people and societies that are secure, but Adler, in his later writings, seemed to realize this also.

This does not mean that our data contradict the Freudian sexual theories in toto. Freud has said, at one place or another, practically everything that may be said about the sexual life, even if this has often seemed to place him on both sides of the fence at the same time. Thus we can contradict specific state-

ments that he has made only to find that he himself has con-
tradicted them elsewhere. We do not mean this to be a carping
criticism, for it seems to mean only that Freud saw clearly *all*
the clinical facts and would not omit mention of them, even if
they did not quite fit into his theoretical constructions. Neither
do we mean to imply that we must accept *either* the Adlerian *or*
the Freudian approach to sexuality. Freud himself has incorporated much of the Adlerian insight into psychoanalysis by
the simple method of translation, and Adler has paid Freud the
same compliment.

9. *Comparison with Animal Data* (See 12)

If we compare the two sets of data we find a series of startling
parallels and similarities. In general it is fair to say that human
sexuality is almost exactly like primate sexuality with the exception that cultural pressures added to the picture, drive a good
deal of sexual behavior underground into fantasies, dreams, and
unexpressed wishes. What we have to dig for in the human
being we can see overtly in the infra-human primate. It should
be noted that the picture of human sexuality that we have drawn
has been mostly of the somewhat insecure type. The closest
analogy is with the sexual behavior of the baboon and the
macacus rhesus. The sexual life of the secure person is more
closely paralleled by that of the chimpanzee, which has a
different quality of dominance from that of the baboon and
macacus rhesus (15).

The most important common conclusion for the two groups,
human and infra-human, is that dominance is a more potent
determiner of, or is more closely related to, sexual behavior than
is sexual drive. In both groups, sexuality may be used as a power
weapon in the Adlerian sense. One form of human homosexuality
may be explained in the same way as in the monkey. This is
also true for one aspect of sadism-masochism, which were
found to go together in the human being as they did in the
macacus. In human beings, as also in monkeys and apes, sexual
position was found to have definite psychological significance. In
both groups, it was found necessary to treat as separate, sexuality
and reproduction. Both groups are relatively free from sexual
cyclicity, the human group even more than the infra-human.
This relative freedom from cyclicity in the human being is cer-

tainly more complex than in the infra-human, for cultural factors are certainly involved as well as biological differences.

The chief difference we wish to point out between the sexuality and dominance of animals and humans is that dominance, and consequently sexual behavior, is determined in the monkey almost wholly by social position. While it was found to be true that there were individual differences in what may be called by analogy dominance-feeling, still this was a minor factor as compared with dominance-status. What this means essentially is that practically all determination and inhibition of behavior in the monkey is due to external, immediately present, social forces (the presence of other animals). In the human being, we have a tremendous expansion of the importance of *internalization* of these social forces, so dominance-feeling becomes far more important and dominance-status far less important in determining attitudes and behaviors in the sexual sphere. We can rate most human beings in our society as generally bold or timid, but for the monkey, we are forced in almost all cases to specify the particular social situation in which he is at the moment. There are human beings who are inhibited in the presence of practically all of their peers, but there exist few such monkeys and these are the products of exceptional circumstances.

Other possible phrasings are in terms of superego or conscience or socialization which are far more highly developed in the human being than in the monkey. Inhibitions for the monkey are practically always external; for the human being they are much more often internal.

F.   SUMMARY AND CONCLUSION

Using a clinical-experimental methodology, combined with certain quantitative ratings, the general conclusion was reached from both quantitative and qualitative data that sexual behavior and attitudes were much more closely related to dominance-feeling than to sheer sexual drive in our subjects. This same conclusion had been drawn for infra-human primates in previous investigations. Other similarities in findings for these two groups were also pointed out. The most important difference pointed out between monkeys and humans was that in the extent of internalization of social inhibitions.

A. H. MASLOW

197

REFERENCES

1. DAVIS, K. B. *Factors in the Sex Life of Twenty-Two Hundred Women.* New York: Harper, 1929.
2. DICKINSON, R. L., and BEAM, L. *One Thousand Marriages.* Baltimore: Williams & Wilkins, 1932.
3. ————. *The Single Woman.* Baltimore: Williams & Wilkins, 1932.
4. FREUD, S. *Three Contributions to the Theory of Sex* (4th ed.). Washington: Nervous and Mental Diseases Publications, 1930.
5. HAMILTON, G.V. *A Research in Marriage.* New York: Boni, 1929.
6. ————. "The Emotional Life of Modern Women," in *Woman's Coming of Age* (ed. by Schmalhausen, S., and Calverton, V.). New York: Liveright, 1931. (Pp. 207-229.)
7. HORNEY, K. *The Neurotic Personality of Our Time.* New York: Norton, 1937.
8. ————. "What Is a Neurosis?" *American Journal of Sociology,* 1939, 45, 426-432.
9. JOHNSON, W., and TERMAN, L. "Personality Characteristics of Happily Married, Unhappily Married, and Divorced Persons." *Character & Personality,* 1935, 3, 290-311.
10. LANDIS, C., *et al. Sex in Development.* New York: Hoeber, 1940.
11. MALINOWSKI, B. *The Sexual Life of Savages.* London: Routledge, 1929.
12. MASLOW, A. H. "The Role of Dominance in the Social and Sexual Behavior of Infra-human Primates: III. A Theory of Sexual Behavior of Infra-human Primates." *Journal of Genetic Psychology,* 1936, 48, 310-338.
13. ————. "Dominance-feeling, Behavior, and Status." *Psychological Review,* 1937, 44, 404-429.
14. ————. "Dominance-feeling, Personality, and Social Behavior in Women." *Journal of Social Psychology,* 1939, 10, 3-39.
15. ————. "Dominance-quality and Social Behavior in Infra-human Primates." *Journal of Social Psychology,* 1940, 11, 313-324.
16. ————. "A Test for Dominance-feeling (Self-esteem) in Women." *Journal of Social Psychology,* 1940, 12, 255-270.
17. ———— and MITTELMANN, B. *Principles of Abnormal Psychology.* New York: Harper, 1941.
18. ROHEIM, G. "Psycho-analysis of Primitive Cultural Types." *International Journal of Psychoanalysis,* 1932, 13, 2-223.
19. TERMAN, L. M. *Psychological Factors in Marital Happiness.* New York: McGraw-Hill, 1938.
20. WEXBERG, I. *The Psychology of Sex: An Introduction.* New York: Farrar and Rinehart, 1931.

XI

Some Considerations Concerning Orgasm in the Female*

BY JUDD MARMOR

> The sexual frigidity of women . . . is still a phenomenon which is insufficiently understood. Sometimes it is psychogenic, and, if so, it is accessible to influence; but in other cases one is led to assume that it is constitutionally conditioned or even partly caused by an anatomical factor.
>
> —SIGMUND FREUD, *New Introductory Lectures on Psychoanalysis*

Although much is known about both the physiology and psychodynamics of the male orgasm, the mechanisms underlying orgasm in the female remain shadowy and obscure. The reasons for this are both physiological and psychological. On the physiological side is the fact that the female orgasm is not accompanied by an objectively perceptible emission as is that of the male, which not only makes it difficult at times for the woman herself to recognize, but also makes it impossible for any external observer to be certain about it. On the psychological side are the taboos which so strongly surround the subject of female sexuality.

* Read before the Society for Psychoanalytic Medicine of Southern California on November 6, 1952.

The conventions of our culture are still so powerful in this respect that women themselves, who might be expected to shed the greatest light on this subject, are for the most part unable or unwilling to do so. One might speculate as to whether their very sensory perceptions of the process, having developed in the crucible of these conventions, have not been affected in such a way as to interfere with an accurate evaluation of their own sexual reactions.

Freud's Concept of Genital Erogenicity

Most psychoanalytical concepts about the physiology of the female orgasm date back to Freud's classic formulation in his *Three Contributions to the Theory of Sex.* In this monograph, Freud advanced the thesis that genital erogenicity in the normal female, although first centered in the clitoris, eventually becomes transferred to the vagina; and that sexual orgasm in the mature, healthy female should be in response to vaginal rather than clitoral stimulation. "We may assume," Freud says, "that in the phallic phase of the girl, the clitoris is the dominant erotogenic zone. But it is not destined to remain so; with the change to femininity, the clitoris must give up to the vagina its sensitivity, and with it, its importance either wholly or in part."[7] Failure of such transfer to take place leads, in Freud's opinion, to sexual frigidity or "anesthesia," a condition which he believed due to "profuse sexual activities in infantile life."[8]

Horney[9] and Lorand[13] among others have suggested that vaginal sensations may be present in early childhood, but the conclusion that clitoral sensitivity must ultimately give way to vaginal sensitivity in the normal female seems never to have been seriously questioned in the psychoanalytical literature.

Freud's hypothesis was based on certain common clinical observations. It is a well-known fact that masturbation in the young female is generally centered around clitoral stimulation. It is also commonly observed that the sexually "frigid" adult female is incapable of having an orgasm through vaginal intercourse, but it often able to achieve an orgasm through direct stimulation of the clitoris. On the other hand, women who seem to have achieved the greatest degree of sexual freedom and responsiveness are able to have orgasms freely through vaginal intercourse.

The intensity of the orgasm, moreover, appears to differ depending on its character. Most observers report that the "clitoral orgasm" is experienced as a localized response, while the so-called "vaginal orgasm" seems to be a more violent, intense, and generalized reaction.

Although these clinical observations seem well authenticated, recent studies of the sexual physiology of women have thrown some doubt on their theoretical interpretation, and specifically upon the hypothesis of the transfer of erogenicity from the clitoris to the vagina. Evidence has accumulated in recent years to indicate that in the normal adult woman clitoral excitation by the penis in the process of intercourse is an important factor in the stimulation leading to orgasm. A clitoris which is located too high above the urinary meatus is believed by some investigators to reduce the capacity of the female for orgasm during intercourse. Landis measured the meatus-clitoris distance in several hundred women and concluded that individuals in whom this distance is greater than one and one-half inches are less likely to experience orgasm during intercourse than are women in whom it is less. Dickinson,[3] on the other hand, questions that the location of the clitoris is the decisive factor, although he too believes that its stimulation is an essential factor in orgasm. In his opinion, the most reliable index to clitoral function is not its location so much as its susceptibility to displacement during intercourse.

Indirect corroborative evidence of this continued function of the clitoris in adult sexual life is offered by the study of the preferred sexual positions in various cultures of the world.[6] Such study reveals that face-to-face coitus, which affords a greater opportunity for the woman to obtain clitoral stimulation, is the position preferred by most people in most societies. Kinsey and his collaborators[11] found that the position which their subjects considered most conducive to orgasm in the female was that in which the man lies on his back and the woman sits or lies above him in a face-to-face position. This is a position which more than any other favors clitoral excitation during coitus. Ford and Beach found that coitus-a-tergo does not occur as a usual or preferred practice in any of more than thirty-five societies which they studied, and they conclude that this may well be due in part to the fact that stimulation of the clitoris is minimal when this position is employed.

Most significant of all, however, are histological studies in females of the sensory cells known as the genital corpuscles, which "are highly specialized end-organs for the perception of this particular sensation (i.e., orgasm) just as the retina is adapted for the sense of sight and the neuro-epithelium of the nose is adapted for the sense of smell."[10] These histological studies indicate that genital corpuscles do not occur in the vaginal mucosa and are confined predominantly to the glans clitoridis.[10] Some are also found in the areas directly adjacent to the clitoris, notably the labia minora.

Importance of the Clitoris

The meaning of these findings is that the chief sensory area for erogenous sensation in women is localized in the glans clitoridis, just as in men it is localized in the homologous glans penis. (The shaft of the penis, like the vagina, is lacking in genital corpuscles.) This does not, of course, mean that these are the only erogenous areas. The importance of the secondary erogenous zones such as lips, breasts, and buttocks is well known. Moreover, there are kinesthetic receptors within the vaginal wall, the stimulation of which by the erect penis contributes voluptuous sensations to the normal woman. There are similar receptors in the bulbocavernosus muscles around the lower end of the vagina which contribute a sense of ejaculation during orgasm by their spasmodic pulsations. The contractions of these same muscles in the male cause actual ejaculation of semen from the penis during orgasm.

How do these observations concerning the importance of the clitoris in the sex life of the normal adult woman fit into the pattern of the previously mentioned clinical observations about "clitoral" and "vaginal" orgasms? Do they not seem to require some revision of the hypothesis concerning the shift of erogenicity from the clitoris to the vagina? If so, what hypothesis can be offered in its place?

Before considering these questions, it may be pertinent to examine, for a moment, our knowledge concerning the anatomy and physiology of orgasm in the male. It is an accepted fact that in the male there is an orgastic spinal center in the sacral segment of the spinal cord. As can be demonstrated from the evidence of neurophysiology, discharges of tension in this orgastic center can be achieved either at a reflex spinal level or by cortical stimulation. In the former instance, this discharge is achieved by simple mechanical stimulation of the genital corpuscles of the glans penis, which eventually causes a rising tension in the spinal center until reflex discharge takes place. In the latter instance, the cortical stimulation is achieved through psychological stimuli, occurring through supraspinal sensory receptors. Thus not only stimulation of secondary erogenous areas (lips, nipples, etc.) but even witnessing exciting scenes, or reading an erotic piece of literature, or merely fantasying, dreaming, or anticipating a particularly exciting or erotic experience can produce orgasm in some males in the total absence of any physical stimulation of the penis itself. In certain neurotic men it has been observed that extreme anxiety or tension of nonsexual origin may occasionally produce sexual orgasm, apparently through the medium of an overflow of cortical excitation which affects the spinal orgastic center.

In the normal masculine orgasm, however (normal from a psychodynamic standpoint), what apparently takes place is a combination of the spinal and cortical mechanisms. The male reaches a high state of sexual excitation through the combination of psychological, tactile, olfactory, and visual stimuli, even in the absence of any direct physical stimulation of the glans penis. This excitation is sufficient to produce erection but not orgasm. For orgasm to take place, a certain amount of supplementary physical stimulation of the glans penis itself, through the process of intercourse, is necessary. This physical excitation is further enhanced in the process of intercourse by the psychological stimulus from the mounting excitement of the partner. Under ideal circumstances this crescendo of excitement occurs in both partners simultaneously, and the combination of physical and psychological stimulation finally results in orgasm.

In considering the parallel mechanism of orgasm in the female, there is no reason to expect from our knowledge of anatomy and physiology that the female has two spinal orgastic centers rather than one. On the contrary, it is fair to assume that the female undoubtedly has an orgastic center located in the sacral segment

of the spinal cord, exactly as the male has. From neurohisto-
logical evidence, it can be shown that the sensory receptors for
this spinal orgastic center are the genital corpuscles, located
predominantly in the glans clitoris, just as the homologous
sensory receptors in the male are confined primarily to the glans
penis. Although one might naturally assume that the tiny clitoris
could hardly play as important a sensory role as the much larger
penis, Dickinson[4] points out:

> The female organ is minute compared with the male organ,
> but the size of its nerves, and the number of nerve endings in
> the glans of the clitoris compare strikingly with the same pro-
> vision for the male. Indeed, Kobelt states that the glans of the
> clitoris is demonstrably richer in nerves than the male glans, for
> the two stems of the dorsalis clitoridis are relatively three to four
> times as large as the equivalent nerves of the penis. Without
> dividing up, they run mostly with three branches to the edge of
> the glans. Here, before their entry, they are so thick one can
> hardly comprehend how such a volume of nerve tissue can find
> room between the numberless blood vessels of the tiny glans.
> Arrived near the surface of the glans they dispose themselves,
> just as in the male glans, in an intricate plexus, running also in
> loops into the tender membrane of the prepuce.

An indirect corroboration of the high degree of erogenicity
implicit in the extremely rich nerve supply of the glans clitoridis
lies in the much greater capacity of the female to have multiple
orgasms as compared to the male.

Orgastic Impotence

Yet, in spite of all the evidence that anatomically and physiologically the female should, at the very least, be fully as able as
the male to have orgastic reactions, the clinical facts are that
women are much more frequently orgastically impotent than are
men. Dickinson and Beam[5] in a study of one thousand married
women, found that only 2 out of every 5 women experience
regular orgasms during intercourse, and these figures are cor-
roborated by other investigators.

The conclusion seems inescapable that when anatomical factors such as described by Landis[12] and Dickinson[3] are ruled out,
the major difficulty must lie primarily in the psychological rather

than in the physiological sphere. This does not in any way gain-say the important effect of the ovarian cycle upon the libidinal reactions of women, as demonstrated by the studies of Benedek and Rubenstein,[2] but frigidity per se, as Benedek herself says, "can be related to the ovarian function only in rare cases of severe hypogonadism. In all other instances, women may have any form and degree of frigidity, and at the same time normal gonadal function."[1] Similar observations have been more recently made by Perloff.[14]

The psychological factors involved in feminine frigidity, on the other hand, are manifold. They have been frequently and amply described in the psychoanalytical literature and do not require repetition here. The complexity of sexual maturation in women, the greater degree of sexual repression and inhibition which our culture impresses upon them, and the envy and hostility to men which stems in part at least from the position of women in an androcentric culture are only a few of the factors which interfere with the capacity of women to enter with un-inhibited pleasure into a sexual relationship. Fears of being injured by the penis, fears of pregnancy and childbirth, and lack of adequate skill, tenderness, or potency on the part of the male partner are other factors which have been commonly described.

We are concerned here, however, not so much with the psycho-dynamics of frigidity as with the mechanisms involved in the orgastic reaction of the woman. The important consideration for our present purpose is the fact that whenever, and for whatever reason, a psychological inhibition of the capacity to enjoy sexual intercourse exists, the woman will usually be capable of re-sponding orgastically only at a spinal level, if at all; that is to say, only through the medium of direct mechanical stimulation of the clitoris itself. On the other hand, if the woman has been able to free herself from the blanket of psychological inhibition, she will be capable of responding through the medium of enhanced cortical excitement (that is, through cortical facilita-tion) to vaginal intercourse.

The conclusion that such a response is the result of vaginal excitability has been due to the implicit assumption that the physical stimulation which is taking place in vaginal intercourse is primarily of the vaginal wall and mucosa. Actually, as has

been pointed out, some stimulation of the clitoris almost invariably occurs in normal vaginal intercourse and is an important
factor in the excitation leading to orgasm. The difference between the so-called clitoral and vaginal orgasms, therefore, is
explicable not in terms of the different origin or location of the
orgastic response, but in the different intensity of it and in the
degree to which cortical factors are contributory. As in the male,
the intensity of orgasm in the female varies with the degree of
psychological excitation present. In a purely spinal reflex, due
only to mechanical stimulation of either the penis or the clitoris,
the orgasm is generally experienced as a localized and limited
reaction. On the other hand, in both the male and female, the
higher the degree of emotional and psychological participation,
the greater the degree of cortical facilitation of the spinal discharge and the more general and intense is the orgastic experience. Where the cortical excitation is of a particularly high
order, the orgastic reaction may be so intense and generalized
as to result in convulsive twitchings which are almost like minor
epileptic seizures, and which probably have a somewhat similar
neurophysiological mechanism in terms of dysrhythmic cortical
discharges. It would be pertinent in this regard to do electro-
encephalographic studies of cortical patterns during intense
orgasm.

Extragenital Orgasm

It should be noted further that there are other analogous reactions in the female which are similar to those observed in
the male. For example, in women, too, orgasm is capable of
taking place without any local genital stimulation at all. To quote
from Dickinson and Beam's study of one thousand marriages,
"The records contain instances of orgasm obtained from nipple
suction, from lying beside another, from nursing a baby, from
pressing (fully dressed) against another, from a shampoo at the
hands of a male hairdresser, from a look, from a kiss, from touching the eye or ear, from a handclasp, and from a picture or
flower which contains no figure and no likeness to any person
or scene."[5] Orgasms, under most of these circumstances, represent a discharge of the spinal center which has been initiated
primarily by cerebral excitation. In the normal woman, more-

over, as in the normal man, the excitement of the partner, and particularly the setting off of his orgastic reaction, constitutes an intense psychological stimulus for her and often acts as a trigger for her own climactic response.

Pursuing the logic of this hypothesis, therefore, we may say that strictly speaking there is no such thing as a "vaginal" orgasm in the female, any more than we might speak of "scrotal," "anal," or "prostatic" orgasm in the male. It seems logical to assume that the actual spinal mechanism of orgasm is identical in all females, but that variations which take place in the nature of female orgasm are due to the degree to which cortical inhibition or cortical facilitation accompanies the spinal reflex. Where cortical inhibition is great, due to long-standing sexual repression or to a high degree of anxiety, hostility, ambivalence, or guilt in relationship to the sexual partner or the sexual act, the spinal mechanism may be completely inhibited, in which event we observe a total incapacity for orgasm, or so-called frigidity. Where the cortical inhibitions are not of such a high order, we observe a capacity to have orgasm only with prolonged stimulation of the clitoris. This is what is ordinarily described as a "clitoral" orgasm. However, where cortical inhibitions do not exist, where there is a freedom from psychological tension or anxiety in the sexual act, and instead there is a high degree of tender affection, love, and psychological excitement, then cortical facilitation takes place. The result is an intense orgastic response in which the intromission of the phallus into the vagina is of major importance. This is both psychodynamically and physiologically the optimum type of response, and represents what is ordinarily characterized as a "vaginal" orgasm.

Conclusions

The question may properly be asked as to what significance, if any, these considerations may have. Their importance lies in the effect which our present theories concerning female sexuality have upon the psychology of many women and upon the physicians who treat such women. Women patients are often encountered who suffer from anxiety because their subjective reactions do not fit the popular hypothesis concerning clitoral and vaginal sensitivity. Such women will often say that they enjoy sex and have orgasms regularly, but worry "because my husband has to stimulate my clitoris first," or because "most of my sensations seem to be clitoral." Obviously one cannot generalize about such reactions, and psychological disturbances are often involved even in such relatively minor limitation of orgastic function. But it may be an error to assume in advance that such reactions are necessarily of serious neurotic import. It is perfectly possible that in some instances they may be, as Freud himself suspected, "constitutionally conditioned or even partly caused by an anatomical factor."

An understanding of the function of the clitoris, moreover, is of importance to men as well as to women. Not infrequently sexual maladjustment of women can be traced to a failure of their male partners to appreciate the importance of clitoral stimulation in sexual foreplay as a factor in preparing the woman for an orgastic reaction. In addition, the woman herself all too often fears, resents, or objects to any form of clitoral manipulation for a variety of unconscious reasons—masturbatory guilt, shame about her genitals, anxiety that such manipulation is "perverse," "unnatural," or "neurotic," etc.

It seems fair to conclude, therefore, that a proper understanding of the role which the clitoris normally plays in adult female sexuality will help the physician in general as well as the psychiatrist more adequately to evaluate and treat the sexual disturbances of their patients as well as to reassure those who suffer from needless anxiety because of misapprehensions based upon faulty knowledge.

Summary

Some considerations have been presented which throw doubt on the popular assumption that genital erogenicity in the female becomes normally transferred from the clitoris to the vagina. There is evidence to indicate that clitoral sensitivity is a continuing factor in adult female sexuality, and that the chief difference between so-called clitoral and vaginal orgasm is explicable not in terms of the different origin or location of the orgastic response, but in the different intensity of it and in the degree to which cortical facilitation of the spinal reaction has taken place.

REFERENCES

1. BENEDEK, T. "The Functions of the Sexual Apparatus and Their Disturbances." In: ALEXANDER, F., *Psychosomatic Medicine*. New York, Norton, 1950.

2. BENEDEK, T., and RUBENSTEIN, B. B. "The Sexual Cycle in Women." *Psychosom. Med. Monog.* Washington, D. C., National Research Council, 1942, vol. 3, nos. 1 and 2.

3. DICKINSON, R. L. In: FORD, C. S., and BEACH, F. A., p. 21.

4. DICKINSON, R. L. *Human Sex Anatomy*. Baltimore, Maryland, Williams & Wilkins, 1933, p. 42.

5. DICKINSON, R. L., and BEAM, L. *A Thousand Marriages*. Baltimore, Maryland, Williams & Wilkins, 1931.

6. FORD, C. S., and BEACH, F. A. *Patterns of Sexual Behavior*. New York, Harper, 1951, p. 24.

7. FREUD, S. "The Psychology of Women." In: *New Introductory Lectures in Psychoanalysis*. New York, Norton, 1933, p. 161.

8. FREUD, S. "Three Contributions to the Theory of Sex." In: *The Basic Writings of Sigmund Freud*. New York, Modern Library, 1938, p. 164.

9. HORNEY, KAREN. "Denial of the Vagina," *Internat. J. Psycho-Analysis* 14:57, 1933.

10. KELLY, G. L. *Sex Manual* (ed. 5). Augusta, Georgia, Southern Medical Supply Co., 1950, pp. 30 *et seq.*

11. KINSEY, A. C., POMEROY, W. B., and MARTIN, C. E. *Sexual Behavior in The Human Male*. Philadelphia, Saunders, 1948.

12. LANDIS, C. In: FORD, C. S., and BEACH, F. A.

13. LORAND, S. "Contributions to the Problem of Vaginal Orgasm," *Internat. J. Psycho-Analysis* 20:432, 1939.

14. PERLOFF, W. H. "Role of the Hormones in Human Sexuality," *Psychosom. Med.* 11:133, 1949.

XII

Womanliness as a Masquerade

By Joan Riviere

Every direction in which psychoanalytic research has pointed seems in its turn to have attracted the interest of Ernest Jones, and now that of recent years investigation has slowly spread to the development of the sexual life of women, we find as a matter of course one by him among the most important contributions to the subject. As always, he throws great light on his material, with his peculiar gift both clarifying the knowledge we had already and also adding to it fresh observations of his own.

In his paper on "The Early Development of Female Sexuality"[1] he sketches out a rough scheme of types of female development, which he first divides into heterosexual and homosexual, subsequently subdividing the latter homosexual group into two types. He acknowledges the roughly schematic nature of his classification and postulates a number of intermediate types. It is with one of these intermediate types that I am today concerned. In daily life, types of men and women are constantly met with who, while mainly heterosexual in their development, plainly display strong features of the other sex. This has been judged to be an expression of the bisexuality inherent in us all; and analysis has shown that what appears as homosexual or heterosexual character traits, or sexual manifestations, is the end result of the interplay of conflicts and not necessarily

[1] Ernest Jones, "The Early Development of Female Sexuality," *International Journal of Psychoanalysis*, Vol. VIII, 1927.

evidence of a radical or fundamental tendency. The difference
between homosexual and heterosexual development results from
differences in the degree of anxiety, with the corresponding
effect this has on development. Ferenczi pointed out a similar
reaction in behavior,[2] namely, that homosexual men exaggerate
their heterosexuality as a "defense" against their homosexuality.
I shall attempt to show that women who wish for masculinity
may put on a mask of womanliness to avert anxiety and the
retribution feared from men.

It is with a particular type of intellectual woman that I have
to deal. Not long ago intellectual pursuits for women were
associated almost exclusively with an overtly masculine type of
woman, who in pronounced cases made no secret of her wish or
claim to be a man. This has now changed. Of all the women
engaged in professional work today, it would be hard to say
whether the greater number are more feminine than masculine
in their mode of life and character. In university life, in scientific
professions and in business, one constantly meets women who
seem to fulfill every criterion of complete feminine development.
They are excellent wives and mothers, capable housewives; they
maintain social life and assist culture; they have no lack of
feminine interests, e.g., in their personal appearance, and when
called upon they can still find time to play the part of devoted
and disinterested mother-substitutes among a wide circle of relatives and friends. At the same time they fulfill the duties of their
profession at least as well as the average man. It is really a
puzzle to know how to classify this type psychologically.

Some time ago, in the course of an analysis of a woman of this
kind, I came upon some interesting discoveries. She conformed
in almost every particular to the description just given; her
excellent relations with her husband included a very intimate
affectionate attachment between them and full and frequent
sexual enjoyment; she prided herself on her proficiency as a
housewife. She had followed her profession with marked success
all her life. She had a high degree of adaptation to reality, and
managed to sustain good and appropriate relations with almost
everyone with whom she came in contact.

[2] "The Nosology of Male Homosexuality," *Contributions to Psycho-
Analysis* (1916).

Certain reactions in her life showed, however, that her stability was not as flawless as it appeared; one of these will illustrate my theme. She was an American woman engaged in work of a propagandist nature, which consisted principally in speaking and writing. All her life a certain degree of anxiety, sometimes very severe, was experienced after every public performance, such as speaking to an audience. In spite of her unquestionable success and ability, both intellectual and practical, and her capacity for managing an audience and dealing with discussions, etc., she would be excited and apprehensive all night after, with misgivings whether she had done anything inappropriate, and obsessed by a need for reassurance. This need for reassurance led her compulsively on any such occasion to seek some attention or complimentary notice from a man or men at the close of the proceedings in which she had taken part or been the principal figure; and it soon became evident that the men chosen for the purpose were always unmistakable father-figures, although often not persons whose judgement on her performance would in reality carry much weight. There were clearly two types of reassurance sought from these father-figures: first, direct reassurance of the nature of compliments about her performance; secondly, and more important, indirect reassurance of the nature of sexual attentions from these men. To speak broadly, analysis of her behavior after her performance showed that she was attempting to obtain sexual advances from the particular type of men by means of flirting and coquetting with them in a more or less veiled manner. The extraordinary incongruity of this attitude with her highly impersonal and objective attitude during her intellectual performance, which it succeeded so rapidly in time, was a problem.

Analysis showed that the Oedipus situation of rivalry with the mother was extremely acute and had never been satisfactorily solved. I shall come back to this later. But beside the conflict in regard to the mother, the rivalry with the father was also very great. Her intellectual work, which took the form of speaking and writing, was based on an evident identification with her father, who had first been a literary man and later had taken to political life; her adolescence had been characterized by conscious revolt against him, with rivalry and contempt of him. Dreams and fantasies of this nature, castrating the husband, were frequently uncovered by analysis. She had quite conscious feelings of rivalry and claims to superiority over many of the "father-figures" whose favor she would then woo after her own performances! She bitterly resented any assumption that she was not equal to them, and (in private) would reject the idea of being subject to their judgment or criticism. In this she corresponded clearly to one type Ernest Jones has sketched: his first group of homosexual women who, while taking no interest in other women, wish for "recognition" of their masculinity from men and claim to be the equals of men, or in other words, to be men themselves. Her resentment, however, was not openly expressed; publicly she acknowledged her condition of womanhood.

Analysis then revealed that the explanation of her compulsive ogling and coquetting—which actually she was herself hardly aware of till analysis made it manifest—was as follows: it was an unconscious attempt to ward off the anxiety which would ensue on account of the reprisals she anticipated from the father-figures after her intellectual performance. The exhibition in public of her intellectual proficiency, which was in itself carried through successfully, signified an exhibition of herself in possession of the father's penis, having castrated him. The display once over, she was seized by horrible dread of the retribution the father would then exact. Obviously it was a step toward propitiating the avenger to endeavor to offer herself to him sexually. This fantasy, it then appeared, had been very common in her childhood and youth, which had been spent in the Southern states of America; if a negro came to attack her, she planned to defend herself by making him kiss her and make love to her (ultimately so that she could then deliver him over to justice). But there was a further determinant of the obsessive behavior. In a dream which had a rather similar content to this childhood fantasy, she was in terror alone in the house; then a negro came in and found her washing clothes, with her sleeves rolled up and arms exposed. She resisted him, with the secret intention of attracting him sexually, and he began to admire her arms and to caress them and her breasts. The meaning was that she had killed father and mother and obtained everything for herself (alone in the house), became terrified of their retribution (expected shots through the window), and defended herself by taking on a menial role (washing clothes) and by *washing off* dirt and sweat, guilt and blood, everything she had obtained by the deed, and "disguising herself" as merely a castrated woman. In that guise the man found no stolen property on her which he need attack her to recover and, further, found her attractive as an object of love. Thus the aim of the compulsion was not merely to secure reassurance by evoking friendly feelings toward her in the man; it was chiefly to make sure of safety by masquerading as guiltless and innocent. It was a compulsive reversal of her intellectual performance; and the two together formed the "double-action" of an obsessive act, just as her life as a whole consisted alternately of masculine and feminine activities.

Before this dream she had had dreams of people putting masks on their faces in order to avert disaster. One of these dreams was of a high tower on a hill being pushed over and falling down on the inhabitants of a village below, but the people put on masks and escaped injury!

Womanliness therefore could be assumed and worn as a mask, both to hide the possession of masculinity and to avert the reprisals expected if she was found to possess it—much as a thief will turn out his pockets and ask to be searched to prove that he has not the stolen goods. The reader may now ask how I define womanliness or where I draw the line between genuine womanliness and the "masquerade." My suggestion is not, however, that there is any such difference; whether radical or superficial, they are the same thing. The capacity for womanliness was there in this woman—and one might even say it exists in the most completely homosexual woman—but owing to her conflicts it did not represent her main development, and was used far more as a device for avoiding anxiety than as a primary mode of sexual enjoyment.

I will give some brief particulars to illustrate this. She had married late, at twenty-nine; she had had great anxiety about defloration, and had had the hymen stretched or slit before the wedding by a woman doctor. Her attitude to sexual intercourse before marriage was a set determination to obtain and experience the enjoyment and pleasure which she knew some women have in it, and the orgasm. She was afraid of impotence in exactly the same way as a man. This was partly a determination to surpass certain mother-figures who were frigid, but on deeper levels it was a determination not to be beaten by the man.* In effect, sexual enjoyment was full and frequent, with complete orgasm; but the fact emerged that the gratification it brought was of the nature of a reassurance and restitution of something lost, and not ultimately pure enjoyment. The man's love gave her back her self-esteem. During analysis, while the hostile castrating impulses toward the husband were in process of coming to light, the desire for intercourse very much abated, and she became for periods relatively frigid. The mask of womanliness was being peeled away, and she was revealed either as castrated (lifeless, incapable of pleasure), or as wishing to castrate (therefore afraid to receive the penis or welcome it by gratification). Once, while for a period her husband had had a love affair with another woman, she had detected a very intense identification with him in regard to the rival woman. It is striking that she had had no homosexual experiences (since before puberty with a younger sister); but it appeared during analysis that this lack was compensated for by frequent homosexual dreams with intense orgasm.

In everyday life one may observe the mask of femininity taking curious forms. One capable housewife of my acquaintance is a woman of great ability, and can herself attend to typically masculine matters. But when, for example, any builder or upholsterer is called in, she has a compulsion to hide all her technical knowledge from him and show deference to the workman, making her suggestions in an innocent and artless manner, as if they were "lucky guesses." She has confessed to me that even with the butcher and baker, whom she rules in reality with a rod of iron, she cannot openly take up a firm straightforward stand; she feels herself as it were "acting a part," she puts on the semblance of a rather uneducated, foolish and bewildered woman, yet in the end always making her point. In all other relations in life this woman is a gracious, cultured lady, competent and well-informed, and can manage her affairs by sensible rational behavior without any subterfuges. This woman is now aged fifty, but she tells me that as a young woman she had great anxiety in dealings with men such as porters, waiters,

* I have found this attitude in several women analysands and the self-ordained defloration in nearly all of them (five cases). In the light of Freud's "Taboo of Virginity," this latter symptomatic act is instructive.

cabmen, tradesmen, or any other potentially hostile father-figures, such as doctors, builders and lawyers; moreover, she often quarrelled with such men and had altercations with them, accusing them of defrauding her and so forth.

Another case from everyday observation is that of a clever woman, wife and mother, a university lecturer in an abstruse subject which seldom attracts women. When lecturing, not to students but to colleagues, she chooses particularly feminine clothes. Her behavior on these occasions is also marked by an inappropriate feature: she becomes flippant and joking, so much so that it has caused comment and rebuke. She has to treat the situation of displaying her masculinity to men as a "game," as something *not real*, as a "joke." She cannot treat herself and her subject seriously, cannot seriously contemplate herself as on equal terms with men; moreover, the flippant attitude enables some of her sadism to escape, hence the offense it causes.

Many other instances could be quoted, and I have met with a similar mechanism in the analysis of manifest homosexual men. In one such man with severe inhibition and anxiety, homosexual activities really took second place, the source of greatest sexual gratification being actually masturbation under special conditions, namely, while looking at himself in a mirror dressed in a particular way. The excitation was produced by the sight of himself with hair parted in the center, wearing a bow tie. These extraordinary "fetishes" turned out to represent a *disguise of himself* as his sister; the hair and bow were taken from her. His conscious attitude was a desire to *be* a woman, but his manifest relations with men had never been stable. Unconsciously the homosexual relation proved to be entirely sadistic and based on masculine rivalry. Fantasies of sadism and *"possession of a penis"* could be indulged only while reassurance against anxiety was being obtained from the mirror that he was safely "disguised as a woman."

To return to the case I first described. Underneath her apparently satisfactory heterosexuality it is clear that this woman displayed well-known manifestations of the castration complex. Horney was the first among others to point out the sources of that complex in the Oedipus situation; my belief is that the fact that womanliness may be assumed as a mask may contribute further in this direction to the analysis of female development.

With that in view I will now sketch the early libido-development in this case.

But before this I must give some account of her relations with women. She was conscious of rivalry of almost any woman who had either good looks or intellectual pretensions. She was conscious of flashes of hatred against almost any woman with whom she had much to do, but where permanent or close relations with women were concerned she was nonetheless able to establish a very satisfactory footing. Unconsciously she did this almost entirely by means of feeling herself superior in some way to them (her relations with her inferiors were uniformly excellent). Her proficiency as a housewife largely had its root in this. By it she surpassed her mother, won her approval and proved her superiority among rival "feminine" women. Her intellectual attainments undoubtedly had in part the same object. They too proved her superiority to her mother; it seemed probable that since she reached womanhood her rivalry with women had been more acute in regard to intellectual things than in regard to beauty, since she could usually take refuge in her superior brains where beauty was concerned.

The analysis showed that the origin of all these reactions, both to men and to women, lay in the reaction to the parents during the oral-biting sadistic phase. These reactions took the form of the fantasies sketched by Melanie Klein[3] in her Congress paper, 1927. In consequence of disappointment or frustration during sucking or weaning, coupled with experiences during the primal scene which is interpreted in oral terms, extremely intense sadism develops towards both parents.[4] The desire to bite off the nipple shifts, and desires to destroy, penetrate and disembowel the mother and devour her and the contents of her body succeed it. These contents include the father's penis, her feces and her children—all her possessions and love-objects, imagined as within her body.* The desire to bite off the nipple is also shifted, as we know, on to the desire to castrate the

[3] "Early Stages of the Oedipus Conflict," *International Journal of Psychoanalysis,* Vol. IX, 1928.

[4] Ernest Jones, *op. cit.,* p. 469, regards an intensification of the oral-sadistic stage as the central feature of homosexual development in women.

* As it was not essential to my argument, I have omitted all reference to the further development of the relation to children.

father by biting off his penis. Both parents are rivals in this stage, both possess desired objects; the sadism is directed against both and the revenge of both is feared. But, as always with girls, the mother is the more hated, and consequently the more feared. She will execute the punishment that fits the crime—destroy the girl's body, her beauty, her children, her capacity for having children, mutilate her, devour her, torture her and kill her. In this appalling predicament the girl's only safety lies in placating the mother and atoning for her crime. She must retire from rivalry with the mother, and if she can, endeavor to restore to her what she has stolen. As we know, she identifies herself with the father; and then she uses the masculinity she thus obtains by *putting it at the service of the mother*. She becomes the father, and takes his place; so she can "restore" him to the mother. This position was very clear in many typical situations in my patient's life. She delighted in using her great practical ability to aid or assist weaker and more helpless women, and could maintain this attitude successfully so long as rivalry did not emerge too strongly. But this restitution could be made on one condition only; it must procure her a lavish return in the form of gratitude and "recognition." The recognition desired was supposed by her to be owing for her self-sacrifices; more unconsciously what she claimed was recognition of her *supremacy* in *having* the penis to give back. If her supremacy were not acknowledged, then rivalry became at once acute; if gratitude and recognition were withheld, her sadism broke out in full force and she would be subject (in private) to paroxysms of oral-sadistic fury, exactly like a raging infant.

In regard to the father, resentment against him arose in two ways: (1) during the primal scene he took from the mother the milk, etc., which the child missed; (2) at the same time he gave to the mother the penis or children instead of to her. Therefore all that he had or took should be taken from him by her; he was castrated and reduced to nothingness, like the mother. Fear of him, though never so acute as of the mother, remained; partly, too, because his vengeance for the death and destruction of the mother was expected. So he too must be placated and appeased. This was done by masquerading in a feminine guise for him, thus showing him her "love" and guiltlessness toward him. It is significant that this woman's mask, though transparent to other

women, was successful with men, and served its purpose very
well. Many men were attracted in this way, and gave her reassurance by showing her favor. Closer examination showed that
these men were of the type who themselves fear the ultra-
womanly woman. They prefer a woman who herself has male
attributes, for to them her claims on them are less.

At the primal scene the talisman which both parents possess
and which she lacks is the father's penis; hence her rage, also her
dread and helplessness.[5] By depriving the father of it and possessing it herself she obtains the talisman—the invincible sword, the
"organ of sadism"; he becomes powerless and helpless (her
gentle husband), but she still guards herself from attack by
wearing toward him the mask of womanly subservience, and
under that screen, performing many of his masculine functions
herself—"for him" (her practical ability and management). Likewise with the mother: having robbed her of the penis, destroyed
her and reduced her to pitiful inferiority, she triumphs over her,
but again secretly; outwardly she acknowledges and admires the
virtues of "feminine" women. But the task of guarding herself
against the woman's retribution is harder than with the man; her
efforts to placate and make reparation by restoring and using
the penis in the mother's service were never enough; this device
was worked to death, and sometimes it almost worked her to
death.

It appeared, therefore, that this woman had saved herself from
the intolerable anxiety resulting from her sadistic fury against
both parents by creating in fantasy a situation in which she became supreme and no harm could be done to her. The essence
of the fantasy was her *supremacy* over the parent-objects; by it
her sadism was gratified, she triumphed over them. By this same
supremacy she also succeeded in averting their revenges; the
means she adopted for this were reaction-formations and conceal-
ment of her hostility. Thus she could gratify her id-impulses, her
narcissistic ego and her superego at one and the same time. The
fantasy was the mainspring of her whole life and character, and
she came within a narrow margin of carrying it through to
complete perfection. But its weak point was the megalomanic
character, under all the disguises, of the necessity for supremacy.

[5] Compare M. N. Searl, "Danger Situations of the Immature Ego,"
Oxford Congress, 1929.

When this supremacy was seriously disturbed during analysis, she fell into an abyss of anxiety, rage and abject depression; before the analysis, into illness.

I should like to say a word about Ernest Jones's type of homosexual woman whose aim is to obtain "recognition" of her masculinity from men. The question arises whether the need for recognition in this type is connected with the mechanism of the same need, operating differently (recognition for services performed), in the case I have described. In my case direct recognition of the possession of the penis was not claimed openly; it was claimed for the reaction-formations, though only the possession of the penis made them possible. Indirectly, therefore, recognition was none the less claimed for the penis. This indirectness was due to apprehension lest her possession of a penis *should be* "recognized," in other words "found out." One can see that with less anxiety my patient too would have openly claimed recognition from men for her possession of a penis, and in private she did in fact, like Ernest Jones's cases, bitterly resent any lack of this direct recognition. It is clear that in his cases the primary sadism obtains more gratification; the father has been castrated, and shall even acknowledge his defeat. But how then is the anxiety averted by these women? In regard to the mother, this is done of course by denying her existence. To judge from indications in analyses I have carried out, I conclude that, first, as Jones implies, this claim is simply a displacement of the original sadistic claim that the desired object, nipple, milk, penis, should be instantly surrendered; secondarily, the need for recognition is largely a need for absolution. Now the mother has been relegated to limbo; no relations with her are possible. Her existence appears to be denied, though in truth it is only too much feared. So the guilt of having triumphed over both can only be absolved by the father; if he sanctions her possession of the penis by acknowledging it, she is safe. By *giving* her recognition, he *gives* her the penis and to her instead of to the mother; then she has it, and she may have it, and all is well. "Recognition" is always in part reassurance, sanction, love; further, it renders her supreme again. Little as he may know it, to her the man has admitted his defeat. Thus in its content such a woman's fantasy-relation to the father is similar to the normal Oedipus one; the difference is that it rests on a basis of sadism. The mother she has indeed killed, but she is thereby excluded from enjoying much that the mother had, and what she does obtain from the father she has still in great measure to extort and extract.

These conclusions compel one once more to face the question: what is the essential nature of fully-developed femininity? What is *das ewig Weibliche?* The conception of womanliness as a mask, behind which man suspects some hidden danger, throws a little light on the enigma. Fully developed heterosexual womanhood is founded, as Helene Deutsch and Ernest Jones have stated, on the oral-sucking stage. The sole gratification of a primary order in it is that of receiving the (nipple, milk) penis, semen, child from the father. For the rest it depends upon re-action-formations. The acceptance of "castration," the humility, the admiration of men, come partly from the over-estimation of the object on the oral-sucking plane; but chiefly from the renunciation (lesser intensity) of sadistic castration-wishes deriving from the later oral-biting level. "I must not take, I must not even ask; it must be *given* me." The capacity for self-sacrifice, devotion, self-abnegation expresses efforts to restore and make good, whether to mother or to father-figures, what has been taken from them. It is also what Radó has called a "narcissistic insurance" of the highest value.

It becomes clear how the attainment of full heterosexuality coincides with that of genitality. And once more we see, as Abraham first stated, that genitality implies attainment of a *post-ambivalent* state. Both the "normal" woman and the homosexual desire the father's penis and rebel against frustration (or castration); but one of the differences between them lies in the difference in the degree of sadism and of the power of dealing both with it and with the anxiety it gives rise to in the two types of women.

XIII

On Women Who Hate Their Husbands*

By David A. Freedman

This report is based on the analysis of three similar young women. Of the many characteristics which they shared, the most striking was the angry contempt in which they held their husbands. Each patient stated within the first session that the essential root of her difficulties lay in her husband. Aside from this complaint, enough about these young women was similar to mark them off in my mind as a group presenting a specific clinical constellation. Of course they were not identical in all respects. Rather, their hatred of and contempt for their husbands appeared to be an element in a definite but restricted psychic constellation which they shared. It is my intention to present this constellation as it appeared to me, note some of the respects in which the patients differed, review some of the salient features of their analyses, and, finally, offer my views as to the genesis of the syndrome.

The Clinical Syndrome: Presenting Features

Each of the three patients—whom I shall call Anne, Barbara, and Claire—was in her middle twenties when she came to treatment. The husbands were seven to ten years older than the wives. All three were physically attractive in what might best

* Read at the meeting of the New Orleans Psychoanalytic Society, April 10, 1959.

be described as a typical young housewife way. That there was no gross distortion of body image, or rejection of femininity, at least at this level of perception, was indicated by the fact that each was well built and obviously concerned about her physical appearance. None was either overdressed or careless about her clothes. They were all, as a general rule, well groomed, they used moderate amounts of cosmetics and jewelry, and they went to the beauty parlor regularly. They belonged to and were reasonably active in women's clubs appropriate to their age and social origins. In brief, in these respects the patients seemed unexceptional.

The same cannot be said of other aspects of their ego function. The poorly concealed contempt in which they held themselves extended to all areas of living and all aspects of behavior. Further, whether primarily or secondarily (of this I cannot be certain), this contempt in all cases ultimately proved to be closely connected with their feelings about themselves as women. That is, for each of these patients, the concept of the role of the female (at least as she was involved in it) as essentially inferior to that of the male was implicitly assumed as valid—as I shall show.

The defect in the executive aspects of their ego function was demonstrated by a series of half-finished projects, and by their tendency to deprecate the significance of anything they had done which could be regarded as a positive achievement.

Their educational histories are illustrative of the half-finished projects. All three are of superior intellectual endowment. Anne, the only one for whom I have test data, has an IQ of 127, and she is, by clinical estimate, the least well endowed of the three. Yet only Claire managed to complete college. Anne barely succeeded in scraping by academically for two years in one university and for another year in a second. She considered herself very intellectual, but studying seemed pointless to her. Although she expressed disdain and contempt for those who did work hard at their studies, the envy and inadequacy she felt was always in her awareness. Barbara completed one year of college at a school on the west coast. Although she made excellent grades, she deprecated her ability to do so and constantly anticipated failure in course work. She approached each examination with severe anxiety, but when she did well, her reaction was that it meant nothing. She also felt extremely uncomfortable and apprehensive in social and interpersonal situations. During the Christmas vacation at home she met her future husband and became engaged. They were married at the end of the school year. Claire, who completed college, did so very successfully—she stood first in her class and received her degree *summa cum laude*. However, she deliberately chose a school she considered to be inferior, and elected to major in medical technology rather than to take the pre-medical course she was really interested in. Having taken her degree, she held, during the four-year period between graduation and entering analysis, no fewer than 20 jobs. In each she insisted on confining herself to the most routine and humdrum of laboratory tasks—for example, urinalyses and blood counts. The least well integrated of the three patients, Claire reacted to requests that she do more complicated work by developing severe headaches—her initial referral was from an internist interested in an evaluation of her headaches—and both obsessive and paranoid reactions. The latter at times assumed a sufficiently bizarre quality to be considered psychotic. She was, for instance, afraid to draw blood from the fingers of male patients because they might have masturbated, semen might be on their hands, and she later in wiping herself might inadvertently be impregnated.

Any positive achievement for these women seemed to be devalued as soon as it became associated with the possibility of enhancement of their self-esteem. The conclusion each held to was that anything she did or achieved, anyone could do. In terms of significant aspects of life, her activities simply did not matter; indeed, she tended to greet with anxiety any evidence that they might matter. Although they had superficially unremarkable associations with other women and women's organizations they all felt inferior and "like outsiders." None felt really accepted by her associates—and this despite all evidence that she was. As Barbara put it repeatedly, "I'm nothing, I'm empty." One of her dreams is illustrative of the feelings of all three both with regard to themselves and men. She dreamed, "I went with J [a friend] to H's office [H is an obstetrician remarkably similar in appearance to the patient's husband, who is also an obstetrician]. The waiting room was crowded with a row of urinals like the ones in men's rooms. I could see H through the door urinating into a bag and pouring it back into his penis over and over again." She thus saw herself in the role of woman as a receptacle of some utilitarian value awaiting the convenience and pleasure of self-contained and uninterested man.

The picture of herself as a person—particularly as it applied to herself in the role of woman—played a determining role in each instance in the patient's selection of a mate. All three had had romances prior to marriage; Anne had had a sexual affair.[1] In each instance the patient broke off the romance because of her doubts concerning her ability to hold someone whom she admired in a sustained relationship. By contrast with the doubts and fears with which these relationships were handled, as well as with the quality of the postmarital relationships, almost dramatic certainty and determination characterized engagement and marriage for each patient.

The courtships varied in duration from six months to three years. That is, on the surface the marriages appeared to be well considered and based on considerable knowledge of the prospective mate. Closer inspection, however, did not support this impression. Barbara, who met her husband-to-be during the Christmas holidays, returned to school, saw him again only during the Easter vacation, and married him the following summer. Anne met her husband while visiting a friend in a remote city. During the nine or ten months which intervened before their marriage they saw one another only on occasional week-ends, *in toto* about five times. Claire met her husband when she was a freshman and he a senior in college. She decided at once that she would marry him and never wavered in this decision or had conscious doubts about it until the wedding ceremony was safely over. It is of parenthetical interest that Claire, a devout and, when I first knew her, even scrupulous Catholic, in reciting her marriage vows found herself thinking, "It is all right about 'love' but *they* aren't really serious about 'honor and obey.'"

In each instance the patient felt convinced that her mother was wholeheartedly in favor of her marriage while her father acquiesced in it only reluctantly.

Another striking similarity in the histories of these patients

[1] This was with a man the patient describes as quite sadistic. In this relationship she was constantly aware of his faults and at no time derived sexual gratification.

was the character of their husbands. They were all competent but not outstanding professional men. In each instance the patient could regard her husband as coming from a social background inferior to her own. The involvement of each man with his own mother was a salient feature of his psychology. Thus the obstetrician is the by no means favored son of a midwife. Anne's spouse apparently had never contemplated marriage until the death of his mother. He met his prospective bride during the period of obligatory mourning, and married her as soon as his religion (orthodox Jewish) would allow. One of Claire's more or less realistic complaints had to do with her husband's refusal to leave New Orleans for more lucrative job offers elsewhere. This reluctance—a literal reluctance to be parted from his mother, who has several other children in the city—coupled with his need to be the one to care for his mother and her home constituted a major source of marital discontent.

In general the criticisms the women made of their husbands were monotonously uniform. The husbands were dull, they were stupid, they were uninterested and undynamic. They didn't question, they weren't curious. Above all, they spent too much time watching television. Each wife's thesis was that if her husband were only more aggressive and interested, everything would be fine. With regard to their way of treating their wives, the latter's principal complaint was directed at passivity and apparent indifference. The wives spent enormous amounts of time and energy goading and needling in deliberate attempts to provoke the husbands into anger. Fantasies of being forcibly restrained or struck were explicit in all three. Like the husband in O. Henry's story, "A Harlem Tragedy,"[2] however, the spouses' responses were to become more placating, more passive, and more "considerate"—or, as the wives saw them, to present themselves as weaker and more childlike. The result, of course, in every case, was to increase the patient's anxiety and manifest scorn, induce more goading behavior on her part, and perpetuate the marital conflict in cycles of ever-increasing intensity.

Each of the patients retreated from the realities of her life into fantasies of some sort of never-never land where everything would be perfect. This uniformly implied something vaguely

[2] W. S. Porter, "A Harlem Tragedy," pp. 1397-1401, in *The Complete Works of O. Henry;* Garden City, N.Y., Garden City, 1937.

described as glamor. The closest approximation Anne and Barbara could find to their dream was the theater. Claire, the more obsessive patient, thought of becoming a doctor and ultimately, of course, a psychoanalyst. Each also was characterized by episodes of impulsive behavior in which she defiantly spent more money than she and her husband could well afford, or did something which could only be construed as deliberately hurtful and inconsiderate of him and the marital relationship.

All three of the women were orgastic although none was consistently so. Doubts about her sexual attractiveness were, as could be expected, close to paramount in the thinking and feeling of each. In addition, they all considered the woman's role in sexuality a degraded one. The fact that it was pleasurable seemed at times to be particularly a source of embarrassment. Anne and Barbara were unable to talk about their sexual feelings for many months. Barbara then denied ever having orgasm. As time went on she indicated that her orgastic response occurred almost immediately upon insertion when, she said, her husband couldn't tell. Claire, who utilized intellectualizing and isolating as defense mechanisms to a much greater extent than the others, discussed her sexual experiences ostensibly in a most dispassionate way. She seemed to attempt to titrate her level of pleasure on one occasion as compared to another—all in the content of a pseudodetachment from the experience. She had been unresponsive for some years prior to initiating treatment, but during the early phase of analysis, when she formed an intense positive transference, orgasm was possible. As the transference relation altered, however, and she again became more oriented to her dependence on her husband, she again became frigid. None of the patients could engage comfortably in foreplay or allow herself any explicit expression of tenderness, verbal or physical. Each was preoccupied with the conviction that her mate only wanted to use her, that to express love or tenderness would only lead to her own embarrassment, discomfort, and ultimately desertion.

To a greater or lesser extent, all of the women interpreted the world around them from what I would call a paranoid position. As adults they felt isolated and different from others. All three couples had reasonably active social lives, but the women felt "on the defensive" in social situations. The intensity of this reaction varied from Anne's complaints about the clannishness and inconsiderateness of New Orleanians, to Claire's frankly delusional ideation concerning her co-workers.

The Anamnestic Data

In the developmental history of these women, again, there seem to me to be definite and striking similarities. In effect each was an only daughter. Claire is an only child. Barbara is the second of four and an only daughter. Anne, the oldest of three, has a sister, but the younger girl is 14 years her junior. The developmental movement of the relations of these girls to their parents seemed to follow almost, but not quite, classical Oedipal lines. Those aspects of their development that I could retrace followed remarkably the course outlined by Jones[3]—in particular, each gave evidence of being enormously interested in and fascinated by her father during the early years of life. For Anne and Barbara this was clearly reciprocated and thus fostered by the father, but in Claire's case, the father's overt interest in the child was apparently choked off by maternal intervention. All three patients ultimately felt deserted by their fathers and left to the mercies of their mothers. Herein, of course, lies the most significant deviation from the classical Oedipal story. The patients did not relinquish their object choice from fear of maternal retaliation; rather, apparently each felt that she had been given up by the object of her affection. The resolution of this situation in each case again followed classical lines in that the patient formed a close identification with the parent of the same sex. The identification in aim, in value system, and in concept of self had the effect of solidifying the patient's image of herself as a woman, but it also had the special characteristic of preventing the patient from even conceiving of herself as capable of adequate performance as a woman, or even as an adult, independent of her mother. She had, after all, been spurned in the mother's favor.

In each instance, furthermore, the mother was quite disturbed. In particular, the concepts that this is a man's world and all men

[3] Ernest Jones, "The Early Development of Female Sexuality," pp. 438-451, in *Papers in Psycho-Analysis* (5th ed.); Baltimore, Williams & Wilkins, 1948.

are selfish were fundamental in the mothers' thinking. Open conflict between the parents characterized all three homes, involving accusations leveled against the father as a selfish, exploiting tyrant. Anne's mother was frankly psychotic and has had several hospital admissions. She was given to towering and destructive rages, during one of which the father said to the patient, his oldest child, "If it weren't for you, I would have left her long ago." Needless to say, however, he ignored repeated opportunities to help the patient in her difficulties with the mother. Claire confirmed the inference made in analyses that her father did not simply desert her as a child, when she was able to see her mother attempt to keep him from making contact with the patient's child.

In all three cases it was clear that the father either was allowed to have little interest or actually did have little interest in the care and raising of the child, so that the child was thrown on the mercies of a maternal figure toward whom her feelings were highly ambivalent. The resolution of this conflictual situation through identification with the mother was clearly evident in the patient's primary family identification. Each thought of herself as her mother's child and the maternal connection as "my family." For Barbara and Claire the identification was fostered by the fact that the fathers were from remote communities and the mothers' families were in New Orleans. Both of Anne's parents were from remote communities. In this case the overvaluation of the psychotic mother revolved around her having received a master's degree from Columbia, in contrast to the father, who was "merely" a successful businessman. Anne accepted the postgraduate degree as clear evidence of her mother's superiority—a superiority which may have overwhelmed her, since she was unable to perform satisfactorily at college despite her IQ of 127. The dilemma posed by the mother's obviously disordered behavior was further complicated by what the child saw as incontrovertible evidence that the mother was the intelligent, dominant, and really significant member of the family.

It should be added that in each instance the father was professionally or financially successful. Further, all three fathers were extremely generous to their children materially.

The families were all characterized by the paucity of relations established outside the immediate family circle. "You are as good as anyone—we are as good as anyone," the plaintive injunction of Barbara's mother to her daughter, summarized the feeling in all three families. The denial involved in the protestation was painfully evident to the child. She felt isolated from and different from her associates. These feelings included her family, which she saw as quite different from those of her contemporaries. While her conscious valuation tended to be that in some ineffable way her family was superior, from the standpoint of ego function she clearly felt inept and inadequate in dealing with other children. She experienced shame concerning the details of her family life and felt unable to bring her friends home. In each instance this feeling was reinforced by experiences in school. The patients all recall social rejections which for them were reaffirmations of their convictions that they were different from others and not particularly attractive to their associates. That these experiences were most certainly self-induced—that is, the result of their ways of handling the world and their associates—is, I think, rather beside the point for the moment. The effect was further to reaffirm their sense of isolation and inadequacy and thus to perpetuate and intensify the self-contemptuous feelings.

THE ANALYSIS

Claire—the least well integrated initially—has successfully completed an analysis. In the past two and a half years (since termination) she has come in to see me five times in order to discuss a specific issue; the need to do this and the problem itself are indicative of the nature of her unresolved feelings in the transference. Working as a volunteer on the psychiatric ward at a hospital, she became involved in an attempt to "help" a rather disturbed, paranoid young man. When she found herself beyond her depth she became anxious and came in for guidance. Evidences of successful analysis are: (1) Freedom from the headaches for which she had been referred and from bizarre obsessive thinking for at least three years. (2) A satisfactory relationship with both parents; this involves her recognition of her significance to them as a person, and her freedom from both her obsessive dutifulness and her anger toward them. (3) A comfortable acceptance of her Catholicism, so that she can recognize its weaknesses and inconsistencies and yet practice it in the context of its significance in the milieu in which she lives without having to resort to scrupulous defenses. (4) A contented marital existence based on a comfortable acceptance of her husband. This, needless to say, involves a recognition of his positive qualities as well as acceptance of the fact that he, like the patient, has his foibles. In brief, she can tolerate his not being omnipotent. (5) The ability to deal with an adopted child for close to two years, without undue anxiety or concern about her efficacy in the role of mother.

Although there are areas in which I might wish for more for this woman, on the basis of the foregoing I feel justified in considering her successfully analyzed.

The two other patients are still in analysis. In both instances I would consider them well advanced in treatment in that each has made significant modifications in her way of life. Anne will terminate treatment shortly. Barbara, who has made the most radical change in her personal life, continues in treatment.

I would like now to review the analyses from the standpoint of what appeared to be the major problems met in dealing with the patients' defenses, particularly as they were experienced in the transference relationships.

The initial reaction of each patient was to treat the analyst as an omnipotent figure who would be on "her side" if she refrained from offending him. During this period each evinced a great deal of interest in the analyst's family, particularly in his wife. In one way or another each managed to get to see her and evolved fantasies about replacing her. With regard to her own life each plunged immediately into a violent indictment of her husband and, in relatively short order, of her family as well. Both were seen as inhibiting and frustrating—the husband because of his passivity, the family more because of the demands for performance that resulted in the patient's feeling a need to be a "good girl" for them. Their positions were, of course, essentially paranoid in that each patient was entirely oblivious to her contribution to the acute stresses and strains in her relationships, and implicitly assumed that she was trapped in her situation, without the capacity either to modify it or to remove herself from it. As each patient began to recognize her contribution to the difficulties, and her capacity for changing the situation, she began to deal with her own sense of inferiority. As the analysis underscored the significance of the patient's behavior in shaping her own and her family's lives, and emphasized her proclivity for discounting her role, the impulsive behavior tended to drop out—as did the tendency to fantasy some glamorous never-never situation which would come true in the nebulous future.[4]

In association with these confrontations, the transference reaction underwent a gradual shift. The therapist was no longer seen as omnipotent and, equally or more important, was no longer seen as inevitably on the patient's side. Rather, the patient reconstructed in the transference situation the relations which had colored her life with her mother. The analyst was seen as an indispensable but demanding and frustrating person. The analyst's indispensability, however, was largely overlooked and time and energy were devoted particularly to the patient's fantasied obligations to him. He forced her to come; she had to do as he demanded; he exploited her; she was at his mercy, and so forth. In brief, these women tended to create an atmosphere that obscured their own vested interests in treatment by projecting their needs on to the therapist in the guise of a demand on his part. That this constituted a continuation in the transference of the fantastic aspect of the relationship with her husband and ultimately the relationship with her mother seems to me, at least, very clear. Progress in therapy has been largely dependent on a working out of the distorted aspects of this conception, particularly in the transference relation, but also in the marital situation. In various ways it was of course pointed out to the patient that her feelings allowed for the perpetuation of an adolescent mode of adaptation in which she gained the security of the presence of a bigger and stronger person than she, but paid for it in terms of frustration of her adult aspirations. In each instance,

---

[4] In this context, it is of interest that all three patients brought up the story of Marjorie Morningstar (Herman Wouk, *Marjorie Morningstar;* New York, Doubleday, 1955). Furthermore, in talking about the book, all three forgot the epilogue—were unaware that it even existed—in which Marjorie is presented as a settled matron involved in a comfortable but unexciting marriage with a man who had taken over his aggressive mother's business.

however, before the analytic work in this area acquired much significance, documentation of specific interpretations and confrontations had to be derived from an acute emotional experience on the part of the patient. The imminent threat of separation was the consistent catalyst. In Claire's case, this occurred in the therapeutic relationship; for the other two, the principal focus was the marital situation.

Claire's experience was by far the most dramatic from the standpoint of the therapist. The combination of her own obsessive-paranoid character and the requirements of her Catholicism served to create a situation in which she accepted her marriage as inevitable. She could rail against her husband but could think of leaving him only in terms of its impossibility. The transference situation, on the other hand, did not admit of this rationalization. Literally for months, however, she devoted herself to castigating the therapist. He exploited her; he made her come to therapy; he was using her to his advantage, and so forth. Numerous suggestions that there were other psychiatrists in the city went unheeded, of course. Ultimately I became sufficiently exasperated to state categorically that she must find another therapist; I offered to help her in getting situated but insisted that we had come to an impasse which was beyond my abilities to cope with. The effect was a complete reversal in her feelings. From an angry, accusing position she became anxious and frightened. The tie to me, which she had seen as my creation, became the most important relationship she had. With considerable and very real reluctance I agreed to continue working with her on a trial basis. During the ensuing nine months the patient was able to work through her feelings in the transference sufficiently so that she could stop therapy.

Anne, by a process of continual provocation and goading, succeeded in bringing her husband to the point of agreement to a divorce. It was only when he arranged an appointment with an attorney that she began to think in terms of both her inability to manage for herself and the threat of emotional separation and isolation. From this awareness of her vested interest in her marriage she has been able to modify her perception of her husband, and also her perception of herself as a person of significance in the marital relation. With less intensity than

Claire, but nonetheless quite clearly, this patient also saw herself as ensnared by the transference relationship. Her particular mode of protest was to be tardy or absent for appointments. When I took a firm position concerning this problem, her reaction was to infer that I disliked her, that I wanted to be rid of her as a patient. That I felt that her therapy was important enough to make it desirable for her to meet her appointments did not seem quite plausible to her. The difference from the situation with Claire seemed to me to be one of degree rather than of quality of the relationship. Anne's increased understanding and acceptance of her role, both in the therapeutic relationship and in her family stiuation, has been sufficient so that she has deliberately become pregnant, which she had avoided for the past five years. Her one other pregnancy occurred "by accident" just when she had made up her mind to leave her husband.

Barbara has actually separated from her husband. Of the three spouses he is undoubtedly the most seriously disturbed. The separation followed his brief and less than half-hearted attempt at analysis. Insofar as my patient's analysis is concerned, the separation has served only to underscore all the more emphatically her motivation in marriage. By far the most gifted of the three women, both physically and mentally, she is plagued with doubts about her ability to get along in the world. She cannot conceive of anyone's ever again being interested in her. At the moment she is torn between her conviction that her marriage can never be satisfactory and her equally strong conviction that it's the best she can ever hope for. The separation has served to intensify her awareness of dependent aspects of the transference relationship, and for the present, at least, the picture of myself as frustrating and exploiting has receded—albeit not disappeared. She is able to contemplate both the intensity of her feelings of need for me and the strength of her fear that she can't really "count on" me. In this context she frequently expresses her temptation to run away and her fear that needing me as she does, she is helpless. In preparing for the future she has returned to college with the intention of completing her education and has recently, in the context of recognition at school, been able to concede some awareness of her own abilities.

DISCUSSION

These three attractive young women, then, had come to analysis ostensibly because of the problems they were having with significantly older husbands, whom they saw as frustrating, inept, and stupid, but who were in reality quite competent, albeit passive, dependent, and involved with their own maternal relations. In each instance, it was possible to demonstrate that the patient's choice of mate had been based on the specific defect of her own ego system implied by inability to see herself as a person of sufficient potential significance and ability to hold a man she really admired. She had chosen someone who combined the contradictory, but for her safe, qualities of substantial but not outstanding ability in his own professional sphere, and a passive, dependent, and placatory orientation to the significant female in his life. Rather than satisfying, the relationship proved inevitably to be fraught with anxiety and frustration.

The defective ego formation seemed to be a derivative of the engrafting of rather specific conditions on to a fairly typical female Oedipus situation. All three patients passed through a phase in which the distinctive feature was the patient's feeling that she had been deserted by her father. That is, in contrast to the classical masculine resolution of the Oedipal conflict by giving up of the love object and identifying with the parent of the same sex, these women appear to have felt that they were given up. Thus, they were thrown back to a homosexual identification not by active, more or less voluntary surrender, but by the desertion of their first heterosexual object. To this extent their development follows closely that postulated as typically feminine by Freud, Deutsch, and Jones, among others.[5] It is in this context that I am inclined to see the explanation for their rather clear identification of themselves as women. Their problems did not involve rejection of femininity, but, rather, revolved around ideas that certain liabilities were inevitable accompaniments of femininity. These ideas appear to derive from the peculiarly ambivalent quality of their homosexual identification. All three

[5] Sigmund Freud, "The Psychology of Women, Lecture XXXIII," p. 153-185, in *New Introductory Lectures on Psycho-Analysis;* New York, Norton, 1933. H. Deutsch, *The Psychology of Women,* Vol. 1; New York, Grune & Stratton, 1944. Jones, *op. cit.*

were, in effect, the only daughters and lacked, therefore, contemporaries who could have diluted the intensity of the identification with the mother. The mothers were all isolated, paranoid women; each tended to explain her own unhappiness in terms of the thoughtlessness and selfishness of her husband. These alleged qualities constituted the major text in many violent family quarrels which the patients witnessed, and served obviously to enhance the patients' feelings about their own desertion. In addition, and presumably as a derivative of the foregoing, none of the patients was able to establish adequate relationships outside of the family situation during her childhood and adolescence. Each, therefore, entered "the marriage mart" in search of someone possessed of an extremely unlikely combination of qualities. He must, on the one hand, be passive and dependent enough in his orientation to the significant female in his life not to repeat the traumatic desertion. On the other hand he must be strong enough to supply the kind of ego function that the patient felt she herself lacked and had had to derive from the maternal relationship. In the day to day routine of married life the husband's passivity was such that the patient's intense anaclitic needs and consequent separation anxiety did not become a conscious consideration. She was thus able to devote her attention exclusively to her chagrin over his failings, both real and fancied. Successful treatment was dependent both on clarifying the real significance of the patient's adult functioning and, more basically, on working through the separation anxiety on which her self-depreciation was ultimately dependent.

Two aspects of these problems have been of particular interest to me. First, chance would dictate that any constellation uncovered three times in the course of a relatively brief analytic practice should be fairly common. Yet I know of no literature dealing with this syndrome as such. It goes unmentioned in such a standard work on female psychology as Deutsch's monograph, and Eisenstein's recent collection of essays, *Neurotic Interaction in Marriage*, is similarly devoid of mention of this problem.[6] Why, if my observations are valid, it should be so overlooked is a provocative question.

[6] See Deutsch, *op. cit.*, Victor W. Eisenstein, editor, *Neurotic Interaction in Marriage;* New York, Basic Books, 1956.

Second, once I began to think along these lines, it seemed to me that I could see elements of this problem in several other female patients. By contrast, I have not observed any heterosexually functioning man who has taken quite the same position —that what he does is of no significance. In certain homosexual males, however, something closely akin to the ego defect I describe does seem to be present. Certainly paranoid men are common enough. Obviously, too, there is no dearth of men who have formed intense anaclitic reactions toward their wives and who have, as a consequence, felt frustrated and enraged by them. Their position, however, seems to me to have been that no matter what they do or how they perform they can't quite satisfy their wives. These women, by contrast, take the position that their behavior has no real significance, that effective dealing with the world must come through some other person— husband, mother, or analyst—to whom they are attached.

The inference is tempting that this orientation is closely related to what are still generally considered appropriate attitudes for women in some areas of Western culture. The lack of literature on the problem may tend to support such an inference: perhaps these phenomena were not considered very unusual when observed in the past.

What relation this type of ego formation has to the fact of femininity is, of course, a moot question. That it is not an inevitable result of the possession of a specific type of anatomy or physiology is fairly clear. The question of whether, as Jones in particular proposes, women are by virtue of their anatomy more vulnerable to aphanisis is also an open one. Certainly anthropological data, such as those of Kardiner and Malinowski and what is known about the pre-Hellenic Mediterranean cultures, point to the conlclusion that anatomic factors are relatively unimportant in the evolution of "feminine" versus "masculine" psychology as thought of in Western culture.[7] The characteristics of homosexuality as it is seen in Western culture certainly also militate against a very close association between personality traits and somatic sexual characteristics. Presumably no one factor in itself is sufficient to explain the differences between typical

[7] A. Kardiner, The Individual and His Society; New York, Columbia Univ. Press, 1939. B. Malinowski, Sex and Regression in Savage Society; New York, Harcourt Brace, 1927.

female and male psychology. Attitudes which are common enough to constitute cultural stereotypes of one sex can be applied in a given family situation to members of the other. A given aspect of an individual's ultimate ego formation seems much more likely to be determined by such family attitudes than by the particular anatomic and physiologic equipment he or she possesses. Given the cultural determinants, women are much more likely than men to develop the sort of ego characteristics described here. However, circumstances that result in a male's feeling deserted by the father figure, with consequent identification with the mother, will eventuate in the same attitudes—if the maternal orientation and all it implies about pre-Oedipal relationships is as described. This, I believe, occurs as part of a homosexual orientation. This is not to minimize the importance of such maturational processes as the evolution of the Oedipal relationship. Rather it is to suggest that the ego development which eventuates from the Oedipal relationship may be more dependent on the environments response to this early expression of active attachment to another person than on the shape of the protagonist's genitals.

XIV

Contribution to the Problem of Vaginal Orgasm

By Sandor Lorand

Results in the therapy of psychosexual difficulties in women are frequently not quite satisfactory. Psychoanalysts particularly interested in feminine psychology have noted this fact. Many have therefore concluded that they must be content if they can help the patient to adjust herself to incomplete sexual gratification and to sublimate the sexual desire by converting the penis envy (which some analysts regard as the central problem) into the wish for a child. Nevertheless we cannot accept this solution as the final aim of therapeutic endeavor—least of all, if we understand the pathogenesis of this inability to attain complete sexual gratification. To assume that one single problem is responsible for all the difficulties is to impede our progress toward a solution from the very start.

Psychoanalytic literature presents a variety of approaches to the problems of feminine psychology and sexuality. The consensus of all the investigators (whose material was gathered from many different patients) indicates that the major factors in the conflicts creating vaginal anesthesia are: Oedipus fixation, unconscious guilt accompanying aggression toward both parents, masculinity strivings, rejection of femininity, and penis envy. Although these investigators have added to the understanding of feminine psychology and helped patients to adjust better to social and sexual life, still, in the treatment of frigidity they have not always succeeded in bringing about pleasurable orgasm. An important reason for this failure, I believe, is the incomplete and undetailed analysis of sensation in the vagina. Patients who complain of sexual anesthesia or inability to reach vaginal orgasm during intercourse can describe in detail vaginal sensations of greatly varying degree, quality and location. If these are to be understood they must be thoroughly analyzed.

In the initial phase of analysis complaints of sexual anesthesia are nearly uniform but as analysis progresses minute yet important differences emerge. For further progress and better understanding, these minute changes in vaginal sensation must receive continuous detailed analysis. The usual complaints are: absence of any sensation in the vagina during coitus, vaginal excitement accompanied by tenseness and irritability, at other times extreme pain during intercourse. At times various feelings are attributed to circumscribed parts of the vagina: for instance, sensations in the upper, but none in the lower region. Or, if at first they confuse the clitoridal and vaginal sensations, later in the course of analysis they learn to distinguish between clitoridal, superficial vaginal, and more deeply vaginal sensations. Sometimes relaxation is attained with no other gratification. As analysis progresses these sensations may change their character as well as location and itching, gripping pulsations, both exciting and irritating, will be described. In advanced analysis pulsations may occur during the analytic hour and also at other occasions. Sometimes they may last for days and be accompanied by an insatiable and even unendurable desire to feel the penis constantly within the vagina. This is felt as a hunger sensation of a sucking nature, with keen excitement before intercourse, but no gratification. The vagina was called a monster, constantly hungry, by one woman who felt that before and during intercourse she was "a great big mouth eating herself up" because she could not attain orgasm. Coitus was always very painful to her, but the desire to have the penis inside her vagina made her endure it. She could not relax from her excited state because she feared she would not be satisfied. Later, when she was able to achieve an orgasm, it was accompanied by angry shrieking and a grasping sensation as if her vagina "reached out like an octopus." The tension just before orgasm was characterized as an "inability to let go."

It became evident that the varied vaginal sensations described by patients were all of an oral type. The inability to cope with the reality of sexual functions had its deepest roots in the earliest mother fixation. The constant hunger for affection, guidance, and dependence, the need to be "filled up," characteristic of all these patients, was mainly responsible for the failure to attain sexual gratification. In all, the equation of "vagina = mouth" was dominant. This problem of orality, the identification of vagina with mouth, is stressed by other authors. The importance of the little girl's attachment to her mother and its relation to the disturbances of female sexuality have been studied by Ernest Jones and others of the British group. In his latest writings Freud again has stressed the significance of the prehistory of women in the understanding of female psychology.

In that early infantile period the eating-up and filling-up tendencies are outstanding and closely linked to the mother. When these patients are grown women their sexual attitude still preserves the desires, distrust, aggression, and fears persisting from these early mother attachments. In adult life they express the same aggression and fear for the mother's body, after frustration of the unconscious desires. They desire to be filled up precisely as they did in childhood, to be big, and, like their mother, to have everything inside of themselves. Such wishes implied possession of the mother so as to monopolize her affection and attention. This was the basis of identification with her. (It is interesting that although all these patients expressed a wish to be as different as possible from their own mother, curiously enough, in most cases they turned out to be exact replicas of their mothers.) In childhood all the body openings served the purpose of being filled up and in the adult patients the same tendency prevails. Their envy and aggression was aimed at the mother's body which contained the father's penis and the other children, all of which made her big and powerful. Childhood envy of siblings' breast-feeding and resentment at it became in adult life a source not only of guilt but also of fear that their own bodies would be destroyed in their eating, coitus, menstruation, pregnancy and childbirth. Ernest Jones has shown that there is more femininity in the young girl than analysts generally recognize, and has stressed the need for analysis of her earliest period of attachment to her mother. Melanie Klein, and others too, have pointed out the consequences of this most significant period. I feel strongly that the success of therapy of neurotic difficulties in women depends on the solution of this decisive infantile attachment. Especially is this so when the fears and aggressions resulting from early frustration by the mother are carried over to the field of adult sexual functions. As a result the entire sexual life of these patients is disrupted. Their flight from sexual pleasures is caused by fear of repeated frustrations as in the early mother attachment. There is fear of losing the penis before achieving orgasm, that coitus will end and they will be compelled to surrender the male organ. This is not, as some analysts think, the same as the desire to have a penis, the wish to be a boy: it is the fear of losing the father's penis which they wanted to acquire but had to renounce. This may be amplified to mean: giving up something they wanted in childhood, as they wanted their mother's body and her love. In this instance the word *love* includes varied objects and emotions: the mother (for affection, dependence, and envy); the other children (as rivals and enviable objects); the penis, breast and food (things desirable to have, to acquire, and not relinquish)—all these are included under the homogeneous heading of *love*. When the orgasm is inhibited, it is because of fear of losing this love (breast, penis, affection, etc.), and of being left alone, apart, and empty.

Some analysts have conjectured that vaginal sensations are present before as well as after puberty, but that they are due to vaginal play. However, even without definite memory of vaginal masturbation, the presence of such sensations in early years can be substantiated from the age of three upwards. Some patients have given definitive evidence of knowledge about the vagina and its functioning at the early age of three. Though this knowledge later became confused, it was never completely repressed or denied. We may assume the presence of an early vaginal phase in the little girl, for the assumption that the little girl does not recognize the existence of the vagina is not borne out by facts; nor is it definitely established that lack of a penis always troubles her, or that possessing one would satisfy her. Some of the patients had thought about having a penis but never actually desired to own one as an appendage outside the body. Certainly they admitted wishing for one, but for an internal one. One patient expressed her childhood desire in this manner: at the age of six she pulled her little brother on top of her, with the wish to put his penis inside her vagina, but then realized that his penis was too small, for she knew it was a big one she wanted.

It should be noted here that the patients' typical attitude was that of wanting to acquire something and then tenaciously holding on to it. This attitude is especially characteristic of their sexuality. The escape from sexual pleasure (exemplified by their frigidity) was an expression of the fear of losing something they have already acquired: possibly their pride and adjustment without the pleasure of coitus. Fearing dependence upon a man's penis for their sexual pleasure, they indulged instead in clitoridal masturbation. In coitus, when they had already experienced all the preliminary pleasure sensations, their excitement (even to the point of climax), the fear of coming to orgasm, their "not letting go"—all reproduced the early pattern of purely oral dependence and oral receptiveness which ended in frustration. It was the repetition of this pattern which they feared.

One patient who suffered from severe anorexia, in addition to many other neurotic and character difficulties, had the symptom of vomiting, associated with the fantasy that she had swallowed her father's penis. In her fantasy it lingered inside her. She described the process as a circular one: swallowing, going into her body, coming out at the bottom, again going up to her mouth, swallowing, etc. In the process of analysis she became afraid to relax on the couch because of sexual feelings in her vagina and fear that the analyst, who was a woman,* might insert something into her vagina. The whole fantasy and its resultant symptom meant: a desire to swallow her father's penis, intercourse with him, becoming pregnant (having it in her stomach), and then finally childbirth (vomiting it out). To incorporate the penis, first by the mouth, later by the vagina, is, as Jones pointed out, the realization of the little girl's primary wish for the penis. Naturally her dependence on her mother and her simultaneous aggressive defiance toward her, were the driving forces behind her neurotic symptoms. She actually and consciously employed vomiting to express hostility to her mother.

In another patient this orality was expressed in her vaginal aims, and was unmistakable in her manner of masturbation and fantasy. She used to masturbate by withholding her urine. The

* This case was supervised for Dr. Margaret Fries for over two years.

pleasure and sensation increased in proportion to the fantasied filling up of the bladder. It was a cavity which she in fantasy tried to fill up from an outside source. Simultaneously in this fantasy a man whom she liked very much was forcibly trying to impregnate her. Although she protested, the protest itself was a pleasurable one. These sensations which she would provoke by fantasy were experienced high up in the vagina. She also experienced a remarkable series of sensations in her mouth, teeth, and speech. At times she awoke at night with pains in her teeth which a dentist could not explain. As analysis advanced she resented the gradual awakening of sensitivity in the vagina. As she put it: when she came to analysis, she had no vagina at all, she was not aware of it. Now she was all vagina. Constantly excited, preoccupied with sexual fantasies, tortured mentally by pulsating feelings in her vagina, she felt she was losing herself by being destroyed with desire. She wished for perpetual intercourse. Incidentally, she was notorious for her prodigious appetite and constant eating. In the advanced stages of her analysis she had pleasurable feelings in coitus but she stopped short of orgasm for she felt rising hatred toward her husband since she feared he might take away his penis and give it to another woman. For this reason she was preoccupied throughout intercourse with the thought that something must not happen. She also resented orgasms because she wanted continued coitus.

These attitudes obviously paralleled her feelings toward her mother whom she resented for taking the breast away from her to give it to the siblings. The fear that something terrible might follow intercourse was connected with her childhood fantasies of destruction of the mother's body because of repeated pregnancies. Worth noting is the fact that this patient had no memory of her mother as pregnant or nursing, although she was old enough to remember. However, she could recall seeing in that same period other pregnant women and other unknown women breast-feeding their babies in the street.

The same early tie to the mother's breast, the same feminine-passive-accepting attitude, and strong feminine identification were exhibited by another patient. She had a vivid recollection of vaginal sensations occurring between the ages of five and six. At that time she had contracted a vaginal infection from another girl and had to use a douche. Following that period she practiced vaginal masturbation. She had been sleeping in the same room with her parents for years and the noises heard of parental intercourse excited her and induced masturbation. In adult life during coitus she displayed violent body movements, screamed and bit her husband (all these were developed in the course of analysis) and could not reach orgasm because of the constant fear that her husband would ejaculate too soon. By working through her dreams, associations, and emotions, interesting and important material revealed a deep attachment to her mother and shocking childhood experiences at her hands. Another patient recalled that she knew all the facts of life at the early age of about five or six. At that time when a sibling was born she heard her mother instruct someone to hide the bloody sheets from the patient's observation. Thus she came to connect childbirth with bleeding and injury to the region of the vagina.

Clinical observation shows us that the problem of feminine sexual anesthesia is much more complicated than is generally understood. Although analysts have long attempted to formulate the causes of these difficulties, their therapeutic results have not kept pace with their theoretic formulations. The period which Freud calls "dim and shadowy," the pre-Oedipal phase of the little girl, is the period in which we must seek the basic cause for the sexual difficulty. We find that all women with such difficulties make their mothers responsible for their own lack of an affectionate disposition. In the analytic process they express it thus: when they develop vaginal sensations and the desire for intercourse, they accuse the analyst of throwing them back upon their husbands, just as in childhood the mother forced them to look to the father for affection. Out of spite and resentment they refuse to enjoy coitus. They look upon a mother as a dangerous person, injurious to everyone. Another important factor in the frigid reaction is the patients' idea that the mother's sexual life with the father cannot be one of pleasure. This is caused by their feeling that their own hostility to their mother may have interfered with her sexual pleasure. In fantasy they actually did try to hinder her enjoyment. Their flight from femininity is a reaction to this aggression and consequent fear of the mother. They cannot identify themselves, or find pleasure in vaginal sensation and intercourse. Only when they accept the idea in analysis that their mother may have enjoyed this relationship can they permit themselves to experience pleasurable sensations. Another reason for their flight from femininity is the feeling of inferiority, which is not only an expression of penis envy but in a much deeper sense involves a comparison of mother and child. They resent having to depend on the penis for gratification and on the possessor of the penis for food and support. It recalls painfully their oral dependence in childhood and its many frustrations. The child feels weak and small compared to the mother, and the penis envy refers to the father's penis (affection) of which the mother was the sole recipient.

From the material and therapeutic results presented by many patients in long analysis one may come to the conclusion that vaginal sensations are primary and that infantile masturbation cannot be described as exclusively clitoridal or labial. It involves clitoris, labia and vagina. The theory that the clitoridal sensations are primary and have to be transferred to the vagina cannot be substantiated. In analysis the vaginal sensations regain their importance because the woman rediscovers and relearns early infantile sensations in the vagina which were repressed, forgotten and could not be enjoyed. The vagina can now be accepted and does not have to be denied because it is "an evil and dangerous organ like the mouth which wants to devour everything and everybody," as Ernest Jones has pointed out.

XV

"Penis Envy" in Women*

By Clara Thompson

Penis envy is a term coined by Freud and used by him to describe a basic attitude found in neurotic women. The term had more than symbolic meaning to him. He was convinced that this envy in women grew out of a feeling of biological lack beginning with the little girl's discovery in early childhood that she lacked something possessed by the little boy. Because of this, according to Freud, she believed she had been castrated, and she dealt with this shock either by sublimating the wish for a penis in the wish for a child; that is, becoming a normal woman, or by the development of neurosis, or by a character change described as the masculinity complex, a type of character which seeks to deny that any lack exists.

Critical evaluations of Freud's theory on the subject have already been published by Horney[1] and myself.[2] In brief, it has been shown that cultural factors can explain the tendency of women to feel inferior about their sex and their consequent tendency to envy men; that this state of affairs may well lead

---

* Presented at the annual convention of the Association for the Advancement of Psychoanalysis, in Boston, 19 May, 1942.

[1] Karen Horney, *New Ways in Psychoanalysis;* New York, Norton, 1939 (313 pp.), Chapter 6.

[2] Clara Thompson, "The Role of Women in this Culture," *Psychiatry,* IV (1941) 1-8. See also, "Cultural Pressures in the Psychology of Women," *Psychiatry,* V (1942), 331-339.

women to blame all their difficulties on the fact of their sex. Thus they may use the position of cultural underprivilege as the rationalization of all feelings of inferiority.

The position of underprivilege might be symbolically expressed in the term "penis envy" using the penis as the symbol of the more privileged sex. Similarly, in a matriarchal culture one can imagine that the symbol for power might be the breast. The type of power would be somewhat different, the breast standing for life-giving capacity rather than force and energy. The essential significance in both cases would be the importance in the cultural setting of the possessor of the symbol.

Thus one can say the term "penis envy" is a symbolic representation of the attitude of women in this culture, a picturesque way of referring to the type of warfare which so often goes on between men and women. The possibility of using the term in two ways; that is as actually referring to a biological lack, or as symbolically referring to a feeling of inferiority, has led to some confusion in psychoanalytic writing and thinking. It would make for greater clarity if the term were used only in representing Freud's concept. However, as psychoanalysis has developed, new meanings and different emphases often have become attached to an old term without any attempt at precise restatement. Consequently, the term "penis envy" is used by many without very exact definition. This may lead one to assume that Freud's concept is meant when the thinking is actually along cultural lines. It therefore seems worthwhile to clarify the present-day meaning of the term.

It seems clear that envy of the male exists in most women in this culture, that there is a warfare between the sexes. The question to be considered is whether this warfare is different in kind from other types of struggle which go on between humans and if it is not actually different, why is there such preoccupation with the difference in sex? I believe that the manifest hostility between men and women is not different in kind from any other struggle between combatants, one of whom has definite advantage in prestige and position. Two things have contributed to giving the fact of sexual difference a false importance. Penis envy and castration ideas are common in dreams, symptoms and other manifestations of unconscious thinking. Body parts and functions are frequent symbols in archaic thought. These ideas then may be only the presentation of other problems in symbolic body terms. There is not necessarily any evidence that the body situation is the cause of the thing it symbolizes. Any threat to the personality may appear in a dream as a castration. Furthermore, there is always a temptation to use some obvious situation as a rationalization of a more obscure one. The penis envy concept offers women an explanation for their feelings of inadequacy by referring it to an evidently irremediable cause. In the same way, it offers the man a justification for his aggression against her.

Sexual difference is an obvious difference, and obvious differences are especially convenient marks of derogation in any competitive situation in which one group aims to get power over the other.

Discrimination because of color is a case in point. Here, a usually easily distinguishable difference is a sign which is taken as adequate justification for gross discrimination and underprivilege. A Negro should feel himself inferior because he has a black skin. Obviously, the black skin is important to the group in power because it is such an easily recognized characteristic with which to differentiate a large number of people from themselves. Everything is done to make it a symbol for all the inferiority feelings Negroes have. Few indeed of the governing class can be so fatuous as to believe that black skin, *per se,* implies an intrinsic inferiority. It is amazing, however, to discover how near to this superficiality many of their rationalizations actually come.

In the same way, the penis or lack of penis is another easily distinguishable mark of difference and is used in a similar manner. That is, the penis is the sign of the person in power in one particular competitive set-up in this culture, that between man and woman. The attitude of the woman in this situation is not qualitatively different from that found in any minority group in a competitive culture. So, the attitude called penis envy is similar to the attitude of any underprivileged group toward those in power.

The clinical picture of penis envy is one in which the woman is hostile. She believes the man wishes to dominate her or destroy her. She wishes to be in a position to do similar things to him. In other words, the penis symbolically is to her a sword for conquering and destruction. She feels cheated that she has not a similar sword for the same purpose. This attitude need not have a specific relationship to the sexual life and genitals as such, but may be found as a part of a more general attitude of envy and may only secondarily affect the sexual life. In fact it may be accompanied by evidences of envy in other relationships. Other women who in some way have more assets and opportunities may also be objects of envy. One may thus find a woman supposedly suffering from penis envy showing a general tendency to envy anyone who has something she does not have and which she desires.

Envy is a characteristic of a competitive culture. It implies comparisons to one's disadvantage. There are three general directions in which character can develop in an effort to cope with this feeling. One outstanding type of character development in Western society is the one where the person tries to excel over others. One does away with envy by achieving success. If one fails in proving that one is as good or better than the envied one, tendencies to revenge may develop. The person seeks then to pull the superior one down and in some way humiliate him. Or a person may withdraw from competition, apparently have no ambition, and desire to be inconspicuous. In such a situation, although there may be a feeling of helplessness and increased dependency, there may also be a secret feeling of power due to being aloof from the struggle.

As has been said, the relationship between men and women has special features not found in the relationship with one's own sex. These special features are of two kinds. They have to do with the attitude of a minority group to a dominant group, and they have to do with the fact that the most intimate type of interpersonal situation, the sexual act, is an important part of and usually exclusively limited to the relationship between the two sexes. Thus any problem of interpersonal intimacy would be accentuated in this relationship.

In a patriarchal culture the restricted opportunities afforded women, the limitations placed on her development and independence give a real basis for envy of the male quite apart from any neurotic trends. Moreover, in an industrial culture in which the traditional family is no longer of central importance, the specific biological female contribution, the bearing of children, loses value co-ordinate with the various factors which encourage a diminishing birth rate. This, although it is not a biological inferiority, acts as if it were in that a woman can feel that what she has specifically to contribute is not needed or desired.

Therefore, two situations in the culture are of importance in this discussion: the general tendency to be competitive which stimulates envy; and the tendency to place an inferior evaluation on women. None miss altogether some indoctrination with these two trends. If the competitive attitude is greatly developed by personal life experiences, the hatred of being a woman is correspondingly increased. The reverse is also true; that is, if there has been emphasis on the disadvantages of being a woman, a competitive attitude toward men tends to develop. Out of either situation may appear character developments which fit into the clinical picture of penis envy, and it is not necessary to postulate that in each case an early childhood traumatic comparison of genital organs took place. Such early experiences do sometimes occur, but it is my impression as well as that of Fromm-Reichmann[3] that they are traumatic only in the setting of other serious traumatic factors and that they derive their importance chiefly from offering a kind of rationalization for the feeling of inferiority and defeat.

One scarcely can overemphasize the fact that the sexual relationship is one of the most important interpersonal situations. Any competitiveness in the personality of either participant is bound to have an effect upon the sexual relationship. Any actual social underprivilege of one partner must also have an effect on the sexual relationship. This should not be confused with any idea that a biological sexual inequality was the cause of the competitive attitude or the condition of underprivilege of one partner. The sexual life is merely one important situation in which the problem appears.

Thus it may be seen that the clinical picture of penis envy has little to do with the sexual life, except secondarily, and that it

---

[3] Frieda Fromm-Reichmann, "Notes on the Mother Role in the Family Group," *Bull. Menninger Clinic,* IV (1940), 132-148.

has to do with all aspects of living. If one rejects the idea that inferiority feelings in women are due to a feeling of biological lack, one must conclude that the term does not describe a clinical entity deriving from a constant origin, but has become a symbol and rationalization for various feelings of inadequacy in women. The situation of cultural underprivilege gives the impression of validity to the rationalization.